HIROKO'S AMERICAN KITCHEN

Other Books by Hiroko Shimbo

The Japanese Kitchen
The Sushi Experience

HIROKO'S AMERICAN KITCHEN

Cooking with Japanese Flavors

HIROKO SHIMBO

Photography by Frances Janisch

Andrews McMeel
Publishing, LLC
Kansas City · Sydney · London

Andrews McMeel Publishing, LLC
an Andrews McMeel Universal company
1130 Walnut Street, Kansas City, Missouri 64106

www.andrewsmcmeel.com
www.hirokoskitchen.com

12 13 14 15 16 SHO 10 9 8 7 6 5 4 3 2 1

ISBN: 978-1-4494-0978-4

Library of Congress Control Number: 2012936725

Design and Art Direction: Ren-Whei Harn
Photography: Frances Janisch
Food Stylist: Michael Pederson

ATTENTION: SCHOOLS AND BUSINESSES
Andrews McMeel books are available at quantity discounts with bulk purchase for educational, business, or sales promotional use. For information, please e-mail the Andrews McMeel Publishing Special Sales Department: specialsales@amuniversal.com

Contents

Curried Tofu Squares, page 87.

INTRODUCTION

This book, *Hiroko's American Kitchen*, was born from my own experience of bridging two vastly different cultures and cuisines: my native Japan and my adopted home, America. It shares with you my discoveries over 12 years as a Japanese cook navigating America's culinary waters, resulting in an exciting new way of cooking that combines the best of both traditions.

While the recipes may be new, they are in the spirit of Japan's culinary history. Our cooking culture has always been flexible and open to the adoption of new ingredients, flavors, techniques, and presentations. A thousand years ago, we learned from the Chinese. We got sushi from Southeast Asia. Our version of Wiener schnitzel, *tonkatsu* pork cutlet, came from Europe. Our most popular comfort food, Japanese curry, came from the British (not from India). Tempura arrived from Portugal, while Japanese-style hamburgers came from "you know where." Like these famous "Japanese" dishes, the ingredients, preparations, and presentations in this book are not the confused products of fusion cuisine; they are *extensions* of Japanese cuisine as a living, continually growing and evolving part of Japanese culinary culture.

The mission of this book is to share with you a collection of recipes that expand and extend Japanese cuisine to encompass today's cooking and food preferences. Using a core family of key stocks and sauces, I have married Japanese ingredients, preparation techniques, and traditional dishes with a rich array of American ingredients while retaining respect for the food cultures of Japan and America. The recipes will create balanced, healthy, and appealing meal options for you, your family, and your friends.

Hiroko's American Kitchen is built around a core of six easily prepared homemade stocks and sauces. These Japanese-style stocks and sauces serve as the central ingredient in each of the recipes, adding a dose of satisfying and surprising flavor to primarily American ingredients. I believe that the dishes presented here will have universal appeal at your table, even for your most unadventurous diners. This is not a volume promoting exotic and unfamiliar foods.

BACKGROUND

The family of handy stocks and sauces has greatly enhanced my own life. I rely on them both in my personal life and in my professional life as a consultant-chef and chef-instructor. When I first moved from Japan to America, it was a struggle. Gone were the familiar ingredients I had grown up with and cherished, including the seasonal array of Japanese produce and wide variety of freshly caught local fish. Instead, I had to confront unfamiliar foods at the market: new vegetables, different cuts of meats, and limited (and at times poor-quality) fish and shellfish. But the initial period of uncertainty gave way to an exciting time of experimentation as I gradually realized that I gained more in this new land than I lost.

Today in this country, there are three times the variety of vegetables that are available in Japan. Large cuts of meat such as pork and lamb shoulder, beef short ribs, and skirt steak can be transformed into flavorful Japanese meat dishes with proper preparation. I have also embraced the limited varieties of fresh and frozen fish, adding variety with inventive preparations. Out of necessity, I have truly learned to do without many of the native ingredients and foods of Japan and to take advantage of the abundance of quality materials here. Today I celebrate mainstream American ingredients using Japanese cooking techniques, and my family of stocks and sauces has made this task easier than ever.

Let me explain how the core concept of this book—the use of a family of homemade sauces—came about. Several years ago, I began storing traditional stocks and sauces in the freezer and refrigerator in order to save time and simplify the process of daily meal preparations. Having the sauces ready, I could rely on consistency of flavor, which also led to innovation and experimentation. By adding Japanese stocks and sauces to readily available American ingredients, I was able to greatly expand my horizons. The result is a collection of Japanese recipes that have the feel and appeal of traditional American cooking using seasonal domestic produce, which is also more affordable.

HOW TO USE THIS BOOK

The chapters are named for each of the stocks and sauces found in this book. Two stocks and four sauces—all part of (or derived from) traditional Japanese cuisine—are used to produce a wide variety of dishes. By using these handy stocks and sauces, the complexity and time required to prepare a Japanese meal is significantly reduced and cooking can be done with ease and enjoyment. These six stocks and sauces are:

- **KELP STOCK**—a simple brew of kelp and water
- **DASHI STOCK**—kelp stock made with dried fish flakes
- **WHITE SUMISO SAUCE**—light miso, rice vinegar, and sweetening
- **SPICY MISO SAUCE**—dark miso with crushed red pepper
- **BEST BASTING AND COOKING SAUCE**—soy sauce, sweetener, sake, and flavorings
- **SUPER SAUCE**—a new blend of soy sauce, mirin, kelp, and fish flakes that I have created

Each chapter of the book leads off with the recipe for the stock or sauce and is followed by a diverse selection of recipes employing the chapter's namesake stock or sauce. You might want to start by preparing one or two of the sauces or stocks, trying some of the recipes that use them, and then proceeding to the remaining stocks and sauces and their accompanying recipes.

You will find some traditional recipes as well as some that are new and unfamiliar. For example, you might consider the miso soup with leek, potato, and bacon (page 40) as presented in this book "unauthentic" because it isn't served at Japanese restaurants in America. Answering the question of what is truly "authentic," however, is a discussion that can consume a lifetime. From my point of view, the clichéd miso soup with mundane and stereotypical Japanese ingredients such as tofu, wakame seaweed, and scallions is boring. I believe it is much more thoughtful, interesting, and appealing to utilize readily available, seasonally changing vegetables. In fact, using local produce in season is a basic concept of Japanese cuisine, and since my miso soup recipe uses Japanese dashi stock and real miso, its flavor and spirit couldn't be more authentic.

Let me cite another example: There is a wonderful recipe for lamb braised with miso sauce in this book (page 132). In Japan, this miso-braising technique is used most often with mackerel. But since good-quality mackerel is difficult to find in America (and this oily fish that I dearly love may not appeal to many American diners), I use lamb—readily available and, as a strongly flavored meat, a perfect companion for the miso sauce. This combination results in a surprisingly light and flavorful authentic Japanese lamb dish. The lamb and the soup are perfect examples of how an adaptable and flexible approach can lead to Japanese cuisine's integration into American kitchens.

You will find these recipes easy and fun to prepare in your own kitchen because of the handy stocks and sauces you will have stored in your refrigerator and freezer. Join me in *Hiroko's American Kitchen* to discover a wonderful world of Japanese cuisine that will satisfy your appetite and all your senses and will contribute to a healthy life.

CHAPTER 1

KELP STOCK

In Japan, kelp stock is the most basic vegetarian stock. When this stock is infused with dried skipjack tuna flakes, *katsuobushi*, it becomes another main stock, dashi. Simple kelp stock is used to prepare vegetarian or delicately flavored dishes in which the pleasant but smoky fish flavor of dashi is too strong. When kelp stock is used as a base for other recipes, it is then usually flavored with a combination of key Japanese seasonings such as sea salt, shoyu, miso, mirin, sake, sugar, and rice vinegar.

Today, chefs working in American kitchens have begun to use kelp stock in their non-Japanese preparations. Its clean and lean appeal and umami-rich flavor (see page 7) produces light, new flavor profiles in an array of different types of dishes.

In this chapter, I will show you how easily you can make this simple, flavorful stock, which you can then use in many recipes. These recipes can become delicious, healthful, and everyday additions to your kitchen repertoire.

First, some tips on sourcing, purchasing, and proper storage of kelp. You can find kelp at nearly every Japanese or Asian market, as well as at some of the larger American supermarkets and online (see page 204). Kelp for stock should have the following characteristics:

- The kelp leaf is as thick as three or four sheets of copy paper.

- It is thoroughly dried. The leaves in the plastic package should feel hard and should not be flexible.

- It is deep black-green in color with a touch of glossiness.

- It has no brown blemishes.

- It is covered evenly with a very faint layer of mannite, a natural white powder that is a carbohydrate and source of sweetness.

After opening the package, close it tightly with a rubber band and store it in a cool, dry cabinet. It will keep stored like this for about a year.

If finding kelp is a problem, you can substitute low-sodium vegetable stock for the kelp stock, which will still give you the chance to learn how to prepare and flavor the dishes in this chapter in the Japanese style.

Kelp Stock: Traditional Easy Method

There are two ways to produce kelp stock: by this Traditional Easy Method and by a newly developed method often used by professional chefs (see page 8). This first method can fit easily into a busy home cook's lifestyle. Please note that you must soak the kelp overnight.

I frequently double or triple stock recipes and refrigerate or freeze unused stock in small plastic containers. To defrost frozen stock, I place it in a small pan with a tight-fitting lid and cook over medium heat. Defrosting 2 cups of frozen stock this way takes about 5 minutes.

MAKES 8 CUPS

8 cups cold water (see page 7)

1 ounce kelp (two 4 by 7-inch sheets)

Pour the water into a large bowl. Wipe the kelp with a moist, clean kitchen towel to remove any sand or impurities. Do not wipe off the white mannite powder. Add the kelp to the bowl (you may need to break the kelp into pieces to fit into the bowl). Cover the bowl with plastic wrap and refrigerate overnight.

Remove the kelp from the water and reserve for a second stock preparation (see page 8). On the ends of the swollen kelp you will see some oozing of a slimy liquid. This is a healthful, dietary fiber and a portion of it has already been dissolved in the stock. If a greenish slimy substance is leaking out into the water and is clouding the stock, it is a sign that you are using poor-quality kelp, as stock prepared from good-quality kelp will be clear in appearance. If necessary, strain the stock through a sieve lined with a moist, sturdy paper towel to remove any impurities. The stock is then ready to be used, or it can be refrigerated for 2 to 3 days or frozen for up to 2 months.

Umami: Savory Flavor

Umami is a Japanese word that describes the fifth taste—after the basic four of sweet, salty, sour, and bitter. It is best described as a savory element. Umami, whose major chemical component is glutamate, was isolated and identified by Dr. Kikunae Ikeda in 1908 at the Imperial University of Tokyo. Glutamate is naturally present in many foods, but the greatest amount is found in kelp. In fact, kelp has eight times the amount of glutamate found in tomatoes and other glutamate-rich foods.

There are two other chemicals that form umami: inosinate and guanylate. Both components were identified by Japanese scientists—Dr. Shintaro Kodama and Dr. Akira Kuninaka. Inosinate is found in meat and fish, while guanylate is found in dried mushrooms such as shiitake. The use of these umami-rich ingredients—kelp, dried fish flakes, and shiitake mushrooms—lends savory flavor and richness to Japanese dishes without the use of oil. It is interesting to note that mother's milk is also high in umami, and this is thought to satisfy the appetite of nursing infants. So if you were breast-fed, you had an early appreciation of umami, and this no doubt gave you a primal and innate understanding of what is tasty and delicious.

Water Hardness

Just as aficionados in America discuss the correct level of water hardness for brewing the best-tasting coffee, some renowned Japanese chefs (especially in the Kyoto region) insist on using only the "right kind of water"—Kyoto's soft water—in order to perfect their stock. Yoshihiro Murata, of Kyoto's legendary Kikunoi restaurant, sends local Kyoto water by truck for 300 miles every day to Kikunoi's Tokyo branch, where the water is only very slightly harder. This way, the Tokyo chefs can produce the same quality of flavorful stock as their colleagues in Kyoto. Chef Murata insists that this is a crucial step to keeping the quality of the cuisine high at Akasaka Kikunoi.

When chefs from Kyoto come to America for a demonstration or event, they do not rely on the local tap water for making stock. They seek out Volvic bottled spring water from Auvergne, France—whose level of hardness is close to that of their home region. While I can't recommend this extravagant practice, try not to use very hard water for stock preparation (sorry, Los Angeles!). I am lucky because our New York City tap water—which comes from streams and granite-lined reservoirs in the Catskill Mountains—is very soft and free of dissolved minerals, making it excellent for stock (and coffee) preparation in my own kitchen.

Kelp Stock: Chef's Method

Recent food science has found that the maximum extraction of umami from kelp takes place by immersing it in water at 140°F for 1 hour. In a busy restaurant kitchen, this process can easily be controlled by the use of a thermal immersion circulator or, like Japanese chefs who have perfected this operation without any special equipment, by being diligent in keeping the water temperature consistent throughout the cooking time.

MAKES 8 CUPS

1 ounce kelp (two 4 by 7-inch sheets)

8 cups cold water (see page 7)

Wipe the kelp with a moist, clean kitchen towel to remove any sand or impurities. Do not wipe off the white mannite powder.

Place the water and kelp in a large pot over medium heat. Heat the water until it reaches 140°F. Adjust the heat to carefully maintain the 140°F temperature and cook for 1 hour.

Remove the kelp from the water and reserve for a second stock preparation (see below).

Technique

SECONDARY KELP STOCK

The kelp that was used in the first round stock preparations (traditional easy and chef's method) can be used to make a second stock. Secondary Kelp Stock is weaker in flavor than the first-round stock, but is perfect for use in braising fish, poultry, and meat. To prepare, place the reserved kelp and 6 cups of water in a large pot and bring to a gentle simmer over medium heat. Decrease the heat to medium-low and cook for 15 minutes. Strain the stock through a sieve lined with a moist, sturdy paper towel to remove any impurities, then discard the kelp. Store Secondary Kelp Stock in the same way as instructed for the first-round kelp stock (page 6).

Kelp from Harvest to Table

Humble-looking dried kelp comes to your kitchen from afar and brings with it an inordinate amount of care by those who harvested and processed it. To make the high-quality kelp stock needed for preparing Japanese cuisine, a cook cannot use just any type of kelp that is simply harvested and left to dry on the beach. Most of the best-quality kelp comes from the cold waters of the northern part of Hokkaido Island. This kelp is typically about 6½ feet long and 4 to 6 inches wide, but some plants can grow as long as 60 feet.

Kelp is harvested in the early morning during a short period from mid-July through August. The harvested kelp leaves are spread out by hand—one after another—on pebble-covered sand beaches. Each day in the afternoon, the partially dried kelp is collected in bundles and brought into a barn for overnight storage before the humidity builds up on the beach. The next morning, the kelp is brought out again into the sunshine, and this drying process is repeated three times (or more if necessary), until the leaves are almost completely dried.

After this initial drying process, the kelp is brought out again, this time into the evening humidity so that the hard dried leaves soften for easy stretching in the next step. After returning the softened kelp to the barn, farmers roll the kelp leaves—one after another—into a tight roll (like a roll of toilet paper), resulting in a stretching of the leaves. Once again, the kelp leaves are stored. The stretched kelp is then unrolled and exposed to the sun for the final drying.

After completing this process, workers trim the kelp to prepare the final product. The finished leaves are sorted by size and quality and packed in designated boxes. This labor-intensive work lasts for about three weeks. When all the work is finished, a government maritime products board visits each kelp farmer to inspect and grade the products. But that's not the end! The wholesalers who purchase the boxed kelp from farmers then place the boxes in storage for about two years to mature and improve the flavor.

Today, in order to cut corners and increase production, much of Japan's kelp is farmed, artificially dried, and stretched by machine. However, kelp made by the traditional natural method provides much better flavor and nutritional value—a Premier Grand Cru class of quality than its modern counterpart. And, of course, as with wine, you pay for that Premier Grand Cru quality. I think it is more than worth it.

From left to right: Chilled
Edamame Soup, page 17; Beet
and Potato Soup, page 15;
Chilled Zucchini and Celeriac
Soup, page 16; White Bean,
Sausage, and Vegetable Soup
with Miso, page 46.

Spring Green Pea Soup

From late spring through early summer, freshly harvested, plump peas are available at my local farmers' market. These ephemeral peas are wonderfully sweet, moist, and crunchy, with a slightly grassy flavor. In this recipe, they are cooked in kelp stock, puréed, and flavored with miso. In Japan we call this type of soup *surinagashi*—similar to a puréed, creamy soup. But the Japanese version does not use dairy products, so the flavor of the peas is unmasked and enhanced by the umami-rich kelp stock.

Choose peas that are plump and bright green in color. Store the peas in their pods in a plastic bag in the refrigerator and use them within 2 days. After that, much of the peas' sweetness is lost, so cook any unused peas (shelled) in salted boiling water for 1 minute, and then shock them in ice water and freeze them for later use. This soup is excellent hot or cold.

MAKES 4 SERVINGS

4½ cups Kelp Stock (page 6) or low-sodium vegetable stock

2 cups fresh or frozen green peas

¾ cup coarsely chopped yellow onion

2 tablespoons medium-aged light brown miso (see page 12)

Sea salt

1 tablespoon chopped fresh parsley or chives or 8 young pea shoot leaves

Place the stock, peas, and onion in a medium pot, cover, and place over medium-high heat. Bring to a boil, reduce the heat to medium-low, and simmer for 20 minutes or until the vegetables are tender.

Working in 3 or 4 batches, transfer the broth and vegetables to a food processor or blender, and purée until smooth. (Note: Be very cautious when puréeing hot liquids. If using a blender, remove the plug in the top and cover the hole with a thick kitchen towel that's folded over. Do not fill the blender or food processor more than half full.) Transfer the first puréed batch to a clean pot and repeat the process. Add the miso to the last batch and process.

Before serving, gently reheat the soup, and divide it into soup bowls. Sprinkle a tiny pinch of salt over each portion (see page 14), garnish with the parsley, and serve.

MISO VARIETIES

Miso is a fermented product, like cheese. There are several varieties. When made from a combination of rice and soybeans, it is called *kome-miso*, while barley and soybean is called *mugi-miso* and soybeans alone, *mame-miso*. Ninety-five percent of the miso sold in America is *kome-miso*. *Kome-miso* and *mugi-miso* have different degrees of saltiness, color, and flavor according to the length of fermentation (very much like cheese). The mildest, pale white miso (*shiro-miso*) is aged for three to four weeks and has a very sweet and mild soybean flavor with mild saltiness. The salt content is about 5 percent, or ⅕ teaspoon of salt per 1 tablespoon of miso. Aged (or long-fermented) brown miso (*aka-miso*) is salty and the flavor is rich, complex, and robust. The salt content is about 13 percent, or ½ teaspoon salt per 1 tablespoon of miso. Medium-aged light brown miso—also called *shiro-miso*—falls between these two types. The salt content is about 10 percent, or ⅜ teaspoon of salt per 1 tablespoon of miso. For *mame-miso* there is only one choice—long aging. *Mame-miso* has a strong, distinctive dark color, like chocolate, and a bean-rich flavor, and it is firmer in texture than other varieties. The salt content is about 13 percent. For the recipes in Chapter 2, I sometimes blend two types of miso to make the flavor of traditional miso soups rich and fuller.

MISO SHOPPING AND STORAGE TIPS

Choosing one brand from among many types of miso at the supermarket or Japanese or Asian food store can be daunting. Most of the containers or bags are covered with detailed information in Japanese. Here is how to solve this problem. First, check the ingredients list on the English nutrition label. It should have this simple, short list: soybeans, rice or barley, and salt. You may sometimes see alcohol as an added preservative. Next, check the price. As with many food products, quality and price tend to correlate. When the item is *too* cheap, I always suspect that something is wrong. Choose a miso whose price is in the middle or somewhat higher range. Good-quality miso has gone through a proper, lengthy fermentation process and is not just salty brown paste. Such high-quality miso has both important nutrients and rich flavor and requires less volume to make flavorful dishes, while poor-quality, salty miso adds sodium and little else to your diet. You may store miso in the freezer for up to 6 months. Freezing does not change its texture or nutritional value.

Creamy Turnip Soup

In the past, I have enjoyed this soup made with a special variety of Japanese turnip called *Hakurei*. The *Hakurei* turnip is moister, sweeter, and more tender than the larger American turnip varieties but may not be as readily available. In adapting this recipe to American turnips, I was pleasantly surprised to discover a delicious yellow-tinged soup with a more robust turnip flavor.

Choose turnips that are plump, firm, and heavy for their size, and topped with crisp greens (if they come with greens). If the turnips do come with greens, immediately cut off the top stems and leaves so that the leaves no longer draw moisture from the bulb. Reserve those flavorful greens for miso soup or a salad.

Adding tofu creates an extra-smooth texture in the soup, and the olive oil contributes to a satisfying feel in the mouth. Japanese mustard adds interesting pungent and bitter flavors, perfect complements to the other flavors in the soup. This soup is excellent served hot or cold.

MAKES 4 SERVINGS

½ lemon

8 medium Hakurei or American turnip bulbs (1 pound), peeled

4 ounces celeriac (2 medium egg–size pieces), peeled

4 cups Kelp Stock (page 6) or low-sodium vegetable stock

½ teaspoon Japanese or Colman's mustard powder

1 teaspoon sea salt, plus more for finishing soup

1 tablespoon medium-aged light brown miso (see page 12)

2 tablespoons olive oil

About ½ block (6 ounces) soft tofu (optional)

½ cup finely shaved fennel bulb

¼ cup finely julienned turnip greens or minced fresh parsley

Squeeze the lemon into a medium bowl of water.

Coarsely chop the turnips and celeriac. As you cut the celeriac, place it in the lemon water to prevent browning.

Place the turnip, celeriac, and stock in a large pot over medium-high heat. Bring the stock to a boil, reduce the heat to medium-low, and simmer for 20 minutes or until the vegetables are tender.

Mix the mustard powder with ½ teaspoon hot water to create a paste. Set aside. Working in 3 or 4 batches, transfer the broth and vegetables to a blender or food processor, and purée until smooth. (Note: Be very cautious when puréeing hot liquids. If using a blender, remove the plug in the top and cover the hole with a thick kitchen towel that's folded over. Do not fill the blender or food processor more than half full.) Transfer the first puréed batch to a clean pot and repeat the process. In the last batch, add the salt, miso, olive oil, and tofu (if using), and process.

Before serving, gently reheat the soup, and divide it into soup bowls. Garnish with the fennel and turnip greens. Drop a tiny dab of mustard paste in the center of each bowl. Sprinkle a tiny pinch of salt over each portion (see page 14). Ask your guests to stir and dissolve the mustard paste into the soup before enjoying it.

How Salty Should It Be?

I always properly salt my food to my taste, including my soup, but my husband, Buzz, comments from time to time that it is under-salted. But I don't change the way I salt the dishes. Today everyone in America seems to expect a big punching flavor—too spiced, too salty, too sweet, and sometimes too acidic—from the start of the very first bite. If your soup tastes salty enough at the beginning, by the time you finish it you may be consuming too much sodium in one soup portion. From my point of view, the worst impact is that because of high salt content you are missing out on the taste of the natural flavors of ingredients in the soup. My trick to remedy this problem is that, after serving the prepared soup in individual soup bowls, I sprinkle in an additional pinch of salt. When the dinner guests take a first sip of the soup, this pinch of undiluted salt hits the tongue and creates the impression that the soup is properly salted to their satisfaction. After this initial experience, they seem to enjoy the true flavor of the soup through sipping the remaining portion with no additional salt. No one has ever complained that the soup needed more salt or was too salty. Try this trick at your table, and, for fun, after the diners finish the soup, ask them about the level of saltiness of the dish.

Technique

USING FINGERS AND EGG SIZE FOR MEASUREMENT

I learned some very convenient measuring tips from my mother, who did not have a kitchen scale or ruler in her kitchen. You can use these tips to speed up your cooking chores. I use my thumb and index fingertips to pick up ⅛ teaspoon salt, and adding my middle finger gives me about ¼ teaspoon. My mother's use of egg size for measuring is even more useful. A large egg weighs about 2 ounces. When she needed 3 ounces of diced onion, she peeled and cut an onion that was equivalent to about 150 percent of the large egg size. This method usually produces quite close enough value to the desired amount. A small egg is about 1½ ounces, a medium one is about 1¾ ounces, and a jumbo (extra-large) egg is about 2½ ounces. One more convenient measuring tip: The tip of my pinkie is a convenient 1-inch length. So when I need to cut food items into 1-inch or 2-inch pieces, my pinkie does the measuring job. My middle finger happens to be 3 inches long. How about yours?

Beet and Potato Soup

Although this soup is faintly reminiscent of Russian borscht, it has a decidedly Japanese character using readily available American ingredients, with the pungent bite of the Japanese mustard powder playing in counterpoint to the earthiness of the beets. I serve this soup with homemade crispy potato chips—a nod to the classical boiled potatoes in borscht—but good-quality bagged potato chips will work if you don't have the time to make any from scratch. This soup can be served hot or cold.

MAKES 4 SERVINGS

- 1 medium Yukon gold potato (about 7 ounces), peeled
- 5 medium red beets (12 ounces), peeled and coarsely chopped
- 4 ounces leeks (white part only) or yellow onions, cut into 1-inch-thick slices (about 1 cup)
- 4½ cups Kelp Stock (page 6) or low-sodium vegetable stock
- Canola oil, for frying
- Sea salt
- 1½ tablespoons medium-aged light brown miso (see page 12)
- ½ teaspoon Japanese or Colman's mustard powder
- 1 tablespoon finely minced fresh parsley

Coarsely chop one-third of the potato (5 ounces). With a mandoline or vegetable slicer, cut the remaining piece of potato into paper-thin slices and soak them in a bowl of cold water for 30 minutes. This process removes starch and makes the potato chips crispier once fried.

Place the chopped potato pieces, beets, leeks, and stock in a large pot, cover, and place over medium-high heat. Bring to a boil, reduce the heat to medium-low, and simmer for 25 minutes or until the vegetables are tender.

Meanwhile, drain the potato slices and dry them well on paper towels. Pour 1 inch of canola oil into a medium skillet and place over medium heat. When the oil reaches 350°F, add the potato slices in several batches and cook them until crisp and golden. Transfer the potato chips to paper towels to drain. Sprinkle a little salt over the potato chips.

Working in 3 or 4 batches, transfer the broth and vegetables to a blender or food processor, and purée until smooth. (Note: Be very cautious when puréeing hot liquids. If using a blender, remove the plug in the top and cover the hole with a thick kitchen towel that's folded over. Do not fill the blender or food processor more than half full.) Transfer the first puréed batch to a clean pot and repeat the process. In the last batch, add the miso and mustard powder and process.

Before serving, gently heat the soup and divide it into soup bowls. Garnish each bowl with a tiny pinch of salt (see page 14) and the parsley. Serve with the potato chips alongside.

Chilled Zucchini and Celeriac Soup

At our neighborhood farmers' market, zucchini comes in more whimsical shapes and colors than those in Japan, and they are bountiful and economical through the summer and into early fall. As with many other summer vegetables, zucchini contains quite a bit of water, which makes this soup particularly refreshing when served chilled on a hot summer day.

Choose zucchini that are young and small, as they are sweeter and contain fewer seeds. The olive oil creates a silky smooth texture. This soup can be served hot or cold.

MAKES 4 SERVINGS

- 2 small green zucchini (10 ounces)
- 2 small yellow zucchini (10 ounces)
- 4 ounces celeriac (2 medium egg–size pieces, peeled)
- 2 cloves garlic, peeled
- 4 cups Kelp Stock (page 6) or low-sodium vegetable stock
- 2 teaspoons sea salt, plus more for garnish
- 2 tablespoons olive oil
- 1 tablespoon finely minced fresh chives or green part of a scallion

Trim the ends of each zucchini. Cut a 2-inch piece off of each zucchini. Cut the 2-inch pieces into 1/8-inch dice (you should have 2 tablespoons of each color) and reserve to garnish the soup. Cut the rest of the zucchini into 1/2-inch slices; you should end up with 2 cups of each color.

Place the zucchini slices, celeriac, garlic cloves, and stock in a large pot, cover, and place over medium-high heat. Bring to a boil, decrease the heat to medium-low, and simmer for 20 minutes or until the vegetables are all tender.

Working in 3 or 4 batches, transfer the broth and vegetables to a blender or food processor and purée until smooth. (Note: Be very cautious when puréeing hot liquids. If using a blender, remove the plug in the top and cover the hole with a thick kitchen towel that's folded over. Do not fill the blender or food processor more than half full.) Transfer the first puréed batch to a clean pot (if serving hot) or a large bowl (if serving chilled) and repeat the process. In the last batch, add the salt and olive oil and process.

If serving hot, gently reheat the soup before serving and divide into soup bowls. If serving the soup chilled, cover the bowl with plastic wrap and place in the refrigerator. When ready to serve, divide into chilled soup bowls.

Garnish the soup with the diced green and yellow zucchini and the chives, sprinkle each bowl with a tiny pinch of salt (see page 14), and serve.

Chilled Edamame Soup

Simply boiled in salted water, fresh edamame, or green soybeans, are a favorite snack in Japan during the hot and steamy summer, and nothing is a better accompaniment to a cold glass of beer. Edamame have in recent years become a favorite in America as well.

I have added cucumber and green bell pepper to make this nourishing soup herbaceously flavorful. Either fresh or frozen edamame will work well in this recipe.

MAKES 4 SERVINGS

2 cups shelled fresh or frozen edamame

4 cups Kelp Stock (page 6) or low-sodium vegetable stock

1 large Kirby cucumber (3½ ounces), plus ¼ cup finely diced, for garnish

1 small green bell pepper (6 ounces), seeded and white ribs removed

1½ tablespoons medium-aged light brown miso (see page 12)

2 tablespoons julienned *shiso* (perilla) leaves or minced fresh chives

Sea salt

Place the edamame and stock in a medium pot, cover, and place over medium heat. Bring to a boil, decrease the heat to medium-low, and simmer for 6 minutes. Cut off both ends of the whole cucumber and cut the cucumber and green bell pepper into rough pieces.

Working in 3 or 4 batches, transfer the broth, edamame, cucumber, and green pepper to a blender or food processor and purée until smooth. (Note: Be very cautious when puréeing hot liquids. If using a blender, remove the plug in the top and cover the hole with a thick kitchen towel that's folded over. Do not fill the blender or food processor more than half full.)

Transfer the first puréed batch to a large bowl and repeat the process. In the last batch, add the miso and process. Stir the soup, cover with plastic wrap, and refrigerate. Divide the soup into chilled soup bowls. Garnish with the diced cucumber and shiso. Sprinkle a tiny pinch of sea salt (see page 14) over each soup bowl and serve.

Spiced Kabocha Squash Soup

This spicy, slightly sweet, and richly textured soup is a wonderful addition to a Thanksgiving meal, but its warming satisfaction can be enjoyed throughout the fall and winter. Kabocha squash is loaded with nutrients, so much so that in Japan there is a saying: "Eating kabocha on the first day of winter keeps you from catching a cold." Because uncooked kabocha squash can be difficult to cut, I bake the whole squash, wrapped in aluminum foil, in the oven for about 1½ hours, until very tender.

MAKES 4 SERVINGS

1 medium kabocha squash (2 to 3 pounds); substitute butternut squash if you cannot find kabocha

1 medium carrot (4 ounces), peeled and cut into 1-inch pieces

1 small leek, white part only (2 ounces), cut into 1-inch pieces (⅔ cup)

4 cups Kelp Stock (page 6) or low-sodium vegetable stock

2 tablespoons ginger juice, from grated 2 thumb–size piece of ginger

½ teaspoon ground cinnamon

¼ teaspoon ground nutmeg

1½ tablespoons medium-aged light brown miso (see page 12)

½ teaspoon sea salt, plus more for finishing soup

¼ cup olive oil

2 tablespoons pumpkin seeds, toasted

Preheat the oven to 400°F.

Rinse the kabocha squash and wrap it in aluminum foil. Put the squash in the oven and bake for 1½ hours. Remove the squash from the oven and carefully remove the foil. Cut the squash in half and remove the seeds with a spoon, removing as little pulp as possible. Scoop out the pulp into a large bowl and measure out 2⅓ cups of cooked squash. Freeze any extra pulp for later use, such as the recipe for Kabocha and Lamb Wonton Pot Stickers on page 197. Reserve ¼ cup of the green skin, julienned, for garnish.

Place the carrot, leek, and stock in a medium pot, cover, and place over medium-high heat. Bring to a boil, decrease the heat to medium-low, and simmer for 25 minutes or until the vegetables are tender.

Working in 3 or 4 batches, transfer the broth and cooked vegetables along with the pulp of the squash to a blender or food processor, and purée until smooth. (Note: Be very cautious when puréeing hot liquids. If using a blender, remove the plug in the top and cover the hole with a thick kitchen towel that's folded over. Do not fill the blender or food processor more than half full.) Transfer the first puréed batch to a clean pot and repeat the process. In the last batch, add the ginger juice, cinnamon, nutmeg, miso, salt, and olive oil and process.

Before serving, gently reheat the soup and divide it into soup bowls. Sprinkle a tiny pinch of salt into each bowl (see page 14), garnish each bowl with the julienned green squash skin and pumpkin seeds, and serve.

Cauliflower and Leek Soup

When I begin to see huge heads of cauliflower at very economical prices at our farmers' market toward the middle of autumn, I think of this soup. I make and enjoy it with my family throughout the autumn and early winter season. Do not throw away the healthy green stems; use them in the soup. For the best quality in future cauliflower dishes, boil any unused cauliflower to a still quite firm level and freeze it, rather than keeping it unused for a long time in the refrigerator.

MAKES 4 SERVINGS

1 medium cauliflower (1 pound)

1½ small leeks, white part only (about 4 ounces), cleaned and cut into 1-inch pieces (1 cup)

4 cups Kelp Stock (page 6) or low-sodium vegetable stock

2 tablespoons medium-aged light brown miso (see page 12)

½ teaspoon sea salt, plus more for finishing soup

1 tablespoon olive oil

Pinch of Japanese curry powder or Madras curry powder

Cut 8 small florets from the cauliflower head and reserve for garnish. Coarsely chop the rest of the cauliflower head, including the healthy green leaves if you have them. Place the cauliflower, leeks, and stock in a medium pot, cover, and place over medium-high heat. Bring to a boil, decrease the heat to medium-low, and cook for 25 minutes or until the vegetables are tender.

Working in 3 or 4 batches, transfer the broth and vegetables to a blender or food processor and purée until smooth. (Note: Be very cautious when puréeing hot liquids. If using a blender, remove the plug in the top and cover the hole with a thick kitchen towel that's folded over. Do not fill the blender or food processor more than half full.) Transfer the first puréed batch to a clean pot and repeat the process. In the last batch, add the miso and salt and process.

Cut the reserved cauliflower florets into thin slices lengthwise. Transfer the cauliflower slices along with any small broken bits to a bowl and toss with the olive oil, curry powder, and a pinch of salt. Heat a medium skillet over high heat until hot. Add the cauliflower and cook until lightly golden, stirring occasionally.

Reheat the soup and divide it into soup bowls. Garnish with the sautéed cauliflower. Sprinkle a tiny pinch of salt (see page 14) over each soup bowl and serve.

How to Cook Rice in a Pot on a Stovetop

I cook all varieties of rice: polished white and unpolished brown; short-, medium-, and long-grain. All rice needs a good rinsing before cooking to remove dust, starch, and any impurities from the milling process, and if possible it should be properly soaked before cooking. The soaking process lets each grain of rice absorb water to some degree. This results in evenly cooked rice that is plump and moist in the center of each grain. Cooking rice on the stovetop is easy, and it takes less time than preparing it in a commercial rice cooker. You will need a 2- or 3-quart heavy pot equipped with a heavy, tight-fitting lid. The pot should be narrow and tall, not fat and shallow. Here are general cooking instructions and tips.

TYPE OF RICE	DRY RICE VOLUME	WATER VOLUME (120% of the volume of dry rice)*
Polished white (short-, medium-, long-grain)	**2¼ cups**	120% of the volume of dry rice **2⅘ cups**
Unpolished brown (short-, medium-, long-grain)	**2¼ cups**	200% of the volume of dry rice **4½ cups**

* When cooking rice with other ingredients, follow the water volume specified in each recipe, not the values in this chart.

MAKES 4 TO 6 SERVINGS

RINSING RICE: Pour the measured rice into a fine-mesh sieve so that the rice grains will not escape during rinsing. Make sure it is large enough to comfortably hold the entire portion of rice. Fill a large bowl in which the sieve can loosely sit with plenty of cold tap water. Lower the sieve into the bowl and submerge the rice completely in the water. Gently rub the rice grains between your palms under the water for 30 seconds. The water will quickly become milky. Remove the sieve from the water and discard the water. Fill the bowl with plenty of fresh cold tap water and repeat the rinsing process two or three times. Drain the rice.

SOAKING RICE: Transfer the drained rice to the pot in which you are going to cook it. Add the measured clean, cold tap water and let it stand for 30 minutes. When you cook rice with other ingredients, you must drain the soaked rice and dry it in a sieve for 20 minutes before cooking in order to obtain firmer-textured rice at the end.

COOKING

TYPE OF RICE	
Polished white (short-, medium-, long-grain)	1. Cook the rice, covered, over high heat for 3 minutes or until the boiling water begins to spill out between the lid and the pot. 2. Immediately lower the heat to medium-low so that the spilling stops. Keep up the brisk cooking inside the pot; the liquid may spill over slightly, but that is okay. If the heat is too low, proper cooking will not occur. Cook the rice for about 7 minutes. **Tip:** Toward the end of the cooking time, you can quickly lift up the lid and check to see whether the water is almost absorbed by the rice. The rice should look shiny and moist. If so, then proceed with Step 3. If the rice is dry, the heat was too high and the bottom may be burnt in the succeeding cooking process. So sprinkle ¼ cup of water evenly over the rice, and follow the next step. 3. Decrease the heat to very low and cook the rice for 10 minutes. 4. Leave the cooked rice, covered, for 5 minutes before serving.
Unpolished brown (short-, medium-, long-grain)	1. Cook the rice, covered, over high heat for 6 minutes or until the boiling water begins to spill out between the lid and the pot. 2. Immediately lower the heat to medium-low so that the spilling stops. Keep up the brisk cooking inside the pot; the liquid may spill over slightly, but that is okay. If the heat is too low, proper cooking will not occur. Cook the rice for 15 to 16 minutes. 3. Lower the heat to very low and cook the rice for 15 minutes. 4. Leave the cooked rice, covered, for 5 minutes before serving.

A RICE COOKER CAN BE A SAVIOR

Using a commercial rice cooker offers a totally different level of comfort when cooking rice. You do not need to constantly watch the pot, adjust the heat, or track the cooking time. Today's high-quality rice cookers are very smart, with sensors and computer-controlled functions. The very latest—and most expensive—models use induction heat technology. If you have a rice cooker with sensors, computer-controlled functions or induction heat technology, omit the soaking step. These advanced rice cookers can cook all varieties of rice: short-, medium-, and long-grain, both polished white rice and unpolished brown rice, and regular or sticky rice (also called sweet rice).

When using a rice cooker, be sure to use the measuring cup that comes with the machine to measure your dry rice. For example, $2\frac{1}{4}$ cups of dry rice equals 3 rice cooker cups of dry rice. After rinsing and soaking, place the drained rice in the bowl of the rice cooker. Pour in the cold cooking liquid (water or stock) to the level shown on the inside of the bowl for the type of rice you are preparing. Close the lid, press the start button, and relax. The musical jingle will tell you when your rice is perfectly done, and most rice cookers will automatically keep the rice warm for many hours without overcooking it. For the sake of satisfaction and sanity, a high-functioning model is a worthwhile expenditure.

Spring Green Pea Rice

Takikomi gohan is a type of comfort food in which rice is cooked together with vegetables, seafood, chicken, and/or meat. It is the Japanese equivalent of Spanish paella, Italian risotto, or Cajun jambalaya, although the Japanese version typically does not use any oil.

Takikomi gohan rice dishes celebrate a particular time of year in which special seasonal delicacies are the focus. In this recipe, the rice is cooked with just-harvested springtime peas, which lend a sweet and delicate flavor and fragrance to the dish. The rice takes on not only the sweet taste and springtime fragrance of the peas but also the energy of the sun and the earth in which the peas were grown.

MAKES 6 SERVINGS

2¼ cups short- or medium-grain polished white rice (for rice cooker: 3 rice cooker cups)

1⅛ cups fresh or frozen green peas

1¾ teaspoons sea salt

2½ cups Kelp Stock (page 6) or low-sodium vegetable stock

1 thumb-size piece ginger (1 ounce), peeled

2 large eggs

2 teaspoons sugar

2 teaspoons canola oil or vegetable oil

1 tablespoon white sesame seeds, toasted

Rinse and soak the rice according to the instructions on page 20. Drain the rice and let it stand in a fine-mesh sieve for 20 minutes to dry.

Place the peas, ⅛ teaspoon of salt, and the stock into a small pot and cook over low heat for 5 minutes (3 minutes for frozen peas). While the peas are cooking, prepare a large bowl of ice water. Transfer the peas and stock to a medium metal bowl and place the bowl in the large bowl of ice water to quickly cool the peas and stock. Drain the peas through a sieve placed over a bowl, reserving the stock in the bowl. Transfer the peas to a cup. Check that you have 2½ cups of the kelp stock in which the peas were cooked. If not, add additional water to make 2½ cups of liquid.

In a medium heavy pot, place the drained rice, the 2½ cups reserved stock, and 1½ teaspoons of the salt. Cover the pot and cook the rice as instructed on page 21. Alternatively, if using a rice cooker, follow the instructions on page 22.

While the rice is cooking, cut the ginger into 1½-inch-long julienne strips. Break the eggs in a bowl and lightly beat them with the sugar, the remaining ⅛ teaspoon salt, and the canola oil. Heat a medium nonstick skillet (do not add oil) over medium-low heat and add the egg liquid. Scramble the eggs until they are fairly dry and crumbled. Turn off the heat and transfer the eggs to a small bowl.

When the rice is finished cooking, carefully remove the lid of the pot and add the peas, julienned ginger, and scrambled eggs on top of the rice. Do not stir the rice at this time. Cover the pot with the lid and let the rice stand for 10 minutes.

To complete the dish, add the sesame seeds and gently stir the rice with a spatula. Divide the rice into small bowls and serve.

Salmon in Fennel Rice

This *takikomi gohan*—rice with a variety of added ingredients—is a complete meal in one bowl. Salmon, fennel bulb, and dill infuse the rice, creating an easy-to-prepare (almost), one-pot delicious dish. For variety, you can substitute sweet young asparagus in the spring, hulled fresh corn during the summer, mushrooms in autumn, and cabbage in winter for the fennel bulb. This dish goes well with a nice salad or bowl of soup.

MAKES 6 SERVINGS

2¼ cups short-, medium-, or long-grain polished white rice (for rice cooker: 3 rice cooker cups)

8 ounces salmon fillet with scaled skin-on

2 teaspoons sea salt

2½ cups Kelp Stock (page 6) or low-sodium vegetable stock

1 teaspoon shoyu (soy sauce)

1½ tablespoons sake (rice wine) or dry white wine

1 tablespoon mirin (sweet cooking wine)

1½ ounces fennel bulb, thinly sliced (½ cup)

1½ ounces ginger, julienned (½ cup)

⅓ cup chopped fresh dill

Rinse and soak the rice according to the instructions on page 20. Drain the rice and let it stand in a fine-mesh sieve for 20 minutes to dry.

Season the salmon on both sides with ½ teaspoon of the salt and let it stand for 20 minutes to extrude excess water. Rinse the salmon under cold water and wipe it dry with paper towels. Heat a medium nonstick skillet over medium heat, then place the salmon in the skillet skin side down, and cook it until the skin side is golden, about 1 minute. Carefully turn the fish over and cook the other side until it is golden, about 1 minute. Transfer the salmon to a plate.

Place the drained rice and stock in a medium heavy pot. Add the soy sauce, sake, mirin, and the remaining 1½ teaspoons salt. Evenly sprinkle the fennel and half of the ginger over the rice. Do not stir. Place the salmon, skin side up, on top of the rice. Cover the pot with a lid and cook the rice as instructed on page 21. Alternatively, if using a rice cooker, follow the instructions on page 22.

After the rice is cooked, remove the lid. Use a fork to remove the salmon skin and discard. Sprinkle the remaining ginger and the dill over the rice, close the lid, and let the rice stand for 10 minutes. Remove the lid and use a fork to break the salmon into small pieces. Then use a spatula to gently toss the rice with the salmon, ginger, and dill. Divide the rice into small bowls and serve.

Corn and Ginger Rice with Shoyu and Butter

The combination of corn, shoyu (soy sauce), and butter in this recipe may make you think I have strayed far from Japanese cooking, unless you're aware that excellent sweet corn and high-quality butter are produced on Hokkaido, the northern island of Japan. This combination—corn, butter, and shoyu—is not at all alien today to my native cuisine. Try the dish with just-harvested moist, sweet summer corn, and I guarantee you and all your fellow diners will love it.

MAKES 6 SERVINGS

2¼ cups short- or medium-grain polished white rice (for rice cooker: 3 rice cooker cups)

2 ears corn

2½ cups Kelp Stock (page 6) or low-sodium vegetable stock

1 teaspoon sea salt

1½ ounces ginger, julienned (½ cup)

1 tablespoon shoyu (soy sauce)

3 tablespoons unsalted or salted butter

Rinse and soak the rice according to the instructions on page 20. Drain the rice and let it stand in a fine-mesh sieve for 20 minutes to dry.

Remove the corn husks and quickly grill the ears over a medium open flame on a gas stove, turning them until the entire surface becomes golden. If you do not have a gas stovetop, boil the corn in salted water for 1 minute. Cut each ear of corn in half. Place each half ear on the cut end in a large, shallow bowl, and use a knife to separate the individual kernels from the cob. Repeat with all the pieces. This will produce about 1½ cups of corn kernels.

Place the drained rice and the stock in a medium heavy pot. Sprinkle the corn kernels, salt, and ginger evenly over the rice. Do not stir the rice. Cover the pot with a lid and cook the rice as instructed on page 21. Alternatively, if using a rice cooker, follow the instructions on page 22.

When the rice is cooked, let it stand undisturbed for 10 minutes. Remove the lid and add the soy sauce and butter. With a spatula, gently and quickly toss and mix the rice. Divide the rice into small bowls and serve.

Hearty Mushroom and Salsify Rice

Salsify is a root vegetable that has the appearance of a thin wooden stick just pulled out of the soil. It has no visual appeal whatsoever, but it is rich in dietary fiber and has a firm texture and pleasant, earthy flavor. In Japan, we use a cousin of this vegetable, called *gobo* (burdock). I have found that salsify at the local farmers' market is somewhat superior in flavor and texture to its Japanese cousin. Select salsify that is heavy for its size and firm to the touch. After purchase, rinse the root with cold water, dry it, wrap it in a moist paper towel, and store it in a plastic bag in the refrigerator. The skin of this root is very thin, so before using it, scrub off the skin; I use a *tawashi* (a Japanese natural bristle brush). A peeler also does a good job, but try not to remove too much skin.

MAKES 6 SERVINGS

2¼ cups short- or medium-grain brown rice (for rice cooker: 3 rice cooker cups)

2 tablespoons dried black trumpet mushrooms or other dried mushrooms

4½ cups Kelp Stock (page 6) or low-sodium vegetable stock (optional)

2 ounces salsify (1 inch in diameter and 8 inches long)

4 large button mushrooms (4 ounces)

5 ounces boneless pork chops

1 teaspoon sea salt

1 tablespoon plus 1 teaspoon canola oil or vegetable oil

½ cup raisins

½ cup chopped yellow onion

2 teaspoons chopped garlic

1 tablespoon Japanese curry powder or Madras curry powder

1 teaspoon shoyu (soy sauce)

1 tablespoon mirin (sweet cooking wine)

¼ cup chopped fresh parsley

Rinse and soak the rice according to the instructions on page 20. Drain the rice and let it stand in a fine-mesh sieve for 20 minutes to dry.

Soak the black trumpet mushrooms in 1 cup of the stock for 10 minutes, or until pliable. With a peeler or hard brush, remove only the thin skin of the salsify, not the core meat. Then use the peeler to slice off long strips of salsify, and cut the strips into 2-inch lengths. Remove the stems of the button mushrooms and cut the mushrooms into thin slices. Drain the black trumpet mushrooms, reserving the soaking liquid, and finely chop them.

Lightly season the pork with ¼ teaspoon of the salt on both sides. Heat 1 teaspoon of the canola oil in a large skillet over medium heat. Place the pork in the skillet and cook it for 1 to 1½ minutes, or until the bottom is lightly golden. Turn the pork over and cook the other side until lightly golden. Transfer the pork to a cutting board (the pork will not be cooked through), and cut it into ⅓-inch dice. Transfer the pork to a bowl and add the raisins. In the skillet that was used for browning the pork, heat the remaining 1 tablespoon canola oil over medium-low heat. When it is hot, add the onion and cook for 1½ minutes, or until soft. Add both types of mushrooms and the salsify, and increase the heat to high. Cook the mixture, stirring constantly, for 2 minutes or until the mushrooms wilt. Add the garlic and curry powder and cook for 20 seconds. Turn off the heat.

Place the drained rice, stock (including the reserved stock used to soak the mushrooms), soy sauce, mirin, and the remaining ¾ teaspoon salt in a medium pot. Sprinkle the onion-mushroom mixture evenly on top of the rice, then follow with the pork and raisins. Do not stir the rice. Cover the pot and cook the rice as instructed on page 21. Alternatively, if using a rice cooker, follow the instructions on page 22.

After the rice is cooked, let it stand for 5 minutes. Remove the lid, add the parsley, and gently stir the rice with a spatula. Divide the rice into small bowls and serve.

Glazed Chicken Meatballs

These flavorful chicken meatballs are quite versatile. They are also used in the Napa Cabbage and Chicken Meatballs in Miso Soup (page 45) and the Spicy Sausage, Chicken Meatballs, and Tomatoes (page 30) to produce quick, easy, and satisfying meals. So when you make the chicken meatballs, double or triple the recipe. Finely mince the carrots, scallions, shiitake mushrooms, ginger, and garlic to produce the best flavor and texture for your meatballs. Use a vegetable chopper, if you have one, for a quick mincing of these vegetables.

**MAKES 4 TO 6 SERVINGS
(18 CHICKEN MEATBALLS)**

1 pound ground chicken, preferably mixture of breast and leg and not too lean

¼ cup finely minced scallions (white and green parts), plus 2 tablespoons thinly sliced green part

2½ tablespoons finely minced shiitake mushrooms

2 tablespoons finely minced carrot

1 tablespoon finely minced ginger

1 tablespoon plus 2 teaspoons finely minced garlic

1¾ teaspoons sea salt

1 large egg, lightly beaten

½ cup rice vinegar

½ cup Kelp Stock (page 6) or low-sodium vegetable stock

2 tablespoons sugar

1 teaspoon shoyu (soy sauce)

½ teaspoon toban jiang (fermented chile bean sauce) or sriracha chile sauce

1 to 2 tablespoons canola oil or vegetable oil

1 tablespoon cornstarch mixed with 1 tablespoon water

In a large bowl with clean hands or a fork, thoroughly mix the ground chicken with 2 tablespoons of the minced scallions, shiitake mushrooms, carrot, ½ tablespoon of the ginger, 1 tablespoon of the garlic, 1¼ teaspoons of the salt, and the egg. Cover the bowl with plastic wrap and let it stand in the refrigerator for 20 minutes for easy handling in the next step.

Bring a large pot of water to a boil and have a small cup of very cold water on hand. Place the chicken mixture next to the pot of boiling water. Dip two soupspoons into the cold water and shake them to remove excess water. With one of the soupspoons, scoop out roughly 2 tablespoons of the chicken mixture. With the other soupspoon, shape the chicken mixture into a ball and gently drop it into the boiling water. Continue to make and add the meatballs until you have 6 or 7 of them. Cook them for 2 minutes, or until the outside is firm. With a slotted spoon, transfer the cooked chicken meatballs to a colander to drain. Repeat until the entire chicken mixture is finished cooking and draining. You can freeze the meatballs at this stage for up to 3 months.

In a small bowl, mix the vinegar, stock, sugar, soy sauce, the remaining ½ teaspoon of salt, and the toban jiang. Heat the canola oil in a large skillet over medium heat. Add the meatballs, turning them from time to time, cooking them until all surfaces are golden, about 4 minutes. Transfer the meatballs to a platter. Add the remaining 2 tablespoons minced scallions, the remaining ½ tablespoon ginger, and the remaining 2 teaspoons garlic to the skillet and increase the heat to medium-high. Cook the scallions and garlic for 20 seconds, stirring. Add the vinegar-stock liquid to the skillet, stirring for 1 minute to dissolve the sugar. Turn off the heat, add the cornstarch slurry to the skillet, and with a whisk mix until thoroughly blended. Turn the heat back to low and cook for 2 minutes, stirring. Return the chicken meatballs to the skillet and toss them with the sauce. Stir in the thinly sliced scallions, divide the chicken meatballs into small serving bowls, and serve.

Chorizo and Shrimp Rice

My teaching trips to Spain have inspired this combination of Spanish chorizo and shrimp *takikomi gohan*. I often make a double batch and freeze some for a quick and satisfying lunch. In this recipe, I use wholesome brown rice, but this dish is also very good with polished white rice. If you are able to buy shrimp in the shell, reserve the shells (and heads) and make a stock by boiling them in 2 cups of water for 25 minutes. Then strain and use as a substitute for the bottled clam juice in this recipe.

MAKES 6 SERVINGS

2¼ cups long- or medium-grain brown rice (for rice cooker: 3 rice cooker cups)

6 ounces uncooked spicy Italian pork sausage or 3 ounces Spanish-style cured chorizo

10 ounces small shrimp, shelled and deveined (19 to 20 shrimp)

2 cloves garlic, peeled

1 tablespoon canola oil or vegetable oil

½ cup chopped yellow onion

Pinch of saffron

1 cup clam juice

3½ cups Kelp Stock (page 6) or low-sodium vegetable stock

1 cup fresh or frozen green peas

1 teaspoon sea salt

¼ cup peeled and thinly sliced ginger

Rinse and soak the rice according to the instructions on page 20. Drain the rice and let it stand in a fine-mesh sieve for 20 minutes to dry.

Place the spicy Italian pork sausage, whole, in a pot of boiling water for 3 minutes (you don't need to precook the Spanish-style cured chorizo), then drain and set aside. Cut the shrimp diagonally into halves crosswise. Cut the garlic into thin slices. Heat the canola oil in a skillet over medium-low heat. When the oil is hot, add the onion, and cook for 2 minutes or until transparent. Increase the heat to medium, add the garlic and saffron, and cook for 20 seconds. Add the shrimp and cook just until the shrimp turns white.

Place the drained rice, clam juice, and stock in a medium pot. Level the surface of the rice and evenly scatter the onion and shrimp mixture on top of the rice, then follow with the whole chorizo, green peas, and salt. Do not stir the rice. Cover the pot with a lid and cook the rice as instructed on page 21. Alternatively, if using a rice cooker, follow the instructions on page 22.

After the rice is cooked, carefully remove the lid and transfer the whole chorizo or sausage to a cutting board. Cut the chorizo or sausage into ½-inch dice. Scatter the chorizo or sausage pieces on top of the rice along with the sliced ginger. Do not stir the rice at this time. Immediately cover the pot and let the rice stand for 10 minutes. Then remove the lid and gently fold the rice and ingredients together with a spatula. Divide the rice into small bowls and serve.

Spicy Sausage, Chicken Meatballs, and Tomatoes

This is a delightful meal-in-one-pot dish. Kelp stock, tomatoes, chicken meatballs, sausage, and shoyu (soy sauce) mingle together to orchestrate a wonderful world of umami-rich flavor. The idea of the dish comes from traditional Japanese hot-pot dishes, *nabemono* (see page 31). *Nabemono* are cooked at the table over a portable gas burner, but this dish is prepared in the kitchen. Fresh Italian pork sausage works best in this recipe, providing rich flavor.

MAKES 6 SERVINGS

2 large beefsteak tomatoes (16 to 18 ounces total)

1 large fennel bulb (about 10 ounces)

1 bunch Swiss chard (about 1 pound)

1½ pounds uncooked Italian pork sausage, hot or sweet or a combination of the two, as desired

2 cups Kelp Stock (page 6) or low-sodium vegetable stock

2 cups water

¼ cup sake (rice wine)

¼ cup plus 2 teaspoons shoyu (soy sauce)

18 meatballs from the Glazed Chicken Meatballs recipe (page 27)

2 tablespoons chopped fresh cilantro

1 large lemon, halved

Bring a medium pot of water to a boil. Cut the tomatoes into 8 wedges and set aside. Cut the fennel bulb crosswise into ¼-inch-thick slices. Cut off the bottom hard stems of the Swiss chard and cut the rest crosswise into 2-inch slices. Boil the Swiss chard and fennel bulb in water for 1 minute. With a slotted spoon, transfer the Swiss chard and fennel to a colander, and quickly rinse under cold tap water.

Prick the surface of the sausage with a toothpick or fork and add it to the boiling water. Cook for 2 minutes. Drain the sausage, discard the cooking liquid, and rinse the sausage with cold tap water.

Place the stock, water, sake, and soy sauce in a large pot over medium heat and bring to a boil. Add the sausage and chicken meatballs, and bring the mixture to a simmer. Decrease the heat to low and cook, covered, for about 15 minutes. Add the tomatoes, Swiss chard, and fennel, and cook for 5 minutes longer.

Transfer the sausage to a cutting board and cut it diagonally into ½-inch slices. Divide the sausage, meatballs, and vegetables into soup bowls. Pour a portion of the broth into each of the bowls. Garnish with the cilantro. Squeeze lemon juice over each bowl and serve.

Nabemono, Winter Favorite

Nabemono refers to a dish in which the diners themselves cook the assorted raw or partially cooked ingredients in stock (either unflavored or lightly flavored) in a large ceramic or iron pot set over a portable stove at the table. Sukiyaki and shabu-shabu, some of the most well-known Japanese dishes in America, are representative of this preparation technique. The ingredients are cut into chopstick-manageable sizes before they are brought to the table. Before being consumed piping-hot, each cooked item is usually dipped in one of a variety of fully flavored sauces. *Nabemono* is winter fare, and each prefecture in Japan boasts its own special variety prepared with its own local winter delicacies; for example, there is crab in Hokkaido, cod and its male organ in Aomori, monkfish in Ibaraki, tuna and naganegi green onion in Tokyo, blowfish in Osaka, oyster and miso in Hiroshima, meat organs in Fukuoka, and jidori chicken (see page 96) in Nagoya. *Nabemono* is the perfect way to enjoy a balanced meal. There is always a main player in the dish, which can be seafood, meat, chicken, or tofu. The main ingredient is cooked with a wide variety of assorted seasonal vegetables. The ultimate joy of *nabemono* dining is to finish the meal by cooking precooked rice or udon noodles in the remaining broth, which has by that point been infused with rich flavors from all the previous ingredients that were cooked.

Technique

RINSING OFF THE FAT

When I braise meat, I first brown it in a skillet, then quickly rinse it with hot water. This process cleans the meat and removes excess fat and burnt bits attached to the surface of the meat. I put the cleaned meat along with its cooking liquid in a clean pot and then braise it. This process surprises my fellow American chefs and cooks, and they say, "Don't rinse off the good flavor from the meat!" But I know better; I'm only rinsing off the bad burnt stuff, not the flavor. An additional benefit of rinsing meat after browning is that it reduces the foam that rises during cooking, and this means fewer off-tasting impurities. The result is food that tastes very clean and light. Try this technique for yourself and see if you agree.

Sake-Braised Short Ribs

The gorgeous appearance of these sake-braised short ribs is reminiscent of the dish's popular sister, American-style braised short ribs. (Sake for cooking, see page 34.) But the flavor of this dish is distinctively Japanese, and the dish is lighter and easier on the stomach than the American version. The traditional Japanese *buta no kakuni*—braised pork belly flavored with sugar and shoyu (soy sauce)—offers a similar flavor experience. In my recipe, I use readily available short ribs and Worcestershire sauce, a staple of Japanese cooking for more than 100 years. By cooking and refrigerating this dish a day ahead of time, you can remove coagulated fat from the top of the meat broth and allow the flavors to mingle. Serve the dish with some crusty bread to enjoy the sauce left on your plate.

MAKES 6 SERVINGS

7 tablespoons shoyu (soy sauce)

5 tablespoons honey

3 tablespoons Worcestershire sauce

1 tablespoon red pepper flakes

5 to 5½ pounds bone-in short ribs (about 6 whole bones)

2 tablespoons canola oil or vegetable oil

1 cup sake (rice wine)

2 cups Kelp Stock (page 6) or low-sodium vegetable stock

2 tablespoons sugar

1 bunch Swiss chard with white stems (about 1 pound)

6 cipollini onions, peeled

12 prunes

1 tablespoon rice vinegar

6 cherry tomatoes

Crusty bread, for serving

In a large bowl, combine 6 tablespoons of the soy sauce, the honey, Worcestershire sauce, and red pepper flakes. Add the short ribs to the sauce and marinate for 2 hours.

Heat the oven to 325°F. Bring a medium pot of water to a boil. Remove the short ribs from the marinade and wipe them with paper towels, reserving the marinade. Place the canola oil in a large skillet over medium heat and add half the meat. Cook the ribs until all sides are golden brown, 4 to 6 minutes total. Transfer the browned short ribs to a sieve, and lower the ribs into the boiling water. Quickly swish the ribs in the water and remove them, discarding the water after both batches of ribs have been cooked and washed (see page 31).

Combine the sake and stock in a large pot over medium heat and bring it to a simmer. Add the sugar and the ribs (in a single layer) and bring the mixture to a gentle boil. Cover the pot with a lid, transfer it to the oven, and cook the short ribs for 1 hour.

Cut the Swiss chard in half lengthwise along the center of the stems, and then crosswise into 2-inch slices. Bring a medium pot of salted water to a boil (see page 14). Add the Swiss chard and cook for 1 minute. With a slotted spoon, transfer the Swiss chard to a colander to drain and air-dry. Add the cipollini onions to the boiling water and cook for 2 minutes. With a slotted spoon, transfer the onions to the colander with the Swiss chard.

Continued

Remove the pot of short ribs from the oven and transfer it to the stovetop. Add the reserved marinade to the pot and cook, covered, over medium-low heat for 15 minutes. Add the prunes and cipollini onions and cook for 15 minutes longer. Toward the end of the cooking time, taste the cooking liquid and, if desired, add the remaining 1 tablespoon soy sauce.

Remove the beef, prunes, and onions from the cooking liquid and place them in a bowl. Transfer the cooking liquid into a gravy separator to remove the excess fat. Return the cooking liquid to the pot (you will have about 2 cups) and add the vinegar. Cook the liquid over medium heat, uncovered, until it is reduced to two-thirds of its previous volume. Return the short rib , prunes, and onions to the pot, and add the Swiss chard and tomatoes. Cook the short ribs and vegetables, covered, over low heat for 5 minutes, or until the ribs and vegetables are heated through. Divide the meat and vegetables among dinner plates and pour the remaining cooking liquid over them. Serve the dish with crusty bread.

Technique

SAKE FOR COOKING

We seem to use alcohol, in the form of sake (rice wine), in Japanese preparations more frequently than French cooks with red or white wine. However, the amount added to each recipe is usually quite small—a couple of tablespoons or so. There are so-called "cooking sakes" available at many Japanese and Asian food stores, but they are the same as very low-quality "cooking wine." They often contain many unnecessary ingredients such as salt to prevent them from being consumed as beverages. So avoid these, and instead use an inexpensive or moderately priced bottle of drinkable sake. The one I use happens to be among the cheapest available. I keep this grade of sake just for cooking. I buy the largest available bottle (1.8 liters) for about $10 at a discount store. I transfer it to several tall, clean bottles for easy storage, refrigerate them, and use the sake within 1½ months. If you want to consume this style of sake, I recommend that you warm it to about 95°F in order to bring out the sweetness and aroma. To warm sake, transfer it to a heat-resistant glass or porcelain flask and then put the container into a pot of gently simmering water. Do not heat sake directly in a pot on the stovetop.

Sake-Steamed Clams

Steaming carefully cleaned clams in kelp broth with sake brings out their best taste and natural sweetness. Look for very fresh clams at the market, and be sure to transport them in an open bag to avoid suffocating them. To clean the clams, prepare a bowl of saltwater that has the same salt content as seawater (3 percent by weight, which is a little less than 1 tablespoon of salt per 2 cups of water). Put the clams in a strainer so they are just covered by the saltwater. Place the bowl in a dark, cool, and quiet place for 2 hours so the clams can relax and expel impurities and sand from their systems.

MAKES 4 SERVINGS

2 pounds littleneck or other hard-shell clams

Sea salt

1 cup sake (rice wine) or dry white wine

1 cup Kelp Stock (page 6) or low-sodium vegetable stock

⅓ cup thinly sliced scallions (white part only), plus ½ cup finely sliced green part

½ cup thinly sliced fennel bulb

1 *akatogarashi* Japanese red chile pepper or pinch of red pepper flakes

A few fennel fronds, for garnish

Prepare the cold salt water (see headnote) and soak the clams for 2 hours. Drain the clams in a colander and scrub the shells with a hard brush under cold water.

Place the sake, stock, white part of the scallions, sliced fennel, and chile pepper in a medium pot over medium heat. Bring the mixture to a simmer, then lower the heat to low and cook, covered, for 3 minutes. Increase the heat to medium, add the clams, and bring the mixture to a boil, covered. Cook the clams for 3 to 5 minutes. During cooking, shake the pot several times to agitate any slow-opening clams.

Remove the lid and discard any unopened clams. Divide the clams into soup bowls. Strain the cooking broth through a paper towel–lined strainer into a bowl, discarding the scallions, fennel, and chile pepper. Divide the clam broth among the soup bowls. Garnish with the scallion greens and fennel fronds and serve.

CHAPTER 2
DASHI STOCK

In this chapter I will introduce you to Dashi Stock, which was briefly mentioned in Chapter 1. Dashi is made by infusing dried skipjack tuna flakes, *katsuobushi* (see page 38), in Kelp Stock. This flavorful dashi is the most frequently used stock in the Japanese kitchen, and the recipes in this chapter can become delicious, healthful, and everyday additions to your kitchen repertoire. Dashi, as is the kelp stock, is usually flavored with a combination of key Japanese seasonings such as sea salt, shoyu, miso, mirin, sake, sugar, and rice vinegar.

First, here are some tips on sourcing, purchasing, and the proper storage of *katsuobushi*. You can find *katsuobushi* in nearly every Japanese or other Asian market, as well as at some of the larger American supermarkets and online. Look for a package with large flakes that are pink and bright, with a glossy color. Aging causes the flakes to oxidize, turning the flakes brown and diminishing their glossiness. After opening the package, gently squeeze it to remove the excess air inside and tightly seal the bag after use. For the best flavor, use the fish flakes within three months.

The prepared Dashi Stock may be frozen for up to three months or kept in the refrigerator for two to three days. If you are unable to find kelp and fish flakes, low-sodium chicken stock is an appropriate substitute. Even if you use the chicken stock, you will learn how to prepare and flavor dishes the Japanese way.

Dashi Stock

MAKES 7½ CUPS

8 cups prepared Kelp Stock (page 6)

4 cups *katsuobushi* (skipjack tuna fish flakes; 2 ounces)

Heat the prepared Kelp Stock in a large pot over medium heat to 176°F. Do not bring the stock to a boil. Add the fish flakes all at once, gently pushing the flakes down into the stock with a spatula. Wait for the stock to come to a gentle simmer and then quickly turn off the heat. Leave the fish flakes in the stock for about 5 minutes.

Strain the stock through a moist paper towel–lined strainer, ensuring that none of the fish flakes pass into your stock. Dashi Stock should be very clean and clear. Reserve the cooked fish flakes for a Second Dashi Stock preparation (page 39). I store the prepared stock in 4-cup plastic containers—one in the refrigerator for use in a day or two, and the other in the freezer for later use.

The Art of Katsuobushi Production

In America, *katsuobushi* comes in plastic bags in the form of shaved flakes—known simply as "fish flakes." Before shaving, *katsuobushi* looks like a hard and inedible piece of wood. The transformation from fresh fish to *katsuobushi* takes half a year, and the magical process that changes raw fish to an umami-rich, completely dry, and safely storable food was perfected in Japan during the Edo period (1600–1868).

Katsuobushi production begins with harvesting *katsuo* (skipjack tuna) in spring through early summer, when the fish has relatively little stored oil. When the harvested fish are brought into processing facilities at the port or, in most cases today, caught in distant waters and flash frozen for quality, no time is wasted. The fish is quickly filleted, boned, and steamed before going through a laborious smoking and drying process. By the end of the entire process, the fish has lost almost 80 percent of its body water. In order to remove additional moisture, thereby allowing safe unrefrigerated storage, the fish is left in a temperature- and moisture-controlled room to allow mold to grow on its surface. After two weeks, the fish is covered with blue mold that is then carefully removed by hand, and the fish is left to dry in the sun. This process is repeated several times. By the end of the procedure, the fish loses an additional 5 percent of its moisture.

During this process the mold also serves to break down the fat, which makes the fish stable for long storage. One of the chemicals responsible for umami, inosinate, also greatly increases during the processing.

Second Dashi Stock

The kelp and fish flakes used to make the first kelp and dashi stocks may be used again to produce this Second Dashi Stock. Because the aroma and taste of these flakes will be somewhat degraded, we add additional fish flakes to the preparation of Second Dashi Stock, greatly improving the flavor. You can use it in any of the recipes in this chapter.

MAKES 5½ CUPS

Reserved kelp from Kelp Stock preparation (page 6)

Reserved skipjack tuna fish flakes from the Dashi Stock preparation (page 38)

6 cups water

1 cup tightly packed *katsuobushi* (skipjack tuna fish flakes; ⅔ ounce)

Place the reserved kelp and fish flakes in a large pot with the water. Bring the mixture to a gentle boil over medium heat, then lower the heat to medium-low and cook for 10 minutes. Add the new fish flakes and turn off the heat. Let the mixture stand for 5 minutes, then strain through a moist paper towel–lined strainer, ensuring that none of the fish flakes pass into your stock. Discard the kelp and fish flakes after this use.

Chunky Potato and Leek Soup with Miso

Please read about Japanese Miso Soup (page 41) and Miso Varieties (page 12) before making any of the miso soup recipes in this chapter. Miso is a wonderful, delicious, natural product made in many varieties, and it is used to produce an equally wide assortment of delicious soups. If your only experience with miso is the salty, yellow-brown miso soup served in many Japanese restaurants, this recipe and those that follow will provide an eye-opening experience and an abundance of new flavors.

Choose leeks that are firm to the touch and have healthy-looking greens with no yellow spots. Younger, thinner stalks seem to have more delicate flavor than their overgrown, thick counterparts. I love to use Yukon gold potatoes in this soup because of their moist texture and distinctive flavor.

MAKES 4 SERVINGS

3 bacon slices (2 ounces)

1 medium Yukon gold potato or other waxy variety (8 ounces), peeled

1⅓ cups thinly, diagonally sliced leeks

¾ cup chopped yellow onion

4 cups Dashi Stock (page 38) or low-sodium chicken stock

2 tablespoons medium-aged light brown miso (see page 12)

Freshly ground black pepper

Boil a kettle of water. Cut the bacon into thin strips crosswise. Transfer the bacon to a sieve, and pour the boiling water over it to remove excess fat. Drain the bacon. Cut the potato into ½-inch cubes.

Place the bacon, potato, leeks, onion, and stock in a medium pot over medium heat and bring it to a simmer. Cover the pot, decrease the heat to medium-low, and cook for 25 minutes.

Add the miso and dissolve it with a whisk. Divide the soup into small soup bowls, garnish with black pepper, and serve.

Japanese Miso Soup

Most miso soup served in America has the same old ingredients: tofu, wakame seaweed, and scallions. In Japan, miso soup is much more exciting and varied. We use a wide variety of ingredients, from vegetables to seafood and often chicken or meat. The selection of ingredients depends on the season. We flavor the basic dashi stock with a single variety of miso or—in order to produce depth of flavor—sometimes blend two different types of miso together; for example, medium-aged light brown miso and aged brown miso (see page 12). Before serving, we garnish the prepared miso soup with seasonally available, often fragrant herbs and spices to further convey a strong sense of the season. Representative herbs and spices include ginger, scallion, shiso (perilla), yuzu (citron), *myoga* (ginger bud), *shichimi togarashi* (Japanese seven-spice powder), sansho pepper, and Japanese mustard. In my American kitchen, I replace these with easily available garnishes such as fresh cilantro, fresh parsley, red pepper flakes, dried thyme, Colman's mustard, and so on.

Miso is frequently criticized because of its high sodium content. However, if you know the salt content of each type of miso and stick to proper portions of high-quality miso using proper methods, you will greatly benefit from its nutritional value and wonderful flavor. Check out the miso sodium content information on page 12.

The volume of miso used in the miso soup recipes in this book is reduced to almost half of the amount that was commonly used in my mother's day. I am able to do this because of the flavorful and umami-rich Dashi Stock (page 38). For delicious miso soup in any season, just choose the ingredients and miso you like from the table below, prepare the soup, and serve it in a small soup bowl (a coffee mug is perfect). Just try to keep to a proper portion size—no matter how delicious it is. Here is a list of seasonal vegetables for your daily miso soup. Preparing miso soup is a wonderful way to clean out your vegetable bin. If you can, mix and match vegetables of different colors, textures, and flavors for the best results.

SPRING	AUTUMN
asparagus, bamboo shoots, cabbage, Chinese chives, fava beans, peas, mushrooms, onions, salsify, soybean sprouts	broccoli, carrots, cauliflower, eggplant, fennel, mushrooms, hard squash, sweet potatoes, celeriac, turnips, string beans
SUMMER	**WINTER**
bell peppers, carrots, collards, corn, eggplant, kale, okra, string beans, Swiss chard, tomatoes, zucchini	brussels sprouts, cabbage, radishes, cauliflower, celeriac, daikon, leeks, carrots, parsnips, potatoes, rutabagas, spinach

Mushroom and Egg Miso Soup

This is another of my favorites for a quick lunch. I mix and match different mushrooms, sauté them in a little bit of oil in a saucepan, add dashi stock, break in one or two eggs, and cook until the egg is softly poached. The mushroom selection can include shiitake, portobello, cremini, maitake (this mushroom looks like a bushy head, its meaty flesh holds its shape during cooking, and it has an excellent aroma and good flavor), *enokitake* (yellowish with long, slender stems topped with tiny caps, this mushroom has a crunchy texture and distinctive flavor), *shimeji* (white, short, plump stems topped with little brown caps and noted for good flavor), and *eringi* (from the Mediterranean area, this mushroom has a thick, plump stem topped with a flat, slightly brownish top and has a meaty and chewy texture). In this recipe, I mix two varieties of miso, but you can do with just one.

MAKES 4 SERVINGS

1 teaspoon canola oil or vegetable oil

1 tablespoon sliced garlic

3 cups thinly sliced assorted mushrooms

1 cup thinly sliced Swiss chard or other greens

3 cups Dashi Stock (page 38) or low-sodium chicken stock

4 large eggs

1 tablespoon aged brown miso (see page 12)

1½ tablespoons medium-aged light brown miso

Red pepper flakes or hot paprika

Heat the canola oil in a medium pot over medium heat until hot. Add the garlic and cook for 20 seconds, or until fragrant. Add the mushrooms and Swiss chard, and stir until the vegetables are slightly wilted. Add the stock, bring it to a simmer, and cook for 2 minutes. Crack and add the eggs to the pot one at a time without breaking or beating. Cover the pot, decrease the heat to medium-low, and cook the soup for 3 to 4 minutes.

Turn off the heat. Transfer 1 cup of the soup liquid from the pot into a small bowl. Add both miso varieties to the bowl and stir with a whisk until dissolved. This will prevent you from disturbing the eggs in the pot. Return the miso liquid to the pot and, without breaking the eggs, gently stir the soup.

Divide the soup, including the eggs, into soup bowls. Garnish with red pepper flakes and serve.

Miso Soup with Brussels Sprouts

Although Brussels sprouts belong to the cruciferous family and have many beneficial health properties, I find that people often shun them because they are frequently overcooked at home and at restaurants. Prepare this recipe, though, and I believe your family and friends will reconsider the value of this delightful vegetable. Choose sprouts that are bright green, tightly closed, and heavy for their size and have a crisp, unwilted appearance.

MAKES 4 SERVINGS

8 large Brussels sprouts (7 ounces)

1 medium carrot or any other root vegetable (3½ ounces), peeled

1 thumb-size piece ginger (1 ounce), peeled

1 teaspoon canola oil

3 cups Dashi Stock (page 38) or low-sodium chicken stock

2 tablespoons aged brown miso (see page 12)

Little dab of mustard paste made with Japanese or Colman's mustard powder (1 teaspoon mustard powder mixed with 1 teaspoon hot water)

Cut off the bottom ends of the Brussels sprouts and then cut them into halves. Cut each half into thin slices lengthwise. Cut the carrot into 1½-inch-long matchstick-size sticks. Cut the ginger into 1½-inch-long julienne strips.

Heat the canola oil in a medium pot over medium heat. When the oil is hot, add the ginger, stirring, and cook it for 20 seconds. Add the Brussels sprouts, carrot, and stock and bring the soup to a simmer. Decrease the heat to medium-low and cook for 5 minutes.

Add the miso and stir with a whisk until it is dissolved. Divide the soup into small soup bowls. Garnish with a dab of mustard paste and serve.

Spicy Kale Miso Soup

Kale, which comes in several varieties—curly leaf, flat leaf, and toothed leaf with purple stems—was an unknown green for me until I moved to America. When I first tasted the tender red Russian kale from our neighborhood farmers' market, I immediately fell in love with it because of its slightly bitter, green, and grassy flavor and its firm texture. During the long season from summer through deep autumn, I use it raw in salads, stir-fried, simmered, and in this miso soup. Do not discard the hard stems of this vegetable; instead, slice them thinly and enjoy the crispiness they add to dishes like this soup. Choose kale with leaves that appear crisp, moist, and heavy. The source of heat in this soup is *toban jiang* (fermented chile bean sauce). Japanese and Asian stores carry this chile bean sauce, but if it is not available, substitute red pepper flakes.

MAKES 4 SERVINGS

½ bunch kale with stems (½ pound)

1 teaspoon canola oil or other vegetable oil

½ cup chopped red onion

¼ cup finely julienned ginger

¼ to ½ teaspoon *toban jiang* (fermented chile bean sauce) or red pepper flakes

3 cups Dashi Stock (page 38) or low-sodium chicken stock

1½ tablespoons aged brown miso (see page 12)

Cut off the very bottom of the hard stems of the kale, and cut the remaining kale, including the stems, into thin slices crosswise. Heat the canola oil in a medium pot over medium heat, then add the onion. Cook it for 1 minute, stirring, until it is slightly translucent. Add half of the ginger and the *toban jiang*, and give it several stirs. Add the kale and cook, stirring, until the leaves are wilted. Pour in the stock and bring it to a simmer. Decrease the heat to low and cook, covered, for 3 minutes.

Add the miso, stirring with a whisk until it is dissolved. Divide the soup into small soup bowls, garnish with the remaining ginger, and serve.

Napa Cabbage and Chicken Meatballs in Miso Soup

This is another meal-in-a-soup-bowl dish. If you have made and frozen extra chicken meatballs for the Spicy Sausage, Chicken Meatballs, and Tomatoes (page 30), this flavorful and satisfying soup can be ready in 15 minutes. Enjoy the soup with a piece of good bread or a bowl of hot steamed rice.

MAKES 4 SERVINGS

⅓ of a medium napa cabbage
(½ pound)

1 teaspoon canola oil or vegetable oil

¼ cup finely julienned ginger

3 cups Dashi Stock (page 38) or
low-sodium chicken stock

8 Glazed Chicken Meatballs
(page 27), fresh or frozen

1½ tablespoons aged brown miso
(see page 12)

¼ cup thinly sliced scallion
(green part only)

Freshly ground black pepper

Cut the cabbage into 1 by 2-inch rectangular pieces. Heat the canola oil in a medium pot over medium heat. When the oil is hot, add the cabbage and cook for 2 minutes, stirring, or until the cabbage pieces are slightly wilted. Add the ginger and give several large stirs. Add the stock and chicken meatballs and cook, covered, over medium-low heat for 10 minutes (if the chicken meatballs are frozen, cook them for 25 minutes).

Turn off the heat. Add the miso and stir with a whisk until it is dissolved. Divide the soup into small soup bowls, garnish with the scallion greens and black pepper, and serve.

White Bean, Sausage, and Vegetable Soup with Miso

This recipe is a good example of a new extension of Japanese miso soup. As a dried bean lover, I once chose an Italian white bean soup as part of a luncheon at a sandwich shop. It was kind of a gooey and oily soup, but I did love the content and flavor—white beans, sausages, and several vegetables. I thought about how I could preserve what I liked about the soup and eliminate the weak parts. The next day I cooked the same tasty contents in dashi stock and flavored the soup with miso. The result was this delicious and very appealing soup without the problems of the restaurant version.

MAKES 4 TO 6 SERVINGS

½ **pound Italian sausage of your choice**

1 **teaspoon canola oil or other vegetable oil**

1½ **cups chopped yellow onion**

½ **cup chopped celery**

½ **cup peeled and diced carrot**

Pinch of sea salt

4 **cups Dashi Stock (page 38) or low-sodium chicken stock**

⅓ **cup plus 1 tablespoon chopped tomato**

1 **(19-ounce) can white kidney beans, rinsed and drained**

½ **teaspoon dried thyme**

2 **tablespoons medium-aged light brown miso (see page 12)**

Freshly ground black pepper

¼ **cup finely chopped fresh parsley**

Prick the sausage in several places with a toothpick or fork. Bring a large pot of water to a boil over medium heat, then add the sausage and cook for 10 minutes. Drain the sausage and cool it in a cold water bath. Cut the sausages into ½-inch slices.

Heat the canola oil in a medium pot over medium-high heat. Add the onion, celery, carrot, and pinch of salt. Cook, stirring, for 2 minutes. Add the stock and bring it to a simmer over medium heat. Add the sausage, tomato, white beans, and thyme. Decrease the heat to low and cook the soup, covered, for 25 minutes. During cooking, skim the foam off the top several times.

Add the miso and stir with a whisk until it is dissolved. Season to taste with black pepper. Divide the soup into soup bowls, garnish with the parsley, and serve.

Omuraisu in Takikomi Gohan Style

Omuraisu—a contraction of the English words omelet rice pronounced in the Japanese way— is a rice dish created in Japan at the turn of the twentieth century, when modern Japan eagerly sought to adopt all things Western. Cooked rice is stir-fried with chopped onion and cubed chicken and well flavored with ketchup and English Worcestershire sauce. The fried rice is then wrapped up in a French-style omelet. In this recipe, I take two shortcuts to simplify the preparation. First, I put all the *omuraisu* recipe elements in a pot and cook and flavor them at the same time. By doing so, I omit the stir-frying process and use no oil. Second, instead of making an omelet, I serve the rice topped with a sunny-side-up egg. Decorate each dish with a little dollop or squeeze of ketchup right out of the bottle, the way we do in Japan. Be sure to read How to Cook Rice in a Pot on a Stovetop (page 20) before starting this recipe.

MAKES 6 SERVINGS

2¼ cups medium- or short-grain polished white rice

½ pound sweet Italian sausage

2 teaspoons canola oil or vegetable oil

1 cup chopped yellow onion

1 teaspoon sea salt plus a pinch

2½ cups Dashi Stock (page 38) or low-sodium chicken stock

1 teaspoon Worcestershire sauce

¼ cup ketchup, plus more for garnish

½ cup fresh or frozen corn kernels

½ cup fresh or frozen green peas

½ cup chopped fresh parsley

6 large eggs

Rinse and soak the rice according to the instructions on page 20. Drain the rice and let it stand in a fine-mesh sieve for 20 minutes to dry.

Prick the sausage in several places with a toothpick or fork. Bring a medium pot of water to a boil, add the sausage, and cook for 2 minutes. Drain the sausage.

Heat the oil in a medium skillet over medium heat. Add the sausage and brown all sides until golden, about 2 minutes. Transfer the sausage to a plate. Add the onion and the pinch of salt to the hot skillet and cook over medium heat, stirring, until the onion is translucent.

Place the drained rice in a medium pot. In a bowl, mix the stock, the remaining 1 teaspoon salt, the Worcestershire sauce, and ketchup with a spoon. Pour the stock mixture into the pot with the rice. With your hands, gently level the surface of the rice. Sprinkle the cooked onion and corn evenly over the rice, then place the sausage on top of the rice. Do not stir. Cover the pot and cook the rice following the rice cooking instructions on page 21.

Five minutes before the rice is finished cooking, add the peas. Once the rice is cooked, transfer the sausage to a cutting board and cut it into ½-inch slices. Return the sausage to the rice pot, add the parsley, and cover the rice.

Heat a thin layer of oil in a large skillet over medium heat. Break the eggs, one after another, into the skillet. After the bottom of the egg white sets (about 30 seconds), add about 3 tablespoons of water to the skillet. Immediately cover the skillet with the lid, decrease the heat to low, and cook the eggs for 2 to 2½ minutes. While the eggs cook, use a spatula to stir the rice with the sausage, corn, peas, and parsley.

Divide the rice onto serving plates. Top each rice portion with a sunny-side-up egg. Garnish with a dollop of ketchup and serve.

Asparagus and Green Tea Rice

It was almost seven years ago that I first tasted a dish called green tea rice. The rice was a part of the *ekiben*, or lunch box, that I purchased at a station (see page 71) when I visited wasabi farmer Yoshihiko Shiratori in the village of Utogi, Shizuoka Prefecture. This prefecture is also known as "the tea plantation prefecture" because it is and has been for centuries the home of many high-quality tea farms. The green tea rice I had that day had a distinctive tea flavor with a slight astringency. Upon my return to New York City, I tried to re-create green tea rice. After several tries, I came to the conclusion that asparagus and squid are a great match with green tea rice. Here is the recipe.

MAKES 6 SERVINGS

2¼ cups medium- or short-grain polished white rice

8 medium asparagus, stemmed and brown frills removed

2½ cups Dashi Stock (page 38) or low-sodium chicken stock

1½ teaspoons matcha (green tea powder)

1½ teaspoons sea salt, plus more as needed

8 medium cleaned squid (½ pound)

1 tablespoon olive oil, plus more as needed

¼ cup chopped yellow onion

Rinse and soak the rice according to the instructions on page 20. Drain the rice and let it stand in a fine-mesh sieve for 20 minutes to dry.

Cut the asparagus into ⅓-inch-thick diagonal slices. Place the stock in a medium pot over medium heat and bring it to a simmer. Add the asparagus and cook until crisp, 30 to 40 seconds. Drain the asparagus over a bowl and let it air-cool, reserving the cooking liquid. Transfer the cooking liquid to a measuring cup and add enough water to make 2½ cups. Add the green tea powder and 1 teaspoon of the salt to the hot stock and stir with a whisk.

Cut the squid into ⅓-inch-wide rings. Transfer the squid to a bowl and toss it with the olive oil and the remaining ½ teaspoon salt.

Place the drained rice in a medium pot with the green tea stock. With your hand, gently level the surface of the rice. Sprinkle the onion evenly over the rice, then scatter the squid rings evenly over the rice. Cook the rice following the rice cooking instructions on page 21.

When the rice is nearly finished cooking, toss the asparagus in a small bowl with a little olive oil and salt. When the rice is finished cooking, carefully remove the lid of the pot and add the asparagus. Return the lid to the pot and let the rice stand for 10 minutes. Remove the lid and gently stir the rice with a spatula. Divide the rice into bowls and serve.

Quickly Simmered Lettuce and Fried Tofu

This is a very classic, humble home-style dish. All of the flavors, including the slightly fatty taste from the deep-fried thick tofu, mingle with each other to create real Japanese-style comfort food. Commercially prepared, deep-fried tofu, *atsuage-dofu*, is readily available in Japan but can be hard to find here in America. So in this recipe, you will learn how to prepare a similar fried tofu using fresh firm tofu from your local market. If you are lucky enough to find *atsuage-dofu* at a Japanese or Asian food store, or something called "tofu-cutlet," a product similar to *atsuage-dofu* that is marketed here in America, go for it.

MAKES 4 SERVINGS

1 block firm or extra-firm tofu (14 ounces)

¼ cup canola oil or vegetable oil

½ head iceberg lettuce (10 ounces)

2 cups soybean sprouts

2 cups Dashi Stock (page 38) or low-sodium chicken stock

2 tablespoons shoyu (soy sauce)

2 tablespoons sake (rice wine) or water

2 teaspoons sugar

Pinch of salt

¼ cup peeled and thinly sliced ginger

Red pepper flakes or *shichimi togarashi* (Japanese seven-spice powder)

Black sesame seeds

Place the tofu between heavy dinner plates. Put a bowl with water weighing about 1½ pounds on top of the upper plate, tilt the plate, and let the tofu stand for 30 minutes. You want to remove about ½ cup of water from the tofu using this process. Remove the tofu from between the plates, discard the water, cut the tofu in half crosswise, then cut each tofu block into 2 thin sheets, each ⅔ inch thick.

Heat the canola oil in a medium skillet over medium heat, and add all of the tofu slices without overlapping. Cook them over medium-low heat for 10 to 12 minutes, or until both sides are golden, turning them over once. Transfer the tofu to a cutting board and cut each sheet into 4 crosswise strips. Cut the lettuce into 1½-inch-thick wedges.

Bring a medium pot of water to a boil. Add the lettuce and soybean sprouts and cook for 1 minute. Drain the vegetables in a colander, and rinse the vegetables under cold tap water. Gently squeeze the vegetables to remove excess water.

Place the dashi stock, soy sauce, sake, sugar, and salt in the medium pot over medium heat and bring it to a simmer. Add the lettuce, sprouts, tofu, and ginger. Decrease the heat to medium-low and cook the tofu and vegetables, uncovered, for 5 minutes. Turn off the heat and let the tofu and vegetables stand in the cooking liquid for 20 minutes. During this resting time the tofu and vegetables will absorb flavors from the stock.

Divide the liquid and vegetables into bowls, garnish with the red pepper flakes and sesame seeds, and serve.

Kale in Peanut Butter–Tofu Sauce

Puréed, creamy tofu and sesame paste dressing flavored with shoyu (soy sauce), mirin (sweet cooking wine), sugar, and salt is a classic favorite that is often used in Japan to dress lightly cooked vegetables. The flavor of this dressing is wonderful, but it has a pasty texture and appearance, making it a hard sell in America. The traditional preparation also requires an unfamiliar set of tools—a Japanese mortar and pestle. So I have revised the preparation to make the texture and flavor more appealing. I break up the tofu with a fork until it is finely crumbled but not pasty (do not process it in a food processor; it will create pasty, sticky dressing), and I pair it with peanut butter to create a different taste and texture. Even people who sometimes shun tofu say this dressing is delightful.

MAKES 4 SERVINGS

3 tablespoons peanut butter or other nut/seed butter

3 tablespoons warm Dashi Stock (page 38) or low-sodium chicken stock, warmed

1 teaspoon shoyu (soy sauce)

1 teaspoon honey

½ teaspoon sea salt

½ teaspoon freshly ground black pepper

½ block extra-firm or firm tofu (7 ounces)

5 cups thinly julienned kale with stems

½ cup chopped roasted unsalted peanuts or white sesame seeds

Using a spatula, mix and soften the peanut butter with the warm stock in a large bowl. Add the soy sauce, honey, salt, and black pepper and mix thoroughly.

Bring a pot of water to a boil. Cut the tofu in half crosswise, add the tofu to the boiling water, and cook for 1 minute. Drain the tofu and wrap each piece in doubled paper towels, squeezing firmly to remove excess water. Do not worry about breaking the tofu, as you are going to crumble it later. Remove the tofu from the paper towels and transfer it to the bowl with the peanut butter. With a fork, crumble the tofu into very small pieces and mix it with the sauce. Add the kale and two-thirds of the peanuts to the bowl and toss the mixture thoroughly.

Divide the salad into small bowls, garnish with the remaining peanuts, and serve.

Chicken and Vegetable Yakisoba

Yakisoba, ramen noodles stir-fried with bits of pork and cabbage on a large steel griddle, is a very popular quick snack or lunch prepared at casual restaurants and homes in Japan. *Yakisoba* also appears everywhere in the country at festivals and fairs as street food. It is so popular that there are commercial *yakisoba* sauces sold in a bottle, but this recipe doesn't require looking for this special sauce. Cook two servings at a time, because adding too many ingredients at one time in a heated wok or skillet slows down the high-temperature cooking process and can produce a poor result. Be sure to read Noodle Cooking Techniques on page 59.

MAKES 4 SERVINGS

- 1 small boneless, skinless chicken breast (about 5 ounces)
- 2 tablespoons sake (rice wine) or water
- ¼ teaspoon salt
- 1 medium egg white, beaten
- 2 teaspoons cornstarch or potato starch
- 1 cup Dashi Stock (page 38) or low-sodium chicken stock
- 1 tablespoon shoyu (soy sauce)
- 1 tablespoon oyster sauce
- 1½ tablespoons Worcestershire sauce
- 2 teaspoons sugar
- Freshly ground white pepper
- 2 tablespoons canola oil
- 2 tablespoons finely julienned ginger
- 1½ cups cabbage, shredded into 3-inch-long strips
- ½ cup green bell pepper, cut into thin 3-inch-long strips
- ½ cup red bell pepper, cut into thin 3-inch-long strips
- ½ cup yellow bell pepper, cut into thin 3-inch-long strips
- 1 pound precooked soft ramen or *chukasoba* noodles for *yakisoba* or precooked Chinese egg noodles

For this part of the recipe, prepare all of the ingredients in one batch. Later it will be cooked in smaller batches. Cut the chicken into 2-inch-long thin strips. In a medium bowl, toss the chicken with the sake, salt, and egg white. Add the cornstarch and toss it again. Cover the bowl with plastic wrap and refrigerate the chicken for 15 minutes.

Bring a large pot of water to a boil over high heat, and add the chicken mixture to the water. Stir the chicken with tongs to separate and cook it for 1 minute, or until the outside becomes white. Drain the chicken and transfer it to a bowl. In a small bowl, combine the stock, soy sauce, oyster sauce, Worcestershire sauce, sugar, and white pepper.

Place a large wok over medium-high heat and add 1 tablespoon of the canola oil. When the oil is hot, add half of the ginger and cook for 20 seconds. Add half of the cabbage and the bell peppers to the wok and cook until the cabbage is wilted, stirring all the time. Add half of the noodles and cook until all are coated with oil. Add half of the chicken and cook for 1 minute, or until it is mixed with the other ingredients. Add half of the stock mixture and cook, stirring, until the liquid is almost absorbed. Divide between dinner plates to make two portions. Repeat with the remaining half of the ingredients to prepare the second batch of noodles.

Lamb and Mushroom Wonton Ravioli in Dashi Broth

Cooked wonton dumplings filled with pork, seafood, and/or vegetables and floated in soup will delight diners with their silky smooth texture and flavor. The square wonton wrapper, found at Chinese and Asian groceries, is thinner and smaller than the wrapper used for Japanese pot stickers, or gyoza. In this recipe I use lamb and kale as a filling, and I serve them in flavored Dashi Stock as a light appetizer dish. You can also enjoy these wontons two other ways: Simmer or steam them, drain them, and serve with BBC Cilantro Sauce (page 137), or deep-fry them and serve them sprinkled with sea salt or Ponzu Sauce (page 171).

MAKES 8 SERVINGS

1 cup stemmed and finely chopped button and shiitake mushrooms

2 cups finely chopped kale leaves

1½ teaspoons salt

7 ounces ground lamb

2 teaspoons plus 1 tablespoon shoyu (soy sauce)

1 clove garlic, minced

2 tablespoons minced fresh cilantro leaves, plus ¼ cup whole leaves

1 teaspoon Dijon mustard

⅛ teaspoon paprika

80 wonton wrappers

3 cups Dashi Stock (page 38) or low-sodium chicken broth

2 tablespoons sake (rice wine)

1 tablespoon mirin (sweet cooking wine)

½ to 1 tablespoon lemon juice

In a large bowl, toss the mushrooms and kale with ½ teaspoon of the salt and let them stand for 10 minutes. Squeeze the mushrooms and kale firmly to remove excess water. In a clean bowl, mix the lamb with the mushrooms and kale, 2 teaspoons of the soy sauce, garlic, 2 tablespoons of the minced cilantro, mustard, and paprika. Divide the lamb and mushroom mixture into 8 portions.

Prepare a tray covered with moist paper towels, and have additional moist paper towels on hand. Have a cup of cold water on hand too. On a cutting board, spread out about 10 wonton wrappers (you are working in batches). Scoop up a teaspoonful of the meat mixture and place it in the center of each wonton wrapper. Moisten the edges of the wrapper by dipping your index finger in the cup of water and running your wet finger over the edges of the wrapper. Place another 10 wrappers on top of the wrappers with the meat mixture, and press the edges together to seal. Transfer the wonton squares to the paper towel–covered tray, and place additional moist paper towels over the wontons to keep them moist while working on the remaining batches. Repeat until you have 40 wontons total.

Place the stock, sake, mirin, the remaining 1 teaspoon of the salt, the remaining 1 tablespoon of the soy sauce, and the lemon juice in a pot over medium heat until simmering. Turn off the heat. In another large pot, bring water to a boil over medium heat, and add the wontons in 3 batches. Boil each batch for 5 minutes. Carefully remove the wontons from the water with a slotted spoon, drain well, and transfer them to soup bowls. Pour the dashi broth into each soup bowl. Garnish with the whole cilantro leaves and serve.

Ramen with Chashu Pork

Ramen is a "Japanized" bowl of Chinese noodle soup. Ramen noodles are yellow-colored wheat noodles, similar to Chinese egg noodles, but contain no egg. The noodles are known for their distinctive chewy bite when they are properly prepared. They are usually served in richly flavored chicken broth or chicken-and-pork-based broth. Professional chefs can spend up to 10 hours preparing their perfect ramen stock. This recipe takes a shortcut by combining commercially available chicken stock and Dashi Stock (page 38). The standard toppings for ramen noodle bowls are *chashu* pork (sweet and salty simmered pork), boiled egg, scallion, and nori seaweed. It is best to prepare the *chashu* pork and eggs the day before serving for a mature flavor. Be sure to read Noodle Cooking Techniques on page 59.

MAKES 4 SERVINGS

2 cloves garlic, peeled

1 thumb-size piece ginger (1 ounce), peeled

5 cups low-sodium chicken stock, plus more if needed

1 cup Dashi Stock (page 38) or low-sodium chicken stock

2 cups water

1 pound pork belly, skin and excess fat removed

½ cup sake (rice wine)

1 cup shoyu (soy sauce)

1 cup mirin (sweet cooking wine)

4 hard-boiled large eggs

½ sheet nori seaweed

2 scallions

2¼ cups shredded red cabbage

10 ounces dried *chukasoba* (ramen) or dried Chinese egg noodles

Crush the garlic with the side of a knife. Cut the ginger into 3 pieces. Heat the chicken stock, Dashi Stock, and water in a large pot over medium heat until boiling. Add the pork belly, garlic, and ginger to the stock mixture and cook for 1 hour. The pork should be completely submerged while cooking.

Remove the pork belly from the stock and strain the cooking liquid through a moist paper towel–lined strainer set over a bowl. Measure the cooking liquid and, if necessary, add additional chicken stock until you have 6 cups. Refrigerate the stock—from this point it will be referred to as ramen stock—overnight.

Place the sake, soy sauce, and mirin in a small saucepan over medium heat and bring it to a gentle simmer. Add the pork belly, decrease the heat to medium-low, and cook for 20 minutes. While cooking, turn the pork belly several times to ensure even flavoring. Remove the pot from the stovetop and let the pork belly and cooking liquid cool for 30 minutes. Then transfer the pork belly with the cooking liquid into a small sealable container (the pork belly should be barely submerged in the cooking liquid) and refrigerate for 2 hours.

Remove the pork belly from the cooking liquid and transfer it into another sealable container, reserving the cooking liquid in the container. Refrigerate the pork belly overnight. Shell the hard-boiled eggs, add the eggs to the reserved cooking liquid, and refrigerate overnight.

Continued

The next day, remove the eggs from the cooking liquid, reserving the liquid. This liquid is used to flavor the ramen stock for your ramen noodle soup bowl, so let us call it ramen sauce. Cut the eggs in half lengthwise. Cut the pork belly into thin diagonal slices, about ¼ inch thick and 2 inches square. You will use 3 to 5 slices per serving of noodles. Any sliced pork belly not used in this recipe can be frozen for later use. Cut the nori into 4 rectangles. Cut the scallions diagonally into thin slices.

Heat serving bowls by filling them with very hot water. Bring a large pot of water to a boil over medium heat and cook the cabbage for 2 minutes. Remove the cabbage with a slotted spoon and drain in a colander. Add the *chukasoba* noodles to the boiling water and cook them according to the directions on the package. While cooking the noodles, in another medium pot add the ramen stock and bring it to a simmer over medium heat. Add 7 to 8 tablespoons of the ramen sauce to the pot and bring it to a simmer. This is the completed ramen broth.

Drain the noodles. Do not rinse the noodles in cold water. Discard the hot water from the noodle bowls and divide the noodles and the hot ramen broth among the bowls. Garnish each bowl with the *chashu* pork slices, half an egg, the cabbage, scallions, and nori. Serve piping-hot.

Kagetsu Ramen Restaurant in Tokyo

My favorite ramen restaurant in Tokyo—among many—is the 37-year-old Kagetsu Ramen shop near Ebisu Station. Kagetsu is memorable not only because of its top-quality noodle dishes but also because of its amazing single waiter and staff. A long line forms from the inside to the outside of the restaurant every day at lunch, dinner, and late into the night, year-round. The restaurant is a mere 350 or so square feet and has a single counter with about 18 seats. Once you finally reach the inside line of about 20 diners, you must stand, waiting at the backs of the diners who are enjoying steaming hot bowls of ramen. Only three chefs work with single-minded devotion behind the counter. Each repeats his one assigned, simple task—part of the noodle cooking and dish assembly process—in silence over and over again.

As you enter the restaurant, a seasoned, middle-aged waiter wearing high boots approaches to take your order. The menu, posted on the wall, is rather simple but allows for hundreds of possible combinations. You choose ramen broth from four flavors—shoyu, salt, miso, or spicy miso—and select your preference of lean or fatty broth and firm or tender cooked noodles. In addition, you can add extra toppings from a list of over a dozen items.

My order is always like this: lean miso broth, firmly cooked noodles, and two or three added toppings that strike my fancy on the particular day. The waiter takes orders without notepad and pen from all the people waiting inside the restaurant. He orally communicates the orders to the three chefs who are busy preparing dishes (ordered 15 to 20 minutes before) for the seated customers. Nothing is written down at any point. Finally, my turn comes and I am offered a seat at the counter, and miraculously the exact bowl of ramen I have ordered 20 minutes before is placed in front of me. And after I finish and walk to the cashier, the waiter tells the cashier exactly what I ordered, perhaps 40 minutes ago.

After many years of patronizing the restaurant, I have never seen a single error in my dish or any served to another customer. I have no idea how they do this. Physical characteristics? Appearance or gender? Clothing? Frankly, I don't want to know. It's better to leave this as a secret mystery of the restaurant. Nowadays, Kagetsu has begun online sales and home delivery of their ramen. I find it sad that I live too far away (about 6,000 miles outside of their delivery zone) to take advantage of this wonderful service.

Fried Udon Noodles

We call stir-fried udon noodles *yaki-udon*. This dish comes from Fukuoka City, Kyushu Island, in southern Japan. The widely accepted story of the creation of *yaki-udon* goes back to just after World War II, when food was scarce. The owner of the noodle restaurant Darumado used udon noodles in popular *yakisoba* preparations because the proper noodles were not available. This substitution unexpectedly resulted in a delicious dish, and the new preparation soon became a proud local specialty. Today it is a national comfort food. Cook two servings at a time, because adding too many ingredients at one time to a heated wok or skillet slows down the cooking process and can produce poor results. Be sure to read Noodle Cooking Techniques on page 59.

MAKES 4 SERVINGS

10 ounces dried udon noodles

½ pound Boston lettuce

2 scallions

½ cup peeled carrot, cut into thin 3-inch-long slices

½ cup green bell pepper, cut into thin 3-inch-long pieces

1 cup stemmed and thinly sliced shiitake mushrooms

¼ cup canola oil or vegetable oil

1 pound medium shrimp, shelled and deveined (about 26 pieces)

2 tablespoons minced garlic

4 medium eggs

¼ cup Dashi Stock (page 38) or low-sodium chicken stock (optional)

1 teaspoon sea salt

1 teaspoon freshly ground black pepper

2 teaspoons shoyu (soy sauce)

Bring a large pot of water to a boil and cook the udon noodles for 1 minute shorter than the suggested cooking time on the package. Drain the noodles in a colander and rinse them under cold water until cold and no longer starchy. Drain and keep the noodles in the colander.

Cut the lettuce into 1 by 2½-inch strips. Cut the scallions diagonally into thin slices and keep the whites and the greens separate in small cups. Divide the lettuce, carrot, green bell pepper, and mushrooms into two bowls.

Heat 1 tablespoon of the canola oil in a wok or large skillet over medium heat. Add half of the shrimp and cook for 4 minutes over medium-low heat, stirring from time to time. Add half of the minced garlic and the white part of the scallion slices and cook for 20 seconds. Transfer the shrimp and garlic to a bowl using a slotted spoon. Add 1 tablespoon of the canola oil to the wok, and when it is hot, break and add 2 eggs to the wok. Turn the heat to medium-high and give several large stirs, breaking the yolks and briefly cooking the eggs. When the eggs are fluffy and still undercooked, quickly transfer them to the bowl with the shrimp. Set the heat to medium and add one bowlful of the vegetables to the wok. Cook the vegetables, stirring all the time, until they are wilted. Add half of the udon noodles, the stock, salt, black pepper, and soy sauce to the wok. Cook the udon and vegetables, stirring all the time, until the liquid is almost absorbed.

Add the reserved cooked shrimp and eggs, and the green scallion slices to the wok and toss and turn all of the ingredients until they are mixed thoroughly. Transfer to a large platter and keep warm while you repeat with the remaining half of the ingredients to prepare the second batch of noodles. Transfer the second batch to the large platter and serve.

NOODLE COOKING TECHNIQUES

For successful preparation and enjoyment of the Japanese noodle dishes in this book, there are four important techniques that will ensure the best results.

1. No salt is added to the boiling water in which the noodles are cooked. Instead, the cooking process removes excess salt that has been added during noodle production.

2. Cook the noodles in plenty of boiling water. For example, if you are cooking 3½ ounces of dry noodles, use at least 5 cups of water. When water is insufficient, pasty starch released from the surface of the noodles accumulates and slows down the movement of the boiling water. Noodles should always be rolling over as they cook.

3. Use the *sashimizu* technique. *Sashimizu* literally means "adding water." After adding dry noodles to a large pot of boiling water, stir them with a fork to separate them. Then, wait for a second boil. Upon the second boiling, add cold water (5 cups of boiling cooking water requires 1 cup of additional cold tap water) to stop the boiling. This contributes to even cooking by preventing the surface of the noodles from becoming too tender and pasty before the heat penetrates into the center of the noodles. After adding cold water, turn the heat to medium and continue cooking the noodles, making sure that the noodles are rolling over in the water.

4. After the noodles are cooked, rinse them briskly in a bowl full of cold water placed under cold, continuously running tap water. This is done regardless of whether the noodles are to be served hot or cold. The rinsing process cools the noodles, stops further cooking, and removes excess starch that accumulates on the surface of the noodles during cooking. This preserves their firm texture, glossy appearance, and pristine flavor. The only exception to this rule is for ramen noodles that are to be served hot, since they are not rinsed in cold water.

Thin Okonomiyaki

Japanese *okonomiyaki,* a kind of stuffed pancake, is usually about 1 inch thick, and can be even thicker. The cabbage, noodles, seafood, meat, and other ingredients added as stuffing push up its height. There is another element that contributes to the thickness, grated *yama-imo,* Japanese yam (see page 61). This *yama-imo* also works to bind all of the other ingredients. Since this yam can be hard to find and is usually limited to Japanese or Asian food stores in America, I replace it with baking powder. Although baking powder does not function in the same way as *yama-imo,* it is a good substitute because it produces a thin pancake that is crispy and more appealing to American tastes.

MAKES 4 TO 6 SERVINGS

2 medium eggs

1 cup cake flour

2 teaspoons baking powder

1 cup Dashi Stock (page 38) or low-sodium chicken broth

1 teaspoon Worcestershire sauce

1 teaspoon rice vinegar

1½ teaspoons sea salt

1 teaspoon sugar

⅛ to ¼ teaspoon ground cinnamon

4 bacon slices (3½ ounces)

½ of a medium Granny Smith apple (2½ ounces)

1⅓ cups finely julienned red cabbage

1⅓ cups finely julienned carrots

¼ to ½ cup vegetable oil

Freshly ground black pepper

Break and beat the eggs in a bowl and add the flour, baking powder, stock, Worcestershire sauce, vinegar, salt, sugar, and cinnamon. Mix all the ingredients thoroughly with a fork until smooth. Let the mixture stand, covered with a kitchen towel, for 30 minutes.

Prepare a kettle of boiling water. Cut the bacon into thin strips crosswise and transfer to a strainer. Pour the boiling water over the bacon to remove excess fat. Drain the bacon well.

Cut the apple into matchstick-size julienne. Add the bacon, the julienned apple, cabbage, and carrots to the egg-flour-stock mixture and fold the ingredients together with a spatula. Divide the pancake dough into four bowls.

Heat 1 to 2 tablespoons of the oil in a 10-inch skillet over medium heat. When the oil is hot, add one bowl of the pancake dough to the skillet and decrease the heat to medium-low. Using a rubber spatula, make the dough into a 10-inch flat disk. As it cooks, run the spatula along the pancake's edge to create a smooth, clean border. Cook the pancake for 4 to 5 minutes, or until the bottom is golden, running the spatula under the edges of the pancake toward the end of the cooking time to loosen the bottom. Flip the pancake over with a spatula and cook for an additional 4 minutes, or until the bottom is golden. If you like, add an additional 1 tablespoon oil to the skillet to make the surface crispier. Transfer the pancake to a cutting board. Add an additional 1 to 2 tablespoons of oil to the skillet and repeat with the remaining ingredients to prepare 3 more pancakes. Cut the pancakes into thin, bite-size wedges, sprinkle with a little black pepper, and serve hot.

True Yam

Yams confuse us. A true yam is not a sweet potato, but a different tuber that takes various shapes and has varying characteristics. Yams are consumed in Africa, Asia, and Japan. Japanese yam is called *yama no imo* (meaning "mountain yam," shortened to *yama-imo*), and there are two noteworthy types. One of them is the long, baseball bat–shaped *naga-imo* (long mountain yam). When peeled, the inside of this yam is snow white in color and has a crisp, watery, and slimy texture. There is no distinctive flavor. We consume it raw, julienned, or grated, or use it in cooking—for example, in simmered dishes. In such dishes the *yama-imo* takes on flavor from the simmering liquid.

The other type of Japanese yam is a large rutabaga-size, semi-flat yam called *icho-imo* (gingko tree leaf mountain yam, named because of its shape). *Icho-imo* has a dense texture and mild, pleasant sweetness, and when it is grated it has a heavy and resilient texture—similar to fresh mochi, the sticky rice cake made from rice flour. We eat it raw, grated, or cooked. Grated and gooey *icho-imo* wrapped up in a small piece of nori or a shiso leaf, dipped in tempura batter, and deep-fried in hot oil is a personal favorite.

Root Vegetables Simmered in the Japanese Way

Nimono, "simmered dish," is one of the most popular cooking techniques in Japan and is used to enjoy the distinctive flavor of seasonally changing vegetables. Vegetables are first briefly cooked in water, then in flavored stock. Since each vegetable requires a different cooking time and has its own unique flavor and texture, we cook and season each of them separately. The cooked vegetables are then assembled and served together. This approach requires too much trouble and time for most home cooks, so in this recipe I combine compatible vegetables and cook them together for quick and easy preparation. One nearly universal characteristic of *nimono* preparation is that we flavor the vegetables with just enough seasonings such as salt and shoyu (soy sauce) to heighten the natural flavor of each ingredient but not mask it. Prepared *nimono* dishes taste best after marinating for 2 hours to overnight (while the vegetables cool down, the flavor concentrates in them). *Nimono* vegetables can be served cold, at room temperature, or warm after being reheated, as in this recipe. Please read Tips for Vegetable Cooking on page 63.

MAKES 6 SERVINGS

6 medium Japanese or American turnips (12 ounces)

6 large sugar snap peas or string peas

2 medium carrots (½ pound), peeled

6 cherry tomatoes

3 cups Dashi Stock (page 38) or low-sodium chicken stock (optional)

1 tablespoon shoyu (soy sauce)

1 tablespoon mirin (sweet cooking wine)

¾ teaspoon sea salt

Peel the turnips, removing the thick peel, and cut them in half. Remove the strings from the snap peas. Cut the carrots into 1½-inch pieces, using the *rangiri* cutting technique (see page 201) or diagonal slices. Prick several spots on the surface of the tomatoes with a toothpick. Place the turnips and carrots in a medium pot of cold water over medium heat and cook until simmering. Reduce the heat to low, cook for 3 minutes, then use a slotted spoon to transfer the carrots to a bowl of cold water to cool. Drain the carrots. When the turnips have cooked for about 9 minutes total, add the tomatoes and snap peas to the pot and cook for 1 minute. Using a slotted spoon, carefully transfer all of the vegetables to a bowl of cold water to cool, then drain the vegetables. Peel the tomatoes.

Place the stock, soy sauce, mirin, and salt in a medium pot over medium-low heat. Add the carrots and turnips and bring it to a simmer for 5 minutes. Turn off the heat and add the tomatoes and snap peas to the pot. Put the pot in a large bowl of cold water and let the vegetables cool quickly in the liquid. Keep the vegetables in the liquid.

Before serving the vegetables, briefly rewarm them in the cooking liquid. First, bring the cooking liquid to a boil. Then add the vegetables and warm them quickly in order to avoid overcooking them. Divide the vegetables into small bowls. Pour 3 to 4 tablespoons of the cooking liquid over each bowl and serve.

TIPS FOR VEGETABLE COOKING

In *nimono* preparation, the vegetables are first briefly cooked in simmering water. The precooked vegetables are then cooked in the stock and seasoned with ingredients such as shoyu (soy sauce), sugar, salt, mirin, and/or sake. Precooking the vegetables has the following benefits:

- It removes harsh or other undesirable flavors from the vegetables.
- It cleans the vegetables.
- It softens the fibers in the vegetables so they can evenly and efficiently absorb the seasoning ingredients in the second cooking process.
- Cleaned vegetables produce less foam during cooking, so there is no or little need to skim foam during the final cooking.

Tips for precooking vegetables:

1. Cook root vegetables starting with cold water.
2. Cook other vegetables starting with boiling water.
3. Add salt to water when cooking green or leafy vegetables, such as broccoli, Brussels sprouts, peas, spinach, kale, or collards; salt raises the boiling point of the water for effective cooking and stabilizes the green chlorophyll color. The recommended amount of salt differs, depending on the individual vegetable, but in general, it is 1 percent by volume of the water volume (for example, 2 teaspoons salt to 4 cups water). Use a ratio of five times water to the volume of vegetables.
4. Add vinegar or lemon juice to cook cauliflower for enhanced white color.
5. Cook daikon radish, turnip, and burdock with raw rice—1½ tablespoons raw rice to 4 cups water—to remove overpowering flavors and to retain whiteness.

Simmered Eggplant and Kabocha Squash

Please pardon me for cooking summer-autumn eggplant with autumn-winter parsnip and kabocha in this recipe. The eggplant in this recipe is so flavorful that I must violate my declaration of using seasonal ingredients at their peak. I discovered the parsnip in America, and it has become one of my favorite American vegetables in the winter. When simmering eggplant, kabocha, and parsnip, I typically use a little bit of cooking oil at the beginning of the preparation to enhance the purple color of the eggplant, to aid the absorption of vitamin A from the kabocha, and to help to achieve a caramelized flavor. Choose younger parsnips whose centers are less fibrous. These cooked vegetables taste better after resting for 2 hours to overnight. If you purchased a whole kabocha, use any remaining kabocha to make Spiced Kabocha Squash Soup (page 18) or Kabocha and Lamb Wonton Pot Stickers (page 197).

MAKES 6 SERVINGS

3 cups Dashi Stock (page 38) or low-sodium chicken stock (optional)

1 tablespoon shoyu (soy sauce)

1 tablespoon mirin (sweet cooking wine)

1 tablespoon sugar

¾ teaspoon salt

2 small, thin, long American eggplant (1½ pounds)

Canola oil or vegetable oil, for frying

½ of a small kabocha squash (½ pound)

3 large parsnips (1 pound)

1 tablespoon sliced scallion (green part only)

Place the stock, soy sauce, mirin, sugar, and salt in a pot over medium heat and bring it to a simmer. Divide the flavored stock into two bowls.

Cut off the stem ends of the eggplant, and then cut into quarters lengthwise. Make many diagonal shallow cuts—⅛ inch wide—on the skin side of the quartered eggplant. Cut each eggplant quarter into 2-inch-long pieces. Heat 1 inch of the canola oil to 340°F in a medium skillet, then add the eggplant pieces and cook them until the white part of the surface is lightly golden and the purple skin shines. Using a slotted spoon, transfer the eggplant to a paper towel–lined plate. Add the eggplant to one of the bowls of the prepared broth and let cool. The eggplant will lose its bright color in the course of marinating, but will absorb the wonderful flavor from the broth. Keep the eggplant in the cold broth.

Cut the kabocha into 6 wedges (1½-inch pieces) and remove the seeds and pulp with a spoon (see page 65). Using a knife, remove about ⅛ inch of the soft flesh side of each wedge. Cut the parsnip into 1½-inch pieces, using the *rangiri* technique (see page 201) or cutting on the diagonal.

Remove nearly all of the canola oil from the skillet in which the eggplant was cooked, leaving a thin layer of oil on the bottom, and return it to medium heat. Add the kabocha and parsnip pieces to the skillet and cook them until the surface of each piece is golden, about 3 minutes, turning the pieces over from time to time. Add the kabocha and parsnip to a medium pot along with the remaining flavored broth and bring it to a simmer over medium heat. Decrease the heat to low and cook for 8 minutes. Turn off the heat and let the vegetables cool in the cooking broth. Keep the vegetables in the cool broth.

Before serving, warm the vegetables in the broth. Avoid overheating to prevent the vegetables from becoming mushy. Divide the vegetables into serving bowls. Pour 2 to 3 tablespoons of the broth into each bowl. Garnish with the sliced scallion and serve.

Kabocha from Kampuchea

Kabocha is a squash and is shaped like a pumpkin. The size varies, but a medium kabocha is generally about 8 inches in diameter and has a thick, tough, dark green skin. It is known for its sweet flavor and silky, creamy texture when cooked. *Kabocha* is the Japanese name for this vegetable, which originated in South America. The name might have come from a language misunderstanding between the Japanese and the Portuguese, who brought the kabocha to Japan by way of Kampuchea (present-day Cambodia) during the sixteenth century. It is thought that when the Japanese asked what this vegetable was, the Portuguese misunderstood, thinking the Japanese were asking, "Where is the vegetable from?" They replied, "Kampuchea," which to the Japanese sounded like "kabocha"—or so the story goes.

When I first moved to New York City more than a decade ago, my beloved kabocha was a hard-to-find "Japanese" vegetable, and I had to travel to a Japanese food store to purchase it. But today kabocha is readily available everywhere, including our neighborhood supermarket and farmers' markets.

Technique

HOW TO CUT A STONE-HARD KABOCHA SQUASH

Cutting into a whole, hard, tough-skinned *raw kabocha* is as difficult as cutting hardwood. It poses a real challenge. One can easily snap a knife blade in the process. Here is a solution: Wrap a whole kabocha squash in aluminum foil and leave it in a heated oven (350°F) for 30 minutes. Transfer the kabocha to a cutting board and remove the aluminum foil. In this state kabocha is still rather firm but is easier to cut. Remove the protruding stem and insert a knife down through the center, holding it perpendicular to the cutting board. When the knife is deeply inserted, push the handle of the knife down to the cutting board to make a cut. Remove the knife from the kabocha and repeat the same process on the other side, resulting in the kabocha being cut in half. After cutting the kabocha in half, cut it into quarters and remove the seeds and pulp. From this point, smaller pieces can be cut to suit your recipe. Use the cut kabocha within 3 days, or cook and freeze it for later use.

Avocado and Salmon in Dill-Daikon Broth

In this recipe, avocado, salmon, and sweet potato are first coated with cornstarch and fried, then served in a piping-hot, flavored broth. This style of preparation is called *age-dashi*. From the description of the dish you may worry that pouring hot broth over fried items may ruin the crispiness. Not to worry! By doing so, the fried vegetables and salmon absorb excellent flavor from the hot broth, while also shedding excess oil from the fried ingredients. Serve this dish immediately after preparation, while hot, and a good deal of crispiness will remain. Be sure to read Frying Guidelines (page 164) before proceeding.

MAKES 4 SERVINGS

1 pound boneless, skinless
   salmon fillet

3½ tablespoons shoyu (soy sauce)

2½ tablespoons mirin
   (sweet cooking wine)

¼ cup cornstarch

1 small Japanese sweet potato or
   American sweet potato (5 ounces)

1 small avocado

2 cups Dashi Stock (page 38) or
   low-sodium chicken stock

¾ teaspoon sea salt

1 medium daikon radish

1 tablespoon chopped fresh dill

Canola oil, for frying

Cut the salmon into 8 pieces. In a bowl, toss the salmon with 1 tablespoon each of the soy sauce and mirin and let them stand for 20 minutes. Drain the salmon and lightly wipe the pieces with a paper towel to dry. Dust the salmon pieces with the cornstarch and let them stand for 20 minutes.

Cut the sweet potato into 1½-inch cubes. Add the sweet potato to a medium pot of cold water and place it over medium heat until it begins to simmer. Then lower the heat to medium-low and cook the potato pieces for 10 minutes. Drain the potato pieces in a colander and air-dry them. Pit, peel, and cut the avocado in half lengthwise. Cut each avocado half into 4 wedges. Dust the sweet potato and avocado with cornstarch and let them stand for 15 minutes.

Place the stock, the remaining 2½ tablespoons soy sauce, the remaining 1½ tablespoons mirin, and the salt in a saucepan over medium heat and bring it to a simmer. Turn off the heat and set aside. Peel and grate the daikon radish using a very fine grater. Transfer the grated radish to a sieve and gently shake—counting to 10—to remove excess water, and discard the water. Transfer the radish to a bowl and toss with the dill.

Add 2 inches of canola oil to a deep skillet and heat it to 340°F. Add the sweet potato and cook for 2 minutes or until all the sides are lightly golden, turning the pieces from time to time. Using a slotted spoon, transfer the sweet potato to a wire rack set over a sheet pan. While the sweet potato is cooking, re-dust the salmon with the remaining cornstarch. Add the salmon to the skillet and cook it in two or three batches for 4 to 5 minutes each, or until the salmon is cooked through and the outside is lightly golden, turning the fish once or twice during cooking. Using a slotted spoon, transfer the salmon to the wire rack.

Increase the temperature of the oil to 350°F and cook the avocado until the outside is lightly golden, about 2 minutes. Using a slotted spoon, transfer the avocado to the wire rack. Divide the salmon, sweet potato, and avocado among soup bowls. Add the daikon and dill mixture to the prepared stock and bring it to a simmer over medium heat. Pour the hot broth over each bowl. Serve immediately, piping-hot.

Japanese Seafood Quenelles in Kuzu Dashi Broth

In the Japanese kitchen we make a quenelle, *shinjo*, similar to the one from the French kitchen. Traditional *shinjo* preparation does not use dairy products, so that you may better enjoy the clean flavor of the seafood used in the preparation. In this recipe, however, I do add a little cream to the seafood to achieve a slightly richer flavor. The key to the success of this preparation is the use of very fresh fish and shrimp even though everything is processed into a pasty form. The broth is loosely thickened with kuzu, arrowroot starch, a thickening agent such as cornstarch and potato starch. Arrowroot starch produces the clearest, and non-starchy tasting result with a hint of slight sweetness among other agents.

MAKES 4 SERVINGS

- ½ pound boneless, skinless cod
- ½ pound medium shrimp, shelled and deveined (13 to 15 pieces)
- 3½ teaspoons sea salt
- 1 medium egg
- ¼ teaspoon ground nutmeg
- ¼ teaspoon paprika
- ¼ cup heavy cream
- 1 medium egg white
- 2 cups Dashi Stock (page 38) or low-sodium chicken stock
- ¼ cup sake (rice wine)
- ½ tablespoon mirin (sweet cooking wine)
- ½ tablespoon plus 2 teaspoons shoyu (soy sauce)
- 1 tablespoon lemon juice
- 1½ tablespoons kuzu starch or cornstarch mixed with 2 tablespoons water
- 6 cups water
- ½ bundle spinach leaves (7 ounces)
- ½ to 1 teaspoon finely grated lemon zest

Cut the fish and shrimp into rough 1-inch pieces and toss them with 1 teaspoon of the salt in a bowl. Transfer the fish and approximately half of the shrimp to a food processor and process for 30 seconds, using the pulse function. Add the whole egg and process for 10 seconds. Add the remaining shrimp and process for 5 seconds (this portion of the shrimp should remain in small pieces—a chunky form). Transfer the processed fish and shrimp to a medium bowl. Add the nutmeg and paprika to the bowl and fold in with a spatula. In another bowl, beat the heavy cream until soft peaks appear. Fold the cream into the fish and shrimp mixture. In another bowl, beat the egg white until soft peaks appear. Fold the egg white into the fish and shrimp mixture and refrigerate for 20 minutes while making the broth.

Place the stock, 2 tablespoons of the sake, the mirin, ½ tablespoon of the soy sauce, and 1½ teaspoons of the salt in a medium pot over medium heat and bring the mixture to a simmer. Add the lemon juice. Turn the heat to low and add the starch water. Cook the broth over low heat, stirring all the time with a spatula, until the broth slightly thickens and becomes transparent. Turn off the heat and set aside.

Place the water, the remaining 2 tablespoons sake, and the remaining 1 teaspoon salt in a large pot over medium heat and bring to a gentle simmer. Decrease the heat to low and keep the liquid simmering. Remove the fish and shrimp paste from the refrigerator. With a table-spoon, scoop up a one-twelfth portion of the paste, and with another tablespoon form it into a quenelle (oval) shape. Gently push the quenelle into the simmering water. Make several more quenelles and place them in the water. Leave 40 percent of the surface of the water uncovered; quenelles expand in volume during cooking. Decrease the heat to low, cover the pot, and cook the quenelles for 10 minutes.

Using a slotted spoon, transfer the quenelles to a plate. Finish cooking all of the quenelles in batches. Cook the spinach in the quenelle cooking water over medium heat for 1 minute. Drain, clean, and cool the spinach under cold tap water. Firmly squeeze the spinach to remove excess water. Transfer the spinach to a cutting board, lay it flat, and sprinkle with the remaining ½ teaspoon soy sauce. Massage the spinach to distribute the soy sauce. Squeeze the spinach again gently but thoroughly to remove the water, forming into a cylinder. Cut the spinach into 4 portions. Divide the spinach among soup bowls and add 3 quenelles to each bowl.

Heat the prepared broth to a simmer over medium heat. Pour the hot broth into the soup bowls. Garnish with the grated lemon zest and serve immediately.

Japanese-Style Braised Pork Shoulder

I was raised to cook ground, thinly sliced, or steak-cut pork in Japan. I had never faced the challenge of cooking a large cut of meat such as a pork shoulder or butt until I moved to America. After enjoying delicious braised pork shoulder dishes at restaurants across the country, I wanted to create a simple, easy-to-prepare pork shoulder dish with Japanese flavors. Just as with my Sake-Braised Short Ribs (page 33), this dish has become a great favorite of our family and friends. Serve with a piece of good crusty bread to enjoy the sauce left on your plate. An easy way to truss the meat is to wrap the pork shoulder around the width in 4 to 5 places with kitchen string and tie, keeping equal spaces. Then wrap around the meat at the length and tie.

MAKES 4 TO 6 SERVINGS

3 tablespoons shoyu (soy sauce)

2 teaspoons hot paprika

5 tablespoons brown sugar

3 tablespoons aged brown miso (see page 12)

3 pounds trussed pork shoulder

1 tablespoon canola oil or vegetable oil

2¼ cups Dashi Stock (page 38) or low-sodium chicken stock (optional)

2 teaspoons Worcestershire sauce

3 tablespoons rice vinegar

3 large parsnips (1 pound), peeled

½ teaspoon sea salt, plus a couple of pinches

1 teaspoon lemon juice or rice vinegar

½ bunch Swiss chard (7 ounces)

In a large bowl, stir together 2 tablespoons of the soy sauce, the hot paprika, 2½ tablespoons of the sugar, and 2 tablespoons of the miso. Add the pork shoulder to the bowl and massage with the marinade. Let the pork shoulder stand, covered, in the marinade for at least 3 hours or up to overnight in the refrigerator.

Preheat the oven to 350°F. Remove the pork shoulder from the marinade and lightly squeeze it to remove any excess marinade. Reserve the marinade. Prepare a kettle of boiling water. Heat the canola oil in a medium skillet over medium heat, then add the pork shoulder and cook it over medium-low heat until all sides are golden brown, about 4 minutes. Transfer the browned pork to a sieve and quickly pour the boiling water over it (see page 33).

Place 2 cups of the stock, the Worcestershire sauce, rice vinegar, the remaining 2½ tablespoons sugar, the remaining 1 tablespoon miso, and the reserved marinade in a large oven-safe pot, and bring it to a simmer over medium heat. Add the pork to the pot, cover with a lid, and cook it in the oven for 2 hours.

Cut the parsnips into ½-inch slices. Transfer the parsnips to a baking dish and add the remaining ¼ cup stock. Cover the dish with doubled aluminum foil and cook it in the oven during the last 35 to 40 minutes of cooking the pork. Remove the parsnips from the oven and carefully remove the aluminum foil. Transfer the parsnips to a blender with a couple of pinches of salt, the lemon juice, and 4 to 5 tablespoons water. Process the parsnips until smooth.

Remove the pork from the oven and transfer to a plate, reserving the cooking liquid in the pot (you will have 2 to 3 cups). Add the ½ teaspoon salt and the remaining 1 tablespoon soy sauce to the pork braising liquid and cook it over medium heat until it is reduced to about 1½ cups.

When the pork is cool, cut it into 4 to 6 portions. Cut off the bottom part of the hard stems of the Swiss chard, and cut the leaves with the remaining stems into halves lengthwise. Pile up the leaves and cut them crosswise into thin strips. Return the pork pieces to the reduced cooking liquid. Add the Swiss chard to the pork and cook, covered, over low heat for 10 minutes.

Divide the pork, Swiss chard, and parsnip puree among dinner plates. Spoon the remaining cooking liquid over each portion of pork and serve.

Ekiben, the Train Station Lunch Box

Japan is a train country. The small island nation has a network of railway lines traversed by frequent passenger trains, including the famous 200-mph "bullet train," the *Shinkansen*. Trains—whether slow or rapid, short or long distance—are often packed with business-people, students, shoppers, the young, and the old. The national railway timetable of Japan is a 700-page book issued every month. The domestic airline service occupies a mere seven or eight pages at the rear of the train timetables. This unique way of living and traveling has produced a colorful culinary tradition—the *ekiben*, or "station lunch boxes" that are sold at platform kiosks at many stations along all the lines. The name comes from *eki* ("station"), and *ben*, short for *bento*, the traditional Japanese lunch box. *Ekiben* often showcases local culinary specialties and uses ingredients that are hallmarks of the region and season.

My favorite *ekiben* is *Masu no Sushi* from Toyama Prefecture on the Japan seaside of the country. Salt-and-vinegar-cured *sakura-masu* (cherry salmon) is packed with sushi rice, to which the salmon is pressed. The finished sushi looks like a 10-inch deep-dish pizza. A small plastic knife is supplied with the *ekiben*. The knife is used to cut triangular wedges of this delicious sushi, just like a pizza. But unlike pizza, *Masu no Sushi* has only two components; sushi rice and cured salmon. When you bite into it you taste an orchestrated combination of flavors—oiliness, saltiness, sweetness, and tartness—that comes from these two ingredients. Today, popular *ekiben* are sold not just at the specific train station from where they originated, but they are also often transported over long distances to food courts in department stores and super-markets across the country to cater to *ekiben* fans (of whom there are millions). At special *ekiben* fairs held in major cities, you can sometimes find "rare" *ekiben* from smaller towns across the country. Naturally, they sell out very quickly!

Chawanmushi Egg Custard with Creamy Mushroom Topping

Chawanmushi is a savory egg custard that is prepared in individual serving cups. The base of *chawanmushi* is a combination of one part egg to three or four parts Dashi Stock. Japanese egg custard has a clean taste and a silky smooth texture. In this recipe, I top the traditional savory custard with sautéed mushrooms. The addition of dried black trumpet mushrooms adds a robust and appealing fragrance to this dish, which can be served hot or cold.

MAKES 4 SERVINGS

- 1 teaspoon dried black trumpet mushrooms
- 1 cup Dashi Stock (page 38) or low-sodium chicken stock (optional)
- 2 large eggs
- 1 teaspoon mirin (sweet cooking wine)
- 1 teaspoon sake (rice wine)
- ½ teaspoon shoyu (soy sauce)
- ¾ teaspoon sea salt
- 5 ounces assorted mushrooms, such as cremini, portobello, chanterelle, or shiitake
- 1 tablespoon olive oil or vegetable oil
- ¼ cup minced yellow onion
- 2 cloves garlic, sliced
- 2 tablespoons chopped fresh parsley
- ¼ cup heavy cream

Preheat the oven to 325°F. Prepare a large pot of boiling water. Have on hand an oven-safe container that is at least 2 inches deep and can hold four 1-cup ramekins without crowding.

In a bowl, soak the dried black trumpet mushrooms in the stock for 20 minutes. Drain the mushrooms, reserving the stock in a bowl. Cut the mushrooms into thin strips.

In another bowl, beat the eggs lightly and thoroughly with a whisk without creating much foam. Add the mirin, sake, soy sauce, ¼ teaspoon of the salt, and the trumpet mushroom–infused stock and stir. Strain the egg mixture through a fine-mesh sieve set over a bowl. Divide the egg mixture among the four ramekins. Transfer the ramekins to the oven-safe container. Add the boiling water to the container until it reaches halfway up the side of the ramekins. Cover the container with aluminum foil and carefully transfer it to the oven. Cook the egg custards for 45 minutes. To test for doneness, insert a toothpick into a custard. When the liquid runs clear, it is done. If it is still cloudy, it is not done.

Rinse the assorted mushrooms in cold saltwater (see page 85) to clean them if necessary. Cut the mushrooms into thin slices. Heat the olive oil in a medium skillet over medium heat, then add the onion and cook for 3 minutes, stirring. Add the garlic to the skillet and cook for 20 seconds. Add all of the mushrooms, the parsley, and the remaining ½ teaspoon of the salt, and cook for 3 minutes. Add the heavy cream and cook until the cream is absorbed.

Remove the cooked custards from the oven. Garnish with the creamed mushrooms and serve.

Tomato-Bacon Omelet

The classic Japanese omelet, *tamagoyaki*, is made from egg, dashi, sugar, and shoyu (soy sauce) and has a distinctive appearance, flavor, and texture. *Tamagoyaki* is prepared in a special rectangular omelet pan called a *tamagoyaki-ki*. Preparation of traditional *tamagoyaki* requires not only this special pan, but also the use of an unusual cooking technique: First make the egg liquid, pour about ⅓ cup of it into the heated *tamagoyaki-ki*, make a thin omelet, and then roll it into a cylinder. Another thin layer of egg liquid is added to the pan, cooked, and then rolled over the previously made egg cylinder. The repetition of this process four or five times produces a thick rolled omelet made up of many thin layers. This recipe provides a solution that allows people to enjoy this wonderful, unique-tasting Japanese omelet without going through all the traditional trouble. The flavored egg liquid is cooked in an American skillet using an easy American omelet-making technique. The bacon and tomato that I have added here are not a traditional *tamagoyaki* stuffing. Try this omelet as a special treat on a weekend morning with family and friends. I'm sure all your guests will be pleased.

MAKES 4 SERVINGS

4 slices bacon (3½ ounces)

⅓ cup chopped tomato

⅓ cup chopped fresh parsley

8 large eggs

2 tablespoons sugar

2 pinches of sea salt

2 teaspoons shoyu (soy sauce)

⅓ cup Dashi Stock (page 38) or low-sodium chicken stock

2 tablespoons olive oil or vegetable oil

Place a medium skillet over medium heat. When the skillet is hot, add the bacon in a single layer. Cook, turning several times, over medium-low heat for 5 to 6 minutes or until lightly golden and crisp. Transfer the bacon to a paper towel–lined plate and let cool. Cut the bacon into ½-inch pieces. Drain the chopped tomato in a sieve and mix it with the parsley and bacon pieces.

Break the eggs into a bowl and add the sugar, salt, soy sauce, and stock, and beat the mixture with a fork. Divide the egg mixture between two bowls. Wipe out the previously used skillet with paper towels to remove excess bacon fat, and place it on the stove over medium heat. Heat 1 tablespoon of the olive oil and add the egg mixture from one bowl. When the bottom of the egg mixture starts to cook, cut up the cooked bottom part of the egg with a fork, swirl, and let the uncooked egg mixture flow underneath the cooked egg. When the egg is about 70 percent done and the top is still runny (after 2½ to 3 minutes of cooking), evenly sprinkle half of the bacon and tomato mixture on the surface of the egg. Fold one-third of the omelet from the far right end (or left if you are left-handed) over the middle one-third of the omelet. Then quickly turn the folded part over onto the remaining one-third of the omelet. Transfer the omelet to a warm platter and finish making an additional omelet using the remaining oil, egg mixture, tomato, bacon, and parsley. Serve immediately.

CHAPTER 3

WHITE SUMISO SAUCE

White Sumiso Sauce is a traditional sauce made from young, pale white miso or medium-aged light brown miso (see page 12), sugar, and vinegar. It has a thick texture and a pleasant soybean flavor with delicious sweet, sour, and salty characteristics. Even though sumiso sauce is popular in Japan, its role in the classic Japanese kitchen is limited, and typically it accompanies raw, blanched, or simmered shellfish and/or vegetables. After several years of living in my adopted country, I have expanded the use of my homemade White Sumiso Sauce. I use it in traditional and modern Japanese preparations and also employ it as a new flavoring element in many popular American recipes, such as salad dressings, marinades, and rubs.

You will find new flavors for both your daily and special-event cooking repertoires throughout this chapter, including Salad Greens with White Miso Dressing (page 80), Curried Tofu Squares (page 87), Sumiso Ham Sandwich (page 81), Succulent Pork Ribs (page 98), Sumiso-Marinated Grilled Chicken (page 97), and Potato and Salmon Salad (page 89).

Freezing will not change the texture of the sauce, and prepared sauce can be stored in the freezer for up to three months. When needed, take it out of the freezer, quickly scoop and transfer the necessary portion to a small bowl, and return the container to the freezer to preserve the quality.

White Sumiso Sauce

MAKES 1½ CUPS

1 cup medium-aged light brown miso
(see page 12)

¼ cup sake (rice wine)

3 tablespoons mirin
(sweet cooking wine)

½ cup plus 1 tablespoon sugar

¼ cup rice vinegar

2 tablespoons lemon juice

2 tablespoons grapefruit juice

Place the miso, sake, mirin, and sugar in a medium pot and stir until smooth. Cook the mixture over medium heat for 4 to 5 minutes, stirring with a whisk. Add the rice vinegar and the juices and cook until the miso sauce is no longer watery, about 8 minutes.

Transfer the sauce to a clean, freezer-proof container. Cover the container with a tight-fitting lid and store it in the freezer for up to 3 months.

Sumiso and Asparagus

Crisply cooked asparagus and tender simmered squid dressed with White Sumiso Sauce is a traditional Japanese use of sumiso sauce. Prepare fresh squid so that it will be tender but not gummy or tough by cooking the whole, cleaned squid in cold water. When using frozen squid, defrost it slowly in the refrigerator overnight.

MAKES 4 SERVINGS

12 thick-stemmed asparagus spears, brown frills removed

8 small (½ pound) squid, cleaned

2 scallions

¼ cup White Sumiso Sauce (page 76)

2 tablespoons Dashi Stock (page 38) or water

Sea salt

Bring a medium pot of salted water (see page 94) to a boil over medium heat. Add the asparagus and cook for 1 minute. Drain the asparagus in a colander and quickly air-dry. Cut each asparagus spear into 3 sections.

Place the squid in a medium pot and cover with 2 inches of cold water. Bring to a simmer over medium heat. Decrease the heat to medium-low and cook the squid for 4 minutes, or until it is plump and white. Turn off the heat and leave the squid in the water for 5 minutes. Drain the squid and pat dry with paper towels. Transfer the squid to a cutting board and cut it into ½-inch-thick rings. Cut the scallions into thin diagonal slices.

In a small cup, whisk the White Sumiso Sauce with the stock. Taste the sauce and if necessary add a little salt. Divide the asparagus and squid rings into bowls, pour the sauce over the top, sprinkle with the scallions, and serve.

Mesclun with Sumiso-Carrot Dressing

Finely grated, bright orange carrot served with sumiso dressing results in an eye-catching presentation and a mild, sweet carrot flavor. Use a grater that produces a very fine grate of the carrot and onion without shredding them. Choose carrots that are moist, juicy, and sweet.

MAKES 4 SERVINGS

5 tablespoons finely grated carrot

1 teaspoon finely grated yellow onion

2 teaspoons peeled and grated ginger

¼ cup White Sumiso Sauce (page 76)

¼ cup rice vinegar or other vinegar

¼ cup olive oil or vegetable oil

2 teaspoons sugar

¾ teaspoon sea salt

¼ teaspoon freshly ground black pepper

¼ small red onion

1 large orange

8 cups mesclun or other salad greens

⅓ cup walnuts, toasted

Add the carrot, grated onion, ginger, White Sumiso Sauce, rice vinegar, olive oil, sugar, salt, and black pepper to a 16-ounce glass jar. Cover the jar with a tight-fitting lid, and shake it until thoroughly blended.

Cut the red onion into thin slices. Peel and section the orange. Divide the mesclun, onion, and orange sections among salad plates, pour a little dressing on each, top with the walnuts, and serve.

Thirty Foods a Day

When I was growing up in Japan, my country was (and still is) instructing its citizens that eating thirty varieties of foods a day is good for one's health. Consuming not just a few—but a large—variety of items truly offers a better, balanced diet. The easiest way to increase the number of food items is to add more vegetables to our diet. I divide vegetables into three categories: roots, such as carrot, parsnip, turnip, and daikon radish; leaves, such as collard greens, Swiss chard, cabbage, spinach, and lettuce; and fruits, such as eggplant, bell pepper, string beans, and peas. The color of vegetables is linked to particular nutrients. Bright orange vegetables are rich in carotene; purple is associated with polyphenol (an antioxidant); and greens have chlorophyll, calcium, foliate, vitamin C, and beta-carotene. So when planning a dish consisting of mixed vegetables, do not stick to just a few types or colors. A large variety is better for you!

Salad Greens with White Sumiso Dressing

This is an easy-to-make and appealing miso-flavored dressing for your salads. It works well with crisp romaine or Boston lettuce tossed with tomato, avocado, and walnuts, or with steamed asparagus and green beans. For a speedy preparation, add each ingredient to a clean jar, cover with a tight-fitting lid, and shake. Delicious dressing in minutes!

MAKES 4 SERVINGS

1 clove garlic

2 tablespoons White Sumiso Sauce (page 76)

2 tablespoons olive oil or vegetable oil

2 tablespoons rice vinegar

1 teaspoon smooth Dijon mustard

Freshly ground black pepper

Sea salt

4 small heads romaine lettuce

1 cup peeled and shredded carrots

1 cup shredded fennel bulb

Roughly crush the garlic using the side of a knife and add it to a clean 12-ounce glass jar. Next, add the White Sumiso Sauce, olive oil, rice vinegar, Dijon mustard, and black pepper. Cover the jar with a tight-fitting lid, and shake until thoroughly blended. Remove the garlic with a fork and add salt to taste.

Halve the romaine lettuce heads and divide them among salad plates. Top with the carrots and fennel, pour the dressing over the salad, and serve.

Sumiso Ham Sandwich

This is a great example of how an exciting Japanese flavor can enhance and become a part of an existing popular American dish. Try this recipe with roast beef, roast turkey, or a variety of cheese—cheddar, American, mozzarella, or Emmental. They all go very well with White Sumiso Sauce.

MAKES 4 SERVINGS

¼ cup White Sumiso Sauce (page 76)

2 tablespoons unsalted butter, softened

2 teaspoons smooth Dijon mustard

8 slices sandwich bread of your choice

4 large leaves iceberg lettuce

4 large slices tomato

4 slices red onion

12 thin slices ham (9 ounces)

Cucumber pickles of your choice

In a small bowl, mix the White Sumiso Sauce, butter, and Dijon mustard with a spatula.

Brush the surface of 4 slices of bread with half of the sumiso-butter mixture. Place the lettuce, tomato, and onion on top of the bread. Cover the vegetables with 3 slices of ham. Spoon the remaining sauce-butter mixture over each portion of ham. Cover the top of the sandwich with the remaining slices of bread. Serve with cucumber pickles.

Vegetables with Sumiso Bagna Cauda

White Sumiso Sauce is delicious served with cooked vegetables. However, the strong soybean flavor and dense texture may be unpalatable for some in my audience. Therefore, I have created a version inspired by one of my favorite sauces, Italian bagna cauda. I thinned the White Sumiso Sauce with Kelp Stock and olive oil and added anchovies and garlic. This new sauce is delicious with steamed vegetables as well as with poached chicken and seafood.

For this recipe, one serving is 7 ounces of vegetables, more than half of the Recommended Daily Allowance by the World Health Organization. If possible, select six different vegetables for this preparation in order to offer not only healthy nutrients but also a colorful presentation. Be sure to read Thirty Foods a Day on page 78.

MAKES 4 SERVINGS

1 small clove garlic

4 salt-packed anchovy fillets

5 tablespoons Kelp Stock (page 6)
   or water

¼ cup White Sumiso Sauce (page 76)

1½ tablespoons olive oil or
   vegetable oil

4 large Brussels sprouts (3 ounces)

4 medium red radishes (5½ ounces)

2 medium turnips (5 ounces), peeled

1 large carrot (5 ounces), peeled

8 string beans

Salt

8 large cauliflower florets
   (regular or Romanesco; 6 ounces)

Press the garlic through a garlic press and add it to a small saucepan. Add the anchovy fillets, stock, White Sumiso Sauce, and olive oil and place the saucepan over medium-low heat. Whisk the sauce until all the ingredients are fully blended and the sauce is no longer watery. Divide the sauce among bowls.

Halve the Brussels sprouts and radishes. Cut each turnip into 4 wedges. Cut the carrot into 4 diagonal slices. Remove the stems of the string beans, leaving the bottom needle-like tips if they are not damaged. Place the turnips, radishes, and carrot in a medium pot. Add enough water to cover the vegetables by 2 inches. Add the salt (see page 63), and bring to a boil. Cook the vegetables for 3 minutes. Without removing the vegetables in the pot, add the Brussels sprouts, cauliflower, and string beans and cook for an additional 3 minutes. Drain all of the vegetables in a colander, shake to remove excess water, and allow the vegetables to air-dry. Divide the vegetables into each bowl of sauce and serve.

Mushrooms and Poached Eggs

Mushrooms and eggs are a universally popular pair. One of the most memorable mushroom and egg dishes I enjoyed was at a small mushroom specialty restaurant, El Cisne Azul in Madrid, Spain. There, an assortment of local, exotic, seasonal, and highly fragrant mushrooms were quickly sautéed in garlic-infused olive oil and served with a runny sunny-side-up egg on top— a very simple and straightforward preparation and presentation, but absolutely delicious.

In my recipe, I pair mushrooms with White Sumiso Sauce, a combination that produces an unforgettable taste experience. Choose ordinary mushroom varieties such as portobello, shiitake, button, and oyster mushrooms for an everyday meal, and add some seasonal specials such as maitake mushrooms (fall), morels (spring, early summer), and chanterelles (summer through winter) for a special occasion. Store mushrooms in a brown paper bag in the refrigerator and use them as soon as possible, or slice, chop, or mince and freeze them (see page 85).

MAKES 4 SERVINGS

10 ounces combination of button, portobello, and shiitake mushrooms, sliced

¼ cup extra-virgin olive oil

Sea salt

3 large cloves garlic

1 scallion

1 tablespoon plus 1 teaspoon rice vinegar or other vinegar

4 large eggs

¼ cup sweet White Sumiso Sauce (page 76)

2 tablespoons Kelp Stock (page 6) or water

Cut the mushrooms into thin slices, place them in a bowl, and toss them with 2 tablespoons of the olive oil and 2 pinches of the salt. Peel the garlic, and cut it into thin slices. Cut the scallion into very thin diagonal slices.

Heat 1 tablespoon of the olive oil in a skillet over high heat, add two-thirds of the garlic and the white part of the scallion, and cook, stirring constantly, for 20 seconds or until fragrant. Add the mushrooms and cook, stirring occasionally, until they are wilted, 2 to 3 minutes. Remove the skillet from the heat and set aside.

Fill a medium pot with water (about 8 cups), add the rice vinegar, and bring to a boil. Decrease the heat to medium-low and maintain the temperature at about 180°F. Break the eggs into separate small cups, and add the first egg to the water. After ensuring that the egg white envelops the egg yolk, drop the second egg into the water. Cook the eggs in the hot water for 3 minutes. Using a slotted spoon, transfer the eggs to a colander and drain. Repeat with the remaining eggs.

Heat the remaining 1 tablespoon olive oil in a small saucepan over medium heat. Add the remaining sliced garlic and cook until fragrant, about 20 seconds. Add the White Sumiso Sauce and stock and cook over low heat for about 1 ½ minutes. Divide the sauce into bowls. Divide the sautéed mushrooms among the bowls and garnish each with a poached egg. Serve immediately.

QUICK FREEZING TIP

If we speed up the freezing time of mushrooms (or any item that you intend to freeze), we can better preserve their quality. To do this, prechill a steel tray that is slightly larger than the intended freezer bag. The ice-cold tray quickly removes the heat from the items to be frozen. In the case of mushrooms, slice, chop, or mince them and put them into the freezer bag. Level the mushrooms flat in the bag and remove the air. Transfer the flattened mushroom bag to the cold tray in the freezer. Do not defrost the mushrooms before cooking them.

WASHING MUSHROOMS

The authoritative food science author of *On Food and Cooking*, Harold McGee, says: "We can wash mushrooms because washing doesn't remove significant amounts of flavor or other materials, and even if they absorb some water (which depends completely on how moist they are to begin with), it will just get cooked out again. In other words, washing doesn't damage mushroom quality, and if anything improves it by removing grit, soil, decaying plant matter, and the other unpleasant creatures that take up residence in mushrooms."

Curried Tofu Squares

Freshly made tofu (see page 88) is packed with the natural sweetness of soybeans and a slight and pleasant astringency. This high-quality tofu should be eaten raw and requires few complementary items, such as chopped scallions, sliced shiso leaf, grated ginger, or good-quality shoyu (soy sauce), for maximum enjoyment. After moving to America, I learned that the tofu here is very different from the tofu in Japan. American tofu has a dense, porous, and firm texture. Since it lacks the sweet flavor of Japanese tofu, I can spice it up and make it much tastier and more interesting. In this recipe, the tofu is marinated in curry-flavored White Sumiso Sauce overnight, then cooked until golden brown in a skillet, like a tofu steak. For a vegetarian appetizer, cut the tofu into 24 small cubes.

MAKES 4 SERVINGS

¼ cup White Sumiso Sauce (page 76)

2 tablespoons sake (rice wine)

2 teaspoons Japanese curry powder or Madras curry powder

1 teaspoon shoyu (soy sauce)

⅛ teaspoon freshly ground black pepper

1 block firm or extra-firm tofu (14 ounces)

¼ cup all-purpose flour

2 tablespoons canola oil or vegetable oil

2 tablespoons water

In a large bowl, mix the White Sumiso Sauce, sake, curry powder, soy sauce, and black pepper with a whisk. Cut the tofu in half crosswise. Cut each tofu block into 2 thin sheets to make 4 tofu sheets. Wrap each piece of tofu in a paper towel and gently squeeze to remove excess water, being careful not to break the tofu. Transfer the tofu sheets to the sauce mixture and toss gently to coat. Cover the bowl with plastic wrap and refrigerate overnight.

Remove the tofu from the marinade, wipe off the excess marinade with a spatula, and reserve the marinade. Lightly pat the tofu dry with paper towels. (If you are making appetizers, cut the tofu into 24 small cubes.) Place the flour in a bowl and dredge the tofu in it. Pat it with your hands to remove any excess flour.

Heat the oil in a medium skillet over medium heat, then add the tofu to the skillet. Reduce the heat to medium-low and cook until the bottom is golden, about 5 minutes. Turn the tofu and cook the other side until golden, about 5 minutes. Cook the remaining edges of the tofu as well by holding each piece of tofu with cooking chopsticks or tongs. Total cooking time is about 18 minutes.

Divide the tofu among plates. Add the reserved marinade and the water to the skillet and mix with a spatula. Return the heat to medium and cook the sauce until it is no longer watery. Pour the sauce into small cups and serve with the cooked tofu.

Artisanal Tofu in Kyoto

A recent trip to Kyoto found me in a hundred-year-old, tiny, family-owned and -operated tofu factory-store called Hirano Tofu, located on Fuyamachi Street. They make some of the best tofu in Japan. The father, mother, and son team starts its operation every day at 5 A.M. so that their customers can purchase freshly made tofu for breakfast. The shop's regular clients include the three most venerable and famous Japanese *ryokan* (inns) in Kyoto—Hiiragiya, Tawaraya, and Sumiya—which have all been in operation for hundreds of years.

Preparing perfect tofu, even in this technologically advanced age, is not an easy task at this very traditional tofu factory. They do not rely on computerized machines but on their own senses and expertise, born from lifelong experience.

For instance, the owner says that the dried soybeans vary in terms of quality from year to year, even though they are supplied through the same route. The sugar content and protein content of the soybeans vary, so he has to carefully adjust the quantity of *nigari* (coagulant) used in production.

The local customers who purchase their tofu every day have the pleasure of chatting with the owner and his wife. Customers always begin such conversations with words of great appreciation for the product. This is followed by any topic, including the weather, food, politics, their health, their kids, a recent ball game or sumo result, and so on. If there is any comment on the tofu itself—such as, "Yesterday's tofu had slight bitterness," the owners take it quite seriously. This relationship is one of the key reasons this small operation has survived and continues to produce quality tofu.

After returning to New York City and shopping at one of my favorite cheese vendors at our neighboring farmers' market, I realized that I enjoy the same kind of conversation with the cheese maker. I believe that in order to keep our food safe and of a high quality in our community, we, the consumers, have to be actively involved.

Potato and Salmon Salad

A can of wild sockeye salmon is handy in my kitchen and frequently turns up in this salad. White Sumiso Sauce replaces mayonnaise in my recipe, so the salad is lighter and more flavorful than the conventional salmon or tuna salad recipe. I always spend an extra dollar or so for better-quality canned salmon for this dish, as poor-quality salmon ruins it.

MAKES 4 SERVINGS

1 pound small red potatoes

Sea salt

3 tablespoons frozen green peas

3 tablespoons frozen corn kernels

¼ cup White Sumiso Sauce (page 76)

¼ cup whole-milk plain yogurt

1 tablespoon olive oil or vegetable oil

1 tablespoon lemon juice

2 teaspoons grainy or smooth Dijon mustard

2 teaspoons sugar

½ cup chopped red onion

1 (6-ounce) can salmon packed in water or oil, drained

4 large romaine lettuce leaves, finely shredded

Place the potatoes and cold water with 1 percent salt by volume in a medium pot (see below). Bring to a simmer over medium heat and cook the potatoes for 20 minutes or until fork-tender. Remove from the heat and set the pot aside.

Bring a small saucepan of salted water to a boil over medium heat. Add the peas and corn and cook for 1 minute. Drain them in a sieve and air-dry.

In a small bowl, whisk the White Sumiso Sauce, yogurt, olive oil, lemon juice, mustard, sugar, and ¼ teaspoon salt.

Drain the cooked potatoes and transfer them to a cutting board. While they are hot, carefully cut them into quarters. Place them in a large bowl and add the red onion and 2 tablespoons of the dressing. Toss the potatoes and onion thoroughly with the dressing. Add the salmon, cooked peas and corn, and an additional 2 to 3 tablespoons of the dressing to the potato mixture. Arrange the lettuce on plates. Spoon the remaining dressing over the lettuce. Spoon the potato and salmon salad on top of the lettuce and serve.

Technique

ADDING SALT TO WATER WHEN YOU COOK POTATOES

Cooking potatoes in salted water takes them to a tender state. I learned this tip a while ago and have since been practicing it without fail. For this book I needed to research the science behind the process, so I called Harold McGee, the guru of cooking science. Harold said, "Adding salt to the cooking water does tend to make potatoes much more tender than without salt, but this can be a disadvantage if you're cooking large chunks—the surface gets fragile and broken while the interior cooks through. For thin slices or small pieces it makes more sense."

Sashimi Tuna with Avocado and Tomato Salad

If you have access to fresh or frozen sushi- and sashimi-quality tuna (this means that they are okay for raw consumption) at your local fishmonger (see page 91), try this recipe. When purchasing frozen tuna, ensure that it has not been gassed with carbon monoxide, a treatment that preserves the bright red color of the flesh but disguises its quality and freshness. Gassed tuna, no matter how old it is, presents with a beautiful reddish pink color. Please also note that not all frozen tuna is suitable for raw consumption. Some packages contain tuna that is meant for cooking only, so be sure to check the instructions for cooking the fish.

In this recipe, I flash-cook the tuna in boiling water for about 30 seconds, or until the outside turns white, then quickly cool it in a bath of ice water. This technique is called *shimofuri* (frosted-look method). Please be sure to read Shimofuri Technique on page 91.

MAKES 4 SERVINGS

3 tablespoons whole-milk
   plain yogurt

2 tablespoons White Sumiso Sauce
   (page 76)

1 tablespoon plus 2 teaspoons olive
   oil or vegetable oil

¼ teaspoon garlic powder

¼ teaspoon grated ginger

¼ teaspoon freshly ground
   black pepper

¾ teaspoon sea salt

10 ounces sushi-grade tuna

1 teaspoon lemon juice

1 medium avocado,
   pitted and peeled

1 small beefsteak tomato

Place the yogurt, White Sumiso Sauce, olive oil, garlic powder, grated ginger, black pepper, and ½ teaspoon of the salt in a clean 12-ounce glass jar. Cover with a tight-fitting lid, and shake until thoroughly blended.

Have a medium bowl of ice water on hand. Bring a medium pot of water to a boil over medium heat. Lower a flat spatula into the boiling water for 30 seconds. (Heating the spatula in advance will prevent the tuna from sticking to the spatula.) Place the tuna on top of the spatula, lower the tuna into the boiling water, and release it from the spatula. Cook the tuna for 30 seconds, or until the thin outside layer turns white. Using the spatula, quickly remove the tuna from the water and carefully drop it into the cold water. When the tuna is cool (do not leave the tuna too long in the water or the fish will lose flavor), transfer it to a cutting board. Pat dry the tuna with a paper towel. Cut the tuna into 1-inch cubes. Transfer the tuna to a clean bowl and gently toss it with the remaining ¼ teaspoon salt and the lemon juice. Refrigerate the tuna while finishing the other ingredients.

Cut the avocado and tomato into ½-inch pieces. Add the avocado and tomato to the bowl with the tuna and gently toss the mixture. Divide the mixture into bowls. Spoon the dressing over each bowl and serve.

Tuna Varieties

I covered tuna intensively in my previous book, *The Sushi Experience*, but here again is a short note on tuna varieties. The Blue Ocean Institute, an organization devoted to promoting sustainable seafood, states that "Tunas (yellowfin and bigeye tunas, poll- and troll [long line]-caught) are fast-growing, prolific breeders, and wide-ranging, but many populations remain depleted."

Bluefin tuna—favored for its meltingly tender belly meat, toro, and attractive deep bright red color—is heavily depleted. You can easily distinguish between the different tuna varieties at your local fishmonger. Yellowfin tuna flesh is water-melon color; bluefin has deep red flesh; and bigeye tuna has a brighter, light red color. The price also reflects the variety. From very expensive to inexpensive, the order is: bluefin, bigeye, and yellowfin. Select the right species for the right recipe, and please consume all tuna in moderation.

Technique

SHIMOFURI TECHNIQUE

The contrast created by blanching tuna fish in boiling water is visually and textur-ally appealing, resulting in a firm-textured white cooked exterior and a tender, red raw interior. You can use the *shimofuri* technique over the open flame of a gas stovetop as well. To do this, first place a block of tuna on three long steel barbe-cue skewers (radiating outward like the ribs of a fan), then hold the fish horizon-tally over an open gas flame set on high and sear it briefly, until the flame-facing side is white and turning lightly golden. Turn the fish over and cook until the other side is white. Immediately cool the fish in a bowl of ice water.

Panko-Dusted Baked Cod

Among the varieties of lean white fish, cod stands out because of its meaty flesh and flaky texture. In this recipe, I bake cod topped with White Sumiso Sauce that has been puréed with collard greens. The beautiful presentation and new flavor of this dish will delight everyone at the table.

MAKES 4 SERVINGS

1½ pounds russet potatoes

3 tablespoons olive oil or vegetable oil, plus more as needed

Sea salt

1½ pounds skinless cod

¼ cup White Sumiso Sauce (page 76)

¼ cup Kelp Stock (page 6) or water

1 cup chopped collard green leaves or spinach

2 large egg yolks

¼ cup panko bread crumbs

2 tablespoons chopped fresh parsley

Freshly ground black pepper

Preheat the oven to 350°F. Clean the potatoes with a hard brush and prick their skin with a fork in several places. Place the potatoes in a pot of salted water over medium heat (see page 89), and bring to a boil. Cook the potatoes for 40 minutes. Remove the potatoes from the water and transfer them to a cutting board. Cut each potato in half lengthwise, then cut each half into 4 wedges. Rub the potatoes with oil and salt and set aside.

Cut the cod fillet into 4 pieces. Lightly salt the cod (see page 94) and let it stand for 15 minutes. Rinse the cod under cold tap water and drain. Wipe the cod dry with a paper towel.

In a blender or food processor, process the White Sumiso Sauce, stock, 2 tablespoons of the olive oil, and the collard green leaves until smooth. Add the egg yolks and process until the eggs are incorporated. In a small bowl, toss the bread crumbs with the remaining 1 tablespoon olive oil, the parsley, and a bit of black pepper.

Lightly coat the bottom of a baking dish that is large enough to hold the fish and potatoes. Arrange the cod in the baking dish and fill the empty spaces in the dish with potato pieces. Spoon the green sumiso over each exposed surface of the cod. Sprinkle the bread crumb mixture over the sauce. Bake the cod for 8 minutes. Increase the oven temperature to 450°F and cook the cod for 2 minutes longer, or until the surface is lightly golden. Divide the cod and potatoes onto plates and serve.

SALTING FISH BEFORE COOKING

Before Japanese cooks grill, bake, or steam fish, we often salt it with about 2 percent of salt to the weight of the fish (for example, 7 ounces of fish requires 1 teaspoon of salt). The purpose of salting is to remove excess water and firm up the surface area of the fish for easier handling. By rinsing the salted fish you can also eliminate any off flavors that may have been present on the surface. In Japan we grill many varieties of seasonal fish—both oily and non-oily types—and in varied forms: whole fish on the bone, smaller whole fish in single-serving portions, or fillets of larger fish. The resting time after salting depends on the variety of fish and whether it is a whole fish with bone and skin or a sliced fillet. Here are the general guidelines for the salted fish resting times for popular fish in America. For oily fish such as salmon, sardines, mackerel, and whole branzino, salt the fish 20 minutes before cooking. For lean fish such as flounder, fluke, halibut, and cod, salt the fish 10 minutes before cooking. Rinse the salted fish under cold tap water to clean it and thoroughly remove the salt. Drain the fish and wipe it dry with paper towels. Before putting the fish over an oiled hot grill or skillet, sprinkle only a little salt on both sides of the fish. This second salting is to flavor the fish properly. Cook the fish through, not rare, since most of the fish that we can buy from our local fishmonger or supermarket is not of sushi or sashimi quality and is not fit for rare or raw consumption.

Chicken Salad

Mayonnaise has been popular in Japan since the beginning of the twentieth century, when a Japanese businessman named Toichiro Nakashima tasted it in Europe and America and decided to begin producing a similar product. In 1925, he began marketing his mayonnaise as a food that would help incorporate oil and egg yolk into the Japanese diet. His Kewpie brand mayonnaise is loved in Japan and well known to many in America. Mr. Nakashima increased the amount of egg yolk in his recipe to suit his Japanese audience. This recipe breaks with tradition and uses White Sumiso Sauce in an American-style chicken salad, resulting in a cleaner-tasting, lighter salad.

MAKES 4 SERVINGS

2 boneless, skinless chicken breast halves (1 pound)

3 tablespoons White Sumiso Sauce (page 76)

2½ tablespoons Dashi Stock (page 38) or water

1½ tablespoons olive oil

1 teaspoon Dijon mustard

1 teaspoon Japanese curry powder or Madras curry powder

1 tablespoon white sesame seeds

Freshly ground black pepper

1 medium Granny Smith apple (6 ounces)

½ cup diced celery

½ cup diced red onion

Bring a large pot of water to a boil over high heat. Decrease the heat to medium-low, add the chicken, and cook, uncovered, for 8 minutes. Cover the pot and turn off the heat. Let the chicken stand in the hot water for 15 minutes.

In a large bowl, whisk the White Sumiso Sauce, stock, olive oil, Dijon mustard, curry powder, white sesame seeds, and black pepper. Core and cut the apple, leaving the skin on, into ⅓-inch pieces.

Remove the chicken from the water and transfer it to a cutting board. When the chicken is cool enough to handle (it should still be rather hot), cut it into ½-inch cubes. Transfer the chicken to the bowl of sumiso dressing and toss it with a large spoon. Add the apple, celery, and red onion to the chicken and mix thoroughly. Divide the salad among bowls and serve.

Poached Chicken with Spinach-Sumiso Sauce

In Japan, we enjoy chicken salted and grilled, rather than masking its flavor with heavy, rich, or spiced sauces. Japanese chicken is very flavorful—especially those that are called *jidori* (see below). To provide better flavor in the finished dish, I usually choose quality over quantity by selecting a small bird with a higher price per pound.

MAKES 4 SERVINGS

4 boneless, skinless chicken breast halves (2 pounds)

4 quarter-size slices peeled ginger

2 scallions

¼ cup White Sumiso Sauce (page 76)

¼ cup Kelp Stock (page 6) or water

2 tablespoons plus ½ teaspoon olive oil or vegetable oil

1 cup chopped spinach leaves, plus 10 large leaves, for garnish

¼ to ½ teaspoon freshly ground black pepper

Pinch of sea salt

Bring a large pot of water to a boil over high heat. Decrease the heat to medium-low, add the chicken, ginger, and scallions, and cook, uncovered, for 8 minutes. Cover the pot and turn off the heat. Let the chicken stand in the hot water for 20 minutes.

Add the White Sumiso Sauce, stock, 2 tablespoons of the olive oil, the chopped spinach, and black pepper to a food processor or blender and process until smooth. Transfer the sauce to a saucepan and warm over medium-low heat.

Cut the spinach leaves for garnish into thin slices. In a small bowl, toss the spinach with the remaining ½ teaspoon olive oil and a pinch of salt.

Using a slotted spoon, remove the chicken from the water and transfer it to a cutting board. Discard the cooking liquid along with the ginger and scallions. Cut each chicken breast crosswise into ½-inch-thick slices. Divide the sumiso sauce among bowls. Add the sliced chicken to each bowl, top with the spinach leaves, and serve.

Jidori: Free-Range Flavorful Chicken

In Japan, many restaurants—including yakitori establishments—advertise the brand name and background story of *jidori* chicken. The original definition of *jidori* referred to the native variety of bird that was raised in Japan before the Meiji period (1868). Nowadays, in order to be identified as *jidori* in Japan, the bird must meet a stringent set of qualifications: It must be 50 to 100 percent pure *jidori*; the age at slaughter is on average 130 days (regular broiler chickens are slaughtered at 50 to 60 days); the birds are fed with no-hormone and no-chemical-additive feed; the birds are allowed free range; and the allotted space for fewer than 10 birds should be no smaller than 1 square meter.

There are over 50 certified *jidori* brands raised all across Japan. The most famous names are *Hinai Jidori* from Akita Prefecture, *Nagoya Kochin* from Aichi Prefecture, and *Satsuma Jidori* from Kagoshima Prefecture. Each of these birds is notable for its own distinctive flavor and texture.

Sumiso-Marinated Grilled Chicken

Miso-marinated fish was conceived in the old capital of Kyoto several hundred years ago as a means of preserving fish in a location that was far from water. A marinade made of miso, sake (rice wine), and mirin (sweet cooking wine) imparts delicious flavor to any fish. Now this fish preparation is one of the most popular dishes at Japanese restaurants in America, but chefs sometimes add too much sugar to the marinade for my taste. In this recipe, I created a different formula using White Sumiso Sauce and chicken, but this is also an excellent preparation for fish. Here I cook the chicken with its skin to add juiciness and flavor. Discard the skin while eating if you wish.

MAKES 4 SERVINGS

6 tablespoons White Sumiso Sauce (page 76)

6 tablespoons whole-milk plain yogurt

1 tablespoon olive oil or vegetable oil

1 tablespoon lemon juice

1 tablespoon sugar, plus more as needed

1 teaspoon garlic powder

8 boneless, skin-on chicken thighs (2 pounds)

1 tablespoon canola oil or vegetable oil

Sea salt

1 large Granny Smith apple

1 tablespoon unsalted butter

In a large bowl, whisk the White Sumiso Sauce, yogurt, olive oil, lemon juice, sugar, and garlic powder. Add the chicken to the bowl and massage with the sauce. Allow some of the sauce to penetrate under the skin by detaching part of the skin and pushing the sauce under it. Cover and marinate overnight in the refrigerator.

Preheat the oven to 350°F. Remove the chicken from the refrigerator. Transfer the chicken to a plate and wipe with a spatula to remove any excess marinade. Reserve the marinade. Heat the canola oil in a medium ovenproof skillet over medium-low heat. Lightly salt the chicken, add it to the skillet, and cook until the skin side is golden, about 2 minutes. (Marinated chicken burns more quickly than unmarinated chicken, so please keep an eye on it.) Turn over the chicken so the skin side is facing up and transfer the skillet to the oven and bake for 20 minutes.

Remove the chicken from the skillet, and divide it onto four plates (two thighs for each guest), keeping it warm. Transfer the cooking juice in the skillet to a small cup, reserving it. Clean the skillet under hot water and wipe dry. Remove the top and bottom parts of the apple, core it and cut it, leaving the skin on, into 4 slices crosswise.

Return the skillet to the stove over medium heat. Add the butter, and when it is sizzling, add the sliced apple. Sprinkle each slice with a pinch of salt and sugar. Decrease the heat to low and cook until the bottom is golden. Turn the apple slices and cook them until the other side is golden. Add an apple slice to each plate next to the chicken. Add the reserved marinade and chicken cooking juice to the same skillet and cook over medium heat until the sauce thickens, about 2 minutes. Divide the sauce over each portion of chicken and serve.

Succulent Pork Ribs

Pork ribs are a beloved barbecue cut in America. My version is a new and delicious flavor experience that combines sumiso sauce, shoyu, and Worcestershire sauce. In this recipe, the pork ribs acquire a golden brown, velvety, mouthwatering appearance. Eating this dish is fun but a bit messy. Have lots of paper napkins and small bowls of lemon water at the table for your guests' fingers.

MAKES 4 TO 6 SERVINGS

¼ cup White Sumiso Sauce (page 76)

1 tablespoon shoyu (soy sauce)

1 teaspoon Worcestershire sauce

1 tablespoon honey

½ teaspoon red pepper flakes

1½ pounds pork spareribs

Preheat the oven to 250°F. In a small bowl, combine the White Sumiso Sauce, soy sauce, Worcestershire sauce, honey, and red pepper flakes.

Place the ribs in the center of a length of aluminum foil that is large enough to wrap around the ribs. With a pastry brush or a spoon, paint the sauce over the ribs, coating both sides. Drizzle extra sauce, if any, over the ribs. Wrap the ribs in the foil, and place them on a baking sheet. Transfer the ribs to the oven and bake for 2 hours.

Carefully remove the ribs from the oven and unwrap the top part of the foil, exposing the meat. Increase the oven temperature to 350°F. Put the ribs back in the oven and cook for about 1 hour, or until the surface is golden brown. During cooking, baste the surface of the ribs with the pan juices several times.

Divide the pork ribs among dinner plates and serve with Cabbage and Red Radish Slaw (recipe follows) on the side.

Cabbage and Red Radish Slaw

This is a quick, pickled vegetable side dish that is perfect with rich meat dishes like Succulent Pork Ribs (page 98), Skirt Steak Meets Spicy Miso Sauce (page 127), Miso-Braised Lamb (page 132), Fried Chicken (page 163), and Chicken Katsu Sticks (page 155). Squeeze salted and rinsed vegetables firmly and thoroughly to remove as much water as possible from the vegetables before seasoning them. Try different seasonal vegetables for added variety, such as turnips and green bell peppers, or fennel bulbs and carrots.

MAKES 8 SERVINGS

½ head napa cabbage (14 ounces)

½ head red cabbage
(1 pound 2 ounces)

3 large red radishes (5 ounces)

3 thumb-size pieces ginger, peeled

3½ teaspoons sea salt

6 tablespoons rice vinegar

3 tablespoons sugar

1 tablespoon white sesame seeds

½ teaspoon red pepper flakes

1 teaspoon sesame oil (optional)

Cut the napa cabbage in half lengthwise, then cut each half crosswise into ⅓-inch-thick slices. Cut the red cabbage into quarters and then cut each quarter crosswise into thin slices. Cut the radishes in half and then into thin slices. Cut the ginger into a fine julienne and set aside. Place the napa cabbage, red cabbage, and radishes in a large bowl that can hold about 16 cups of sliced vegetables. Toss and massage the vegetables with 2 teaspoons of the salt, then let the vegetables stand for 10 minutes.

Pick up a handful of the vegetables, squeeze firmly to remove excess water, and transfer them to a medium bowl. Repeat the process, and finish squeezing water from all of the vegetables. The squeezed vegetables should have only a very faintly salty flavor. If too much salt remains, rinse the vegetables in a colander and repeat the squeezing process.

Add the ginger, rice vinegar, sugar, the remaining 1½ teaspoons salt, the sesame seeds, red pepper flakes, and sesame oil, if using, to the well-squeezed vegetables and toss thoroughly. Cover the bowl with plastic wrap and refrigerate for at least 2 hours before serving.

CHAPTER 4
SPICY MISO SAUCE

Spicy Miso Sauce, made from aged brown miso (see page 12), is rich tasting, sweet, and tangy. This style of miso sauce is used to prepare such classic Japanese dishes as deep-fried eggplant, *nasu no dengaku*, grilled tofu, *dengaku-dofu*, grilled fish, *sakana no miso-yaki*, and simmered-until-tender, sweet winter daikon radish, *furofuki daikon*. Two of these popular classics, Eggplant with Spicy Miso Sauce (page 115) and Traditional Braised Daikon (page 113), are presented in this chapter. As with the White Sumiso Sauce in Chapter 3, I have extended the role of Spicy Miso Sauce to familiar dishes from the American kitchen. My version of this sauce includes red pepper flakes, and it is great for stir-frying, braising, grilling, and as a component of unique and delicious dressings.

The robust character of my Spicy Miso Sauce is a nice complement to vegetables and proteins that have strong flavor characteristics, such as Brussels sprouts, broccoli, cauliflower, bell peppers, kale, daikon radish, sweet potatoes, and beef. The recipes presented in this chapter will introduce you to great new flavors, and they provide health benefits from the nutrients found in miso (see page 12).

Freezing will not change the texture of the sauce, and prepared sauce can be stored in the freezer for up to three months. When needed, take the jar out of the freezer, quickly scoop and transfer the necessary portion to a small bowl, and return the jar to the freezer to preserve the quality.

Spicy Miso Sauce

MAKES 1½ CUPS

1 cup aged brown miso (see page 12)

½ cup plus 1 tablespoon sugar

¾ cup mirin (sweet cooking wine)

¼ cup plus 2 tablespoons sake
(rice wine)

¼ cup lemon juice

1 to 2 teaspoons red pepper flakes

Place the miso, sugar, mirin, and sake in a medium pot and whisk until smooth. Place the pot over medium heat and bring it to a simmer. Cook the mixture, stirring constantly, for 4 to 5 minutes. Add the lemon juice and cook for 8 minutes, stirring occasionally. Turn off the heat, add the red pepper flakes, and stir. Transfer the sauce to a clean freezer container. Cover the jar with a lid and store it in the freezer.

Miso's Great Power

Miso is a product of the fermentation of soybeans, often with added grains such as rice or barley. It is rich in so many important nutrients—vitamins, including E, K, B_1, B_2, B_3, B_5, B_6, B_9, and B_{12}; minerals, including calcium, sodium, potassium, magnesium, phosphorus, iron, zinc, and copper; and essential amino acids. Aged brown miso has more nutritional value than young white miso (see page 12). The longer the fermentation, the more nutrients are produced. The health benefits of miso include improving the flexibility of blood vessels, helping to lower blood cholesterol, and alkalizing the blood. It is also said to possess anti-carcinogenic properties and is thought to strengthen the body's immune system.

Peanut Butter–Miso Sauce

Miso sauce and sesame paste are traditional partners in the Japanese kitchen, but in this recipe I use peanut butter instead of sesame paste. To make the sauce a little spicier, I add whatever hot spice or sauce I have on hand, such as *akatogarashi* (whole dried red chile), *toban jiang* (fermented chile bean sauce), red pepper flakes, Tabasco sauce, or sriracha sauce. You can adjust the amount of warm black tea added to the sauce to produce the desired consistency. Peanut Butter–Miso Sauce is a nice accompaniment to raw vegetable sticks, poached chicken, fish, or tofu.

MAKES ½ CUP

2½ tablespoons brewed hot English Breakfast tea

2 tablespoons smooth or chunky peanut butter

2 tablespoons Spicy Miso Sauce (page 102)

½ to 1 teaspoon *toban jiang* (fermented chile bean sauce) or sriracha sauce

Pinch of sea salt

Mix all of the ingredients in a small bowl with a whisk until well blended. Store the sauce in a clean lidded jar in the refrigerator. Use the sauce within 3 days for best flavor.

Stir-Fried Rice and Sausage with Spicy Red Miso

This is a rice dish that I enjoy making with leftover rice and any fresh vegetables that I have in my refrigerator or freezer. If you use freshly cooked rice in this recipe, place the cooked rice in a strainer and run it under cold tap water to remove any pasty starch that may remain on the surface of the rice. Rinsing also cools and firms up the rice for easy handling.

MAKES 4 TO 6 SERVINGS

3 scallions

7 ounces Spanish-style chorizo or similar hard cured sausage

1 tablespoon canola oil

1 cup carrots, cut into ¼-inch pieces

½ teaspoon sea salt

¾ cup onion, cut into ¼-inch pieces

2 teaspoons minced garlic

2 teaspoons minced ginger

3 tablespoons plus 1½ teaspoons Spicy Miso Sauce (page 102)

5 cups day-old cold rice or newly cooked and rinsed rice (short-, medium-, or long-grain)

½ cup frozen corn kernels

½ cup frozen green peas

½ teaspoon freshly ground black pepper

Cut the scallions diagonally into thin slices and separate the green and white parts. Cut the sausage into ⅓-inch dice.

Heat a wok or deep skillet over medium-high heat and add the oil. When the oil is hot, add the carrots and ¼ teaspoon of the salt, and cook for 2 minutes, stirring, or until the carrots are lightly golden. Add the onion and the remaining ¼ teaspoon salt, and cook for 1 minute, stirring continuously. Add the sausage and cook, stirring constantly, for 2 minutes. Add the garlic, ginger, and the white part of the scallions and cook, stirring, for 30 seconds. Add the Spicy Miso Sauce and stir.

Remove the wok from the heat and add the rice, stirring thoroughly to ensure that the rice and miso sauce are well mixed. Return the wok to medium heat and cook the rice, stirring, for about 3 minutes. Add the corn and green peas to the rice mixture and cook for 2 minutes. Add the black pepper and green part of the scallions. Divide the rice mixture into bowls and serve.

Quick Miso Ramen

Today there are more than 38,000 ramen restaurants in Japan. If you want to understand the drama and Zen of ramen culture in Japan, watch the classic movie *Tampopo*, made in 1985 and directed by Juzo Itami. The movie, available with English subtitles, depicts the story of a widowed woman's single-minded determination and struggle to create a tiny, but excellent, ramen restaurant in her town. It is a story told with delightful humor about the obsession with and dedication to the cult of ramen. The movie is about love, human relationships, perseverance, and Japanese culture.

The original ramen broth from the early twentieth century was flavored with salt or shoyu (soy sauce). In the 1950s, a new ramen flavored with miso appeared in the city of Sapporo, on the northern island of Hokkaido. Since then, it has become a favorite all across the country, and many other variations of this national dish have been created, accepted, and enjoyed in Japan. Pork bone–based broth has been the most suitable and familiar stock for miso ramen, but in this quick recipe I blend a can of chicken stock with Japanese Dashi Stock (page 38) for the base, and add Spicy Miso Sauce to produce a rich and appealing flavor. Prepare the *chashu* pork in advance of the ramen preparation. Be sure to read Noodle Cooking Techniques on page 59.

MAKES 4 SERVINGS

4 cups low-sodium chicken stock

1 cup Dashi Stock (page 38) or low-sodium chicken stock

½ cup Spicy Miso Sauce (page 102)

1 tablespoon aged brown miso (see page 12)

2 teaspoons shoyu (soy sauce)

1 teaspoon *toban jiang* (fermented chile bean sauce) or red pepper flakes (optional)

1 cup fresh or frozen corn kernels

12 slices prepared *chashu* pork (see page 66)

⅓ small seeded red bell pepper (2 ounces)

2 medium eggs, hard-boiled

10 ounces dried *chukasoba* noodles (sometimes called ramen noodles) or dried Chinese egg noodles

2 scallions, thinly sliced

½ sheet of nori seaweed, cut into 4 rectangles

2 tablespoons unsalted or salted butter, cut into 4 cubes

Place the chicken stock and Dashi Stock in a medium pot over medium heat and bring it to a simmer. Add the Spicy Miso Sauce, miso, soy sauce, and toban jiang and stir to dissolve the miso. Add the corn, turn the heat to low, and cook, covered, for 5 minutes. Turn off the heat, add the chashu pork slices, and cover the pot. This is the miso ramen broth.

Bring a large pot of water to a boil over high heat. Cut the red bell pepper into thin slices and place it in the boiling water for 1 minute. Using a slotted spoon, transfer the bell pepper to a sieve and air-dry. Keep the water boiling. Cut the hard-boiled eggs in half lengthwise.

Fill the serving bowls with very hot water to heat them. Add the noodles to the boiling water, then decrease the heat to medium and cook them as instructed on the package. Drain the noodles in a colander.

Discard the hot water from the noodle bowls and divide the noodles among the warmed bowls. Remove the chashu pork from the miso ramen broth and add it to the noodle bowls. Reheat the miso ramen broth over medium heat and bring it to a simmer. Pour the hot broth with corn kernels over the noodles. Top with the red bell pepper, eggs, scallions, nori, and butter cubes and serve.

Udon with Miso-Eggplant Ragu

While eating hot udon (wheat) noodles in broth or cold noodles dipped in sauce is a delicious experience, it is also a very messy operation even for experienced Japanese eaters. In order to keep one's clothes clean, Japanese mothers advise bending your body forward and bringing your mouth close to the hot noodle bowl or holding the dipping sauce up to your mouth. Westerners are always reminded by their mothers to "sit up straight and bring the food from the table to your mouth"—a recipe for disaster for udon eating. In this recipe I serve the udon in an untraditional way, with miso eggplant ragu. If you want to have the traditional udon experience, try the Fried Udon Noodles (page 58), Cold Udon Noodles with Ginger-Walnut Butter Sauce (page 173), Udon Noodles in Hot Broth with Kakiage Pancake (page 181), or Chicken and Egg Udon Noodles (page 183). Be sure to read Noodle Cooking Techniques on page 59.

MAKES 4 SERVINGS

¼ cup canola oil or vegetable oil

½ cup chopped onion

½ teaspoon sea salt

2 tablespoons minced ginger

3½ ounces mixed portobello and shiitake mushrooms

½ pound eggplant, cut into ⅓-inch pieces (2½ cups)

¼ cup Spicy Miso Sauce (page 102)

2 tablespoons sake (rice wine)

1 teaspoon aged brown miso (see page 12)

1 teaspoon shoyu (soy sauce)

1 tablespoon tomato paste

¼ cup plus 2 tablespoons chopped fresh parsley

¼ cup white sesame seeds, toasted

Red pepper flakes (optional)

1 pound dried udon noodles or spaghetti

Place 2 tablespoons of the oil in a skillet over medium heat. When the oil is hot, add the onion and ¼ teaspoon of the salt, then decrease the heat to medium-low and cook, stirring, for 8 minutes or until lightly golden. Add the ginger and cook for 20 seconds. Add the mushrooms and the remaining ¼ teaspoon salt and cook for 2 minutes, or until the mushrooms are wilted. Add the remaining 2 tablespoons oil, and when it is hot, add the eggplant and cook, stirring continuously, for 5 minutes, or until the eggplant is tender. Add the Spicy Miso Sauce, sake, miso, soy sauce, and tomato paste and cook the mixture for 2 minutes, stirring continuously. Add the ¼ cup parsley, the sesame seeds, and red pepper flakes, if using. Remove the skillet from the heat.

Prepare a kettle of boiling water. Bring a large pot of water to a boil over medium heat and cook the noodles as instructed on the package. Drain the noodles in a colander and rinse them under cold tap water until they are cold and any remaining surface starch is removed. Pour the boiling water from the kettle over the rinsed noodles in the colander to rewarm them. Return the skillet with the eggplant sauce to medium heat, and, when it is heated, add the drained noodles. Thoroughly toss the noodles with the sauce. Divide the noodles among serving bowls. Garnish with the remaining 2 tablespoons parsley and serve.

Miso-Beef Ragu and Udon Noodles

Ground beef cooked and flavored with shoyu (soy sauce), miso, and mirin (sweet cooking wine) is known as *niku-miso*, and it was my "comfort sauce" when my mother served it with steaming hot white rice. Today I prepare a similar sauce using my Spicy Miso Sauce and additional ingredients. This flavorful sauce is perfect served with steaming hot rice, udon noodles, Italian pasta, or as a pizza topping. Be sure to read Noodle Cooking Techniques on page 59.

MAKES 4 TO 6 SERVINGS

6 tablespoons Spicy Miso Sauce (page 102)

¼ cup water

3 tablespoons sake (rice wine)

1 teaspoon sugar

3 tablespoons olive oil or vegetable oil

1 cup chopped onions

¼ teaspoon sea salt

2 tablespoons minced ginger

1 pound ground beef

½ teaspoon freshly ground black pepper

1 tablespoon tomato paste

1 cup chopped tomatoes

14 ounces dried udon noodles

½ cup minced fresh parsley

1 tablespoon white sesame seeds

Place the Spicy Miso Sauce, water, sake, and sugar in a small bowl and mix well. Heat the olive oil in a medium pot over medium-low heat, add the onions and ⅛ teaspoon of the salt, and cook, stirring from time to time, for 3 minutes or until the onions are translucent. Add the ginger and cook for 1 minute. Add half of the ground beef, the black pepper, and the remaining ⅛ teaspoon salt to the pot and cook for a minute or two, breaking and crumbling the beef into small pieces with a fork. Add the remaining half of the ground beef, increase the heat to medium, and repeat the crumbling process. The whole cooking time should be 3 to 4 minutes.

Add the tomato paste, tomatoes, and Spicy Miso Sauce mixture and cook for 12 minutes, until the beef is cooked through. Turn off the heat.

Prepare a kettle of boiling water. Bring a large pot of water to a boil over high heat, add the udon noodles, and cook for 1 minute less than the time instructed on the package. Drain the udon noodles in a colander and rinse them under cold water until they are cold and any remaining surface starch is removed. Pour the boiling water from the kettle over the rinsed noodles in the colander to rewarm them.

Return the miso beef mixture to medium heat and, when it is heated, add the drained noodles. Toss the noodles thoroughly with the miso beef. Turn off the heat and add the parsley and sesame seeds. Divide the noodles among serving bowls and serve.

Miso-Flavored Cold Soba

The idea for this soba noodle dish comes from *hiyashi chukasoba* (see page 109), a summertime favorite in Japan. Cooked and chilled ramen noodles (not soba noodles) are served with various toppings and dressed with a refreshing, gingery sweet and sour sauce. This recipe calls for readily available soba noodles (not ramen noodles). Enjoy this cold noodle dish during hot summer days, as they do in Japan, or any time you want a chilled noodle dish with a wide variety of satisfying tastes and textures. Be sure to read Noodle Cooking Techniques on page 59.

MAKES 4 SERVINGS

1⅓ cups low-sodium chicken stock

6 tablespoons Spicy Miso Sauce (page 102)

2 teaspoons shoyu (soy sauce)

1 tablespoon plus 1 teaspoon sugar

2 teaspoons rice vinegar

2 teaspoons sesame oil

2 teaspoons ginger juice from freshly grated ginger

2 tablespoons white sesame seeds

10 ounces dried soba noodles

4 slices Canadian bacon or other ham variety (3½ ounces)

1 small Kirby or other cucumber (3½ ounces)

8 cherry tomatoes

2 large eggs

Pinch of sea salt

Canola oil

1 tablespoon hot mustard paste

Place the chicken stock, Spicy Miso Sauce, soy sauce, 1 tablespoon of the sugar, the rice vinegar, sesame oil, and ginger juice in a large pot over medium heat and bring to a simmer. Transfer the sauce to a bowl and let cool. Add the sesame seeds to the sauce and refrigerate until chilled.

Bring a large pot of water to a boil over medium heat, add the noodles, and cook them as instructed on the package. Drain the noodles in a colander and rinse them under cold water until they are cold and any remaining surface starch is removed. Transfer the noodles to a large bowl and toss them with ½ cup of the chilled prepared sauce.

Cut the bacon into thin 2½-inch-long strips. Remove and discard both ends of the cucumber and cut it (skin on) into thin 2½-inch-long strips. Cut the cherry tomatoes into quarters. Break and beat the eggs in a small bowl. Add the remaining 1 teaspoon sugar and a pinch of salt to the bowl and mix.

Heat a thin layer of canola oil in a medium skillet over medium-low heat, add the egg liquid, and cook it, finely scrambling it with a fork as it cooks. Remove the skillet from the heat. Divide the noodles among serving bowls. Pour the remaining chilled prepared sauce over the noodles. Top with the bacon, cucumber, tomatoes, and scrambled eggs. Add a dab of mustard paste on the edge of the bowls and serve.

Hiyashi Chukasoba, Chukasoba, and Soba: A Guide through Linguistic Confusion

Soba noodles are made from buckwheat. But the dish called *chukasoba* is not made from soba noodles. *Chukasoba* is made from wheat flan. When Chinese-style noodles—prepared by Chinese cooks in the Chinatown of Yokohama City—were introduced to Japan at the end of the nineteenth century, a recognizable name was created for this new dish. So, *chuka*, which means "Chinese style," was added to *soba*, the word for one of the most popular and familiar Japanese noodles. Hence the birth of the name *chukasoba:* Chinese-style noodle dishes that are not made from soba noodles.

Over the next hundred years, *chukasoba* passed through an evolution of cooking techniques, flavors, and presentations in order to suit Japanese tastes and food culture. In this process *chukasoba* was transformed into ramen. To this day, however, some traditional restaurants still call their Chinese-style noodles *chukasoba* rather than ramen. To confuse matters even more, cold ramen noodle dishes (a summertime favorite) are still called *hiyashi* ("chilled") *chukasoba*. And, dried packages of Chinese-style noodles used for making ramen sometimes carry the name *chukasoba* on the label. Yet they are ramen noodles! There is, in fact, some argument over the origin of the word *ramen*. It is largely (but not universally) accepted that it is a corruption of the name for Chinese pulled noodles, *la mian*, a specialty of western China.

Spicy Miso Dressing with Frisée and Orange

Spooning miso straight from the plastic bag or tub into an oil and vinegar preparation does not produce a miso dressing as appealing as this recipe, which uses Spicy Miso Sauce. The robust flavor of this dressing goes very well with strongly flavored vegetables and meats.

MAKES 4 SERVINGS

2 tablespoons Spicy Miso Sauce (page 102)

2 tablespoons rice vinegar

3 tablespoons olive oil or vegetable oil

Sea salt

1 medium head frisée or other salad greens that have a somewhat bitter flavor (7 ounces)

¼ large head of romaine lettuce (4 ounces)

1 large orange

⅓ cup unsalted roasted walnuts

Sugar

In a clean 12-ounce glass jar, combine the Spicy Miso Sauce, rice vinegar, 1 tablespoon of the olive oil, and a pinch of salt. Cover the glass jar with a tight-fitting lid and shake it until thoroughly blended.

Separate the frisée into small sections and transfer to a large bowl. Cut the romaine lettuce crosswise into ½-inch-wide slices and add it to the bowl. Add 1 tablespoon of the olive oil to the bowl and toss with the greens. Peel the orange, section the wedges, and reserve in a cup.

Place the walnuts in a small bowl and toss with the remaining 1 tablespoon olive oil. Add a pinch of salt and a pinch of sugar. Place a skillet over medium heat, add the walnuts, and cook for 2 minutes, or until crisp, turning the walnuts over several times.

Toss the greens with the spicy miso dressing. Divide the greens among salad plates. Top with the orange wedges and walnuts and serve.

Curried Miso Peanuts

There are many varieties of flavored nut products available at food stores. Why not prepare your own delicious and more healthful variety with Spicy Miso Sauce? You will not find this tasty version at any store. They are a great snack and an excellent garnish for any salad.

MAKES 1 CUP

1 tablespoon Spicy Miso Sauce
(page 102)

1 tablespoon sugar

½ teaspoon sea salt

1 teaspoon Japanese curry powder
or Madras curry powder

¼ teaspoon hot paprika

1 teaspoon water

1½ cups unsalted roasted peanuts

Preheat the oven to 250°F. Place the Spicy Miso Sauce, sugar, salt, curry powder, paprika, and water in a small bowl and mix until well blended. Add the peanuts and coat them with the miso sauce. Transfer the peanuts to a baking sheet and bake them in the oven for 40 minutes. Remove the peanuts from the oven, stir them, and return the peanuts to the oven for an additional 20 minutes. Let them cool on the baking sheet and then transfer them to a serving bowl.

Traditional Braised Daikon

The name of this dish is *furo-fuki daikon*, and it is enjoyed in the winter, when daikon radish is the sweetest. The direct translation is "slowly bathed daikon radish" because the daikon first simmers in a hot bath of water and then simmers in kelp stock for about an hour of total cooking time. This makes the daikon tender enough that it can be cut with chopsticks, but not so soft that it becomes mushy. Daikon is typically cooked in water that has been used to rinse rice in order to remove any unpleasant or strong radish flavors. In this recipe, I put raw rice in the cooking pot with the daikon to serve the same purpose.

MAKES 4 SERVINGS

1 pound daikon radish

1½ tablespoons polished white rice

3 cups Kelp Stock (page 6) or
   low-sodium vegetable stock

¼ cup Spicy Miso Sauce (page 102)

1 to 2 teaspoons black sesame seeds

1 tablespoon thinly sliced scallion
   (green part only)

Peel the daikon radish and cut out 4 disks measuring 2½ inches in diameter and 2 inches thick. Place the daikon disks in a medium pot with enough cold water to cover them by 2 inches. Wrap the rice in a double layer of cheesecloth, create a sack by tying the neck with kitchen string, and add it to the pot. Bring the water to a simmer over medium heat, then decrease the heat to medium-low, and cook the daikon, uncovered, for 30 to 45 minutes.

Using a slotted spoon, carefully remove the daikon disks, discard the water and rice, and rinse the disks in a bowl under cold water. Change the water several times. Drain the daikon disks again.

Place the kelp stock in the cleaned pot over medium heat and bring it to a simmer. Add the daikon disks, decrease the heat to low, and cook the daikon for 30 minutes. While the daikon is cooking, mix the Spicy Miso Sauce with 2 tablespoons of the stock from the pot to loosen the sauce.

Using a slotted spoon, transfer the daikon to serving bowls, and reserve the stock for later use in other dishes (like a base for miso soup). Using a spoon, pour the spicy sauce over the daikon disks. Garnish with the sesame seeds and scallion and serve. Warn your guests that the daikon radish may be quite hot in the center.

String Bean and Toasted Cashew Salad

It is fun to experiment with different types of nut butters in combination with my Spicy Miso Sauce. In this dish, cashew butter and cashew nuts bring sweet, nutty flavor and crunchy texture to the salad. Choose string beans that are very fresh by selecting beans with a crisp, green, and undamaged "needle" at the tip of each bean. In Japanese preparation, the bottom part of the string bean is very important—not just to suggest super-fresh quality but for aesthetic appearance as well.

MAKES 4 SERVINGS

14 ounces string beans

3 tablespoons Dashi Stock (page 38) or water, warmed

2 tablespoons Spicy Miso Sauce (page 102)

1½ tablespoons cashew butter

¼ cup roasted, unsalted chopped cashews

Prepare a bowl of ice water. Cut off the stem end of the string beans, but preserve the bottom needlelike parts if they are fresh and attractive. If not, cut them off. Bring a medium pot of salted water to a boil over medium heat, add the string beans, and cook them for 2 minutes. Drain the string beans and transfer them to the ice water. When the string beans are cool, drain them and transfer them to a cutting board. Cut the string beans diagonally in half.

Whisk the stock, Spicy Miso Sauce, and cashew butter in a bowl until well blended. Add the string beans and half of the cashews to the miso sauce and gently toss. Divide the string beans among serving bowls, garnish with the remaining 2 tablespoons cashews, and serve.

Eggplant with Spicy Miso Sauce

This is a popular home and casual restaurant menu item in Japan. In this preparation, eggplant is usually deep fried, then served with richly flavored miso sauce. Eggplant prepared using the traditional recipe absorbs a great deal of oil during cooking and offers a wonderfully creamy texture and a heavenly bite. In my recipe, I use less oil and more steam to cook the eggplant. This provides a healthier option without sacrificing texture or flavor. Choose an American eggplant that has a thinner, more tender skin.

MAKES 4 SERVINGS

1 medium American eggplant
(14 ounces)

¼ cup canola oil or vegetable oil

¼ cup Spicy Miso Sauce (page 102)

2 teaspoons white or black sesame
seeds, toasted

1 tablespoon scallions, sliced into
rings (green part only)

Trim the eggplant, and cut it into 4 disks, about 1½ inches thick. Make fine checkerboard cuts on both surfaces of each slice by making ¼-inch-deep cuts with a knife.

Heat 2 tablespoons of the oil in a skillet over medium heat, add the eggplant disks to the skillet, and drizzle the remaining 2 tablespoons of the oil over the eggplant. Decrease the heat to low and cook the eggplant until the bottom is golden, about 5 minutes. Turn the eggplant and cook, covered, for about 2 minutes. Remove the lid and paint the top of each disk with the Spicy Miso Sauce. Cook, uncovered, for 2 to 3 minutes.

Divide the eggplant among serving plates. Garnish with the sesame seeds and scallion rings and serve.

Spicy Miso-Rubbed Corn

After moving from Tokyo to New York City, the list of my favorite Japanese *shun* vegetables (see page 117) was completely replaced by American varieties. Upon leaving Japan, I sadly said good-bye to early spring mountain vegetables, fresh bamboo shoots, gooey mountain yams, and many others. Fortunately, in New York City, I quickly found more vegetables than I had lost, and to my delight, I found that many of them were locally grown, less than 200 miles from my home. I now eagerly await my newly adopted *shun* vegetables each season, especially the extremely sweet and moist local corn. I hope that you, too, can find this glorious gift of summer in your town. In this recipe, I go beyond the typical butter dressing and enjoy my *shun* corn with Spicy Miso Sauce.

MAKES 4 SERVINGS

4 freshly harvested and shucked ears of corn

2 to 3 tablespoons Spicy Miso Sauce (page 102)

Sea salt and freshly ground black pepper

Place the corn directly on a mesh grill over a medium-hot gas flame or on a medium-hot barbecue grill. Grill the ears, turning them every 30 seconds, until the outside becomes bright yellow with some charred spots. Remove the corn from the fire and rub each ear with the Spicy Miso Sauce. Put the corn back over the fire and cook over high heat for about 5 seconds. Sprinkle salt and black pepper over the corn and serve.

Shun: The Peak of Flavor

Shun is a Japanese word given to food items that are at the peak of their seasonal availability and quality. The word *shun* has no equivalent in the English language and shows our near religious obsession with what we eat in each season. Japan's geography and climate surely helped to shape this unique food culture. For example, asparagus becomes *shun* in early summer. *Shun* asparagus is bursting with flavor and has a tender and moist texture. In order to enjoy *shun* asparagus, we apply the absolute minimum cooking time and minimal flavoring ingredients. The *shun* concept applies not only to fruits and vegetables but to seasonal seafood as well.

Our obsession with the concept of *shun* leads us to further divide the peak season itself into three subdivisions. They are *hashiri*, *sakari*, and *nagori*. *Hashiri* is the quality attributed to *shun* food products that have just come into season. These *hashiri* food items are usually smaller in size and less flavorful than later, at the height of the season. Despite these deficiencies, *hashiri* products fetch a high price because they have just come back onto the market after a full year's absence. They are rare and exciting, and regardless of price, they attract ravenous "early adopters" who will pay any price to obtain these foods. An extreme example is recounted in "*Katsuo* Is Worth More Than My Wife" in my book *The Sushi Experience*. There I describe a famous story about a man back in the Edo period (1600–1868) who pawns his wife to savor the first catch of skipjack tuna.

Sakari describes food items that are at the very pinnacle of their season. They are larger, meatier, mightier, and more flavorful and nutritionally superior than at any other time of year. They are also bountiful, and therefore more economical.

Nagori is the term given to the *shun* food whose harvesttime has nearly ended. *Nagori* foods no longer excite, but consuming them gives us a final chance to offer thanks and say good-bye until the *shun* season next year.

These days when I think of the concept of *shun*, I think of the lifespan of human beings—*hashiri* represents teenagers, *sakari* the middle-aged, and *nagori* the generation after them. But in the case of human beings, I firmly believe that *nagori* people are the most exciting because of their accumulated knowledge, wisdom, and experience.

Spicy Bacon Potatoes

This version of potatoes with bacon and Spicy Miso Sauce is delicious; the tender texture and mild flavor of the potatoes is enhanced by the miso sauce and bacon flavors. I like it so much that I have made it for a light lunch, accompanied by a small salad and a piece of fruit. Waxy, low-starch potatoes such as Yukon gold work best in this recipe.

MAKES 4 SERVINGS

2 large Yukon gold potatoes (2 pounds)

8 bacon slices (5 ounces)

3 tablespoons Spicy Miso Sauce (page 102)

3 tablespoons water

½ cup chopped fresh parsley

Clean the potatoes with a hard brush under cold water. Cut each potato in half lengthwise, and then again in half lengthwise. Cut each quarter into 3 pieces crosswise. Place the potatoes and cold water to cover in a large pot over medium heat until it begins to simmer, decrease the heat to medium-low, and cook the potatoes for 10 minutes, or until tender. Drain the potatoes in a colander.

Cut the bacon into ¼-inch-wide crosswise slices. Heat a skillet over medium heat and add the bacon. When the bacon has warmed, decrease the heat to low and cook the bacon until the edges of each bacon piece begin to crisp. Using a slotted spoon, transfer the bacon to a small bowl. Increase the heat of the skillet with the remaining bacon fat to medium and add the potatoes, cooking them until all of the cut surfaces are lightly golden. Return the bacon to the skillet and cook the bacon and potatoes together for 1 to 2 minutes. In a small cup, whisk the Spicy Miso Sauce and water until blended. Add the prepared miso sauce and parsley to the skillet and give several large stirs for 1 minute. Serve the potatoes on a platter.

Spicy Miso Chicken Wings

Crispy fried chicken wings seem to please any crowd. This recipe adds Spicy Miso Sauce to an American-friendly dish that will be both familiar and delightful to your guests. I first coat the wings with a cornstarch and flour mixture, then deep fry them. The cornstarch and flour mixture creates a rather chewy but pleasant texture on the outside. I then quickly toss the juicy chicken wings with ginger- and paprika-spiked Spicy Miso Sauce. Your guests will need a large supply of paper napkins. A strongly flavored lager beer makes an excellent accompaniment for these wings.

MAKES 4 TO 6 SERVINGS

1½ pounds chicken wings

2 teaspoons onion powder

¾ teaspoon sea salt

1 medium egg, lightly beaten

1 tablespoon sake (rice wine) or water

6 tablespoons cornstarch

¼ cup all-purpose flour

2 tablespoons ginger juice from freshly grated ginger

¼ cup Spicy Miso Sauce (page 102)

2 teaspoons rice vinegar

1 teaspoon shoyu (soy sauce)

2 to 3 teaspoons hot paprika

1 scallion (green part only)

Canola oil or vegetable oil, for frying

Separate the chicken wings at the joints and dispose of the outer sections. Combine the onion powder, salt, egg, sake, cornstarch, flour, and 1 tablespoon of the ginger juice in a large bowl. Add the wings, coat with the mixture, and let stand for 20 minutes.

In another large bowl, combine the Spicy Miso Sauce, vinegar, soy sauce, paprika, and the remaining 1 tablespoon ginger juice. Cut the scallion into very thin slices diagonally and set aside.

Heat 3 inches of the canola oil in a wok or deep skillet to 330°F. Add the wings in 2 batches and cook them for 6 minutes, turning them from time to time. Transfer the wings to a wire rack set over a baking sheet. Increase the heat of the oil to 350°F. Return the wings in 3 batches to the hot oil and cook them for 1 minute, or until the outside is crisp. Remove the wings from the oil and drain on the wire rack.

While the wings are hot, toss all of the cooked wings in the spicy miso sauce mixture until well coated. Transfer the chicken wings to a large platter. Garnish with the scallion and serve.

Baked Tuna with Miso and Mustard

I have no memory of my mother and I ever purchasing tuna to cook in Japan. This is largely because there are numerous other very flavorful fish available all through the year and because tuna was reserved for raw consumption as sushi and sashimi. In America, I have learned that tuna is one of the most popular fish for cooking, so here is the tuna recipe that I have developed to incorporate my Spicy Miso Sauce.

When you purchase tuna, please choose a species that is harvested using sustainable practices (see page 91). Please make sure that the tuna you purchase is a very fresh piece, or flash-frozen and properly defrosted in your refrigerator. Smell the fish, and if there is any indication that it is slightly off, please cook it thoroughly.

MAKES 4 SERVINGS

¼ cup Spicy Miso Sauce (page 102)

2½ tablespoons canola oil or vegetable oil

2 tablespoons honey

1½ tablespoons sake (rice wine)

1½ tablespoons grainy mustard

¼ teaspoon sea salt

⅛ teaspoon freshly ground black pepper

1½ pounds very fresh yellowfin or bigeye tuna steak (sushi-grade tuna), cut into a 1-inch thickness

2 tablespoons all-purpose flour

2 tablespoons water

½ lemon

8 cups mesclun

Whisk the Spicy Miso Sauce, 1½ tablespoons of the oil, the honey, sake, mustard, salt, and black pepper in a small bowl until well blended. Cut the tuna steak into 4 slices and transfer them to a flat container. Rub 4 tablespoons of the prepared miso sauce on the tuna. Refrigerate the tuna for 30 minutes.

Remove the tuna from the container and scrape off the marinade with a spatula, reserving it. Place the flour in a sieve and shake it over the tuna slices, evenly dusting the steaks with flour. Turn the tuna and dust the other side.

Heat the remaining 1 tablespoon oil in a skillet over medium heat, add the tuna, and cook for 3 minutes, or until the bottom is golden. Turn the tuna and cook for 3 minutes. Transfer the cooked tuna to serving plates.

Return the skillet to medium heat and add the water, the reserved miso sauce used for marinating, and the remaining miso sauce mixture and cook the sauce for 1 minute or until it is no longer watery. Squeeze in the lemon juice and stir. Pour the sauce over the tuna.

Turn the heat off under the skillet, add the mesclun, and stir quickly for 10 seconds, using the sauce residue to season the mesclun. Top the fish with the mesclun salad and serve.

Cooking Fish Medium-Rare?

At restaurants, I sometimes overhear exchanges about the doneness of fish that make me feel uneasy. The waiter often asks the customer if he or she would like the grilled fish cooked rare or medium-rare, or the customer addresses the waiter with a similar request. Cooking fish medium-rare has become fashionable, probably because of the impact of sushi dining, but you must exercise great caution in this area. The only fish that is fit for rare or medium-rare consumption is superbly fresh fish that has gone through a proper process during the catch, transport, handling, filleting, and storage, as is done for sushi and sashimi fish. Typically cut fish pieces or fillets, not processed especially for sushi or sashimi, may be allowed to sit on crushed ice at a fishmonger or in the restaurant. Such fish are covered with bacteria and the bacterial decay of excreted products. The fish is not fit for rare or medium-rare consumption. It *must* be cooked through for safety.

So with this in mind, when you have a conversation with a waiter and you wish your fish to be rare or medium-rare, ask about the quality of the fish you are ordering. Has it been handled from start to finish—from the catch to the chef preparing your meal—using the strict standards for sushi- or sashimi-grade seafood? One clue to the answer of this question is the price of the dish. If it is too cheap (use your judgment), then it has likely not been handled with the high standards required for rare or medium-rare consumption. Don't expect a bargain.

Miso Shrimp Scampi

This is not the typical garlic butter sauced shrimp dish that we all know. In this delightful variation of an old standard, shrimp (see page 28) are cooked and coated with Spicy Miso Sauce that has been highly seasoned with fragrant ginger, garlic, and scallion. The resulting dish is absolutely delicious. When you can buy fresh shrimp in shells with the head attached, cook them whole without shelling or beheading.

MAKES 4 SERVINGS

1 pound medium shrimp, shelled and deveined, with tail attached

2 teaspoons cornstarch

2 teaspoons plus 2 tablespoons cold water

½ teaspoon sea salt

3 tablespoons Spicy Miso Sauce (page 102)

¼ cup sake (rice wine) or water

4 teaspoons sugar

3 scallions

2 teaspoons canola oil or vegetable oil

1½ tablespoons minced garlic

2 teaspoons minced ginger

Place the shrimp with the cornstarch, 2 teaspoons of the water, and salt in a large bowl and toss well to coat. Let stand for 10 minutes. Mix the Spicy Miso Sauce, sake, sugar, and the remaining 2 tablespoons water in a small bowl. Cut the scallions into very thin slices, separating the white and green parts.

Heat the canola oil in a skillet over medium-high heat, add the shrimp, and cook for 1 minute on each side, being careful not to move them so that they will brown a bit. Add the garlic, ginger, and white part of the scallions to the skillet and cook for 20 seconds, or until fragrant, stirring. Add the prepared miso sauce mixture to the skillet, reduce the heat to medium-low, and cook the shrimp for 1 more minute. Transfer the shrimp to a large platter. Garnish with the green part of the scallions and serve.

Technique

SHRIMP OR PRAWNS?

Shrimp or prawns—does it matter? People often call large shrimp "prawns," but that is not strictly correct. Shrimp and prawns are different. By checking the shell of each variety, you can tell which one is which. A shrimp's middle shell overlaps both the next section forward and the next section to the rear and the female shrimp carries fertilized eggs on her body for a long period. For prawns, the forward shell overlaps the one after it—from front to rear. Typically, shrimp have a distinctive sweetness. Many of the "shrimp" that we enjoy at the restaurant or purchase at the fishmonger are really prawns.

Here in New York City I wait for the season of wild, sweet Maine shrimp in winter. They come and go in a period as short as eight weeks or so. After a quick, thorough rinsing I simply cook them very briefly in salt water with added sake (rice wine) for a minute or two, until they are just done. I drain them well and serve with lemon wedges.

Hoba Miso Steak

Hoba miso (see page 125) is a unique dish in which seasoned miso sauce, alone or sometimes with added mountain vegetables, is cooked on top of a dried leaf called *hoba*. In English, *hoba* is known as the leaf of the *Magnolia obovata*, or Japanese bigleaf magnolia. The leaf, soaked before use, is placed directly over an open flame for cooking. In this recipe I do not use this very special leaf or any other leaf substitute. But even using this quick-fix method, you can experience the flavor of a true *hoba* miso dish.

MAKES 4 SERVINGS

1 small tomato (5 ounces)

1 medium zucchini (7 ounces)

1 medium Italian eggplant (7 ounces)

3 scallions

16 large cauliflower florets
(7 ounces each)

½ cup canola oil or vegetable oil

1½ pounds rib eye steak, excess fat
trimmed and reserved

Sea salt

1 teaspoon sesame oil

½ cup Spicy Miso Sauce (page 102)

Cut the tomato into 8 wedges. Cut the zucchini and eggplant into 16 small pieces each using the rangiri cut (see page 201). Cut the scallions into very thin slices diagonally. Reserve 2 tablespoons of the sliced green part for garnish.

Bring a medium pot of water to a boil over high heat, add the cauliflower and zucchini and cook for 3 minutes. Transfer the cauliflower and zucchini to a colander, drain, and air-dry. Heat the oil in a deep skillet over medium heat, add the eggplant, and cook for 4 minutes, or until all sides are lightly golden and tender. Drain the eggplant in a paper towel–lined bowl, and remove excess oil from the skillet.

Heat the reserved beef fat in the skillet over medium-low heat. Salt the beef liberally and add it to the skillet. Cook the beef for 4 minutes or until the bottom is golden. Turn the beef over and cook it for an additional 4 minutes, or close to medium-rare in doneness (see page 143). Transfer the steak to a cutting board.

Heat the sesame oil in a saucepan over medium heat. Add the scallions (except for the 2 tablespoons of reserved greens) and cook for 30 seconds. Add the Spicy Miso Sauce, turn the heat to low, and cook for 1 to 2 minutes, stirring, until the sauce is soft and bubbly. If the sauce becomes too thick, loosen it with 1 tablespoon water. Divide the miso sauce among serving plates. Cut the beef into 1½-inch cubes. Divide the beef and all the vegetables on top of each portion of miso sauce. Garnish with the reserved scallions and serve.

Hoba Miso: The Most Humble Preparation

Hoba miso was born deep in the mountainous region of Hida, located in Gifu Prefecture on Honshu, the main island of Japan. The region is dominated by the high mountain ranges called the Japan Alps. Because of this geography, even today's advanced Japanese railroad system cannot shorten the travel time from Tokyo (only 144 miles away). It takes a little over four hours with one transfer to reach this remote area. In contrast, *Shinkansen* bullet trains travel the 321 miles between Tokyo and Kyoto in a bit over two hours.

Winter finds the village of Hida covered with deep and lasting snow. These geographical and climactic hardships have contributed to preserving the essence of this old historical village, which has remained nearly untouched for hundreds of years. Being far from the water, foraged mountain vegetables and grains such as millet have always been (and remain) important food sources for the locals, even though shopping centers and supermarkets are now easily accessible by car. When available, wild animal protein and freshwater fish enrich these staples. Under these harsh conditions it was natural that this very humble *hoba* miso dish was born centuries ago. A large, dried magnolia leaf is soaked in water before being placed over an open flame. The soaked leaf is very durable and does not catch fire during cooking. The wisdom and skill of the locals, who discovered and employed the leaf for cooking, is remarkable.

Today, however, this quaint rural dish and technique has been adopted as a popular cooking method and is found on the menus of upscale restaurants in big cities like Tokyo. There, simple mountain vegetables have been replaced by expensive ingredients such as *wagyu* beef. The times have certainly changed, as have the preparation of the *hoba* miso dishes beyond the region of its origin. However, when you visit the old village you will still find the true, everlasting beauty of nature as well as traditional village life. On my next trip to Japan, Hida will be my destination.

Skirt Steak Meets Spicy Miso Sauce

Skirt steak and its closely related counterpart, flank steak, are bonus cuts. Skirt steak is flavorful and economical and is indispensable for dishes like Mexican fajitas and Chinese stir-fries. Here is my Japanese-flavored version of this cut. It is excellent for cooking in the oven or on the grill. Serve the cooked meat, thinly sliced, with baked sweet potato or simple steamed rice.

MAKES 4 SERVINGS

4 small sweet potatoes (1½ pounds)

1 pound skirt steak or flank steak

¼ cup Spicy Miso Sauce (page 102)

Sea salt and freshly ground black pepper

2 tablespoons canola oil or vegetable oil

¼ cup water

1 tablespoon white sesame seeds

1 tablespoon thinly sliced scallion

Preheat the oven to 350°F. Place the sweet potatoes in a medium pot, add enough water to cover, and bring to a simmer over medium heat. Cook the potatoes for 13 to 15 minutes or until they are soft but not mushy. Remove the potatoes from the water, wrap each potato in aluminum foil, and bake them for 30 minutes.

Rub the beef with 2 tablespoons of the Spicy Miso Sauce and let it stand for 30 minutes, up to 2 hours. Wipe the beef with a paper towel to remove excess sauce. Season the steak with salt and pepper. Heat the canola oil in an oven-proof medium skillet over medium-low heat, add the steak, and cook for 3 minutes or until the bottom is golden. Turn the meat over and cook until golden. Transfer the skillet to the oven and bake the steak for 2 to 3 minutes for medium-rare (see page 143). Transfer the beef to a warm plate.

Add the water and the remaining 2 tablespoons Spicy Miso Sauce to the skillet and cook until it is reduced and slightly thickened. Transfer the beef to a cutting board and cut it into ¼-inch-thick strips crosswise. Divide the beef slices and potatoes among serving plates, then pour the sauce over the meat. Garnish with the sesame seeds and scallion and serve.

Stir-Fried Colorful Vegetables

One of the best uses of my Spicy Miso Sauce is in stir-fry dishes. I use it with rice, vegetables, chicken, shrimp, beef, or tofu. In this preparation, I gather some of the colorful summer vegetables. Cooking time for each vegetable in the recipe varies, so follow the instructions precisely.

MAKES 4 SERVINGS

½ medium red onion (4 ounces)

10 large Brussels sprouts (10 ounces)

½ small red bell pepper (3 ounces)

½ small yellow bell pepper (3 ounces)

1 tablespoon canola oil or vegetable oil

2 tablespoons peeled and finely julienned ginger

1¼ cups shredded red cabbage

¼ cup Dashi Stock (page 38) or water

¼ cup Spicy Miso Sauce (page 102)

¼ to ½ teaspoon freshly ground black pepper

Cut the onion into thin slices crosswise. Cut off the bottom ends of the Brussels sprouts and cut each sprout into 6 wedges. Cut the red and yellow bell peppers into 1½-inch chunks.

Heat the canola oil in a large skillet over medium heat, add the onion slices, and cook, stirring continuously, for 2 minutes. Add the ginger and cook for 20 seconds. Add the Brussels sprouts and cook for 2 minutes, stirring. Add the cabbage and cook for 2 minutes. Add the stock and increase the heat to high. Cook the vegetables, stirring continuously, until the stock is about 80 percent absorbed. Decrease the heat to medium-high, add the red and yellow bell peppers, and cook for 1 minute. Add the Spicy Miso Sauce and cook for 1 to 2 minutes, or until the vegetables are thoroughly coated with the sauce and all of the stock is absorbed. Add the black pepper and give several large stirs. Serve the vegetables on a large communal platter.

Chicken and Cashews

I have a recipe for Chicken, Cashews, and Miso in a Wok in my book *The Japanese Kitchen.* In this tastier version, I use my Spicy Miso Sauce to enhance the flavor. When you toss the chicken with salt, sake, egg white, cornstarch, and sesame oil, please follow the order of ingredients specified in the recipe. The chicken should first be flavored with salt and sake before it is coated with egg white and cornstarch. The latter two produce a protective coating on the surface of the chicken during cooking.

MAKES 4 SERVINGS

2 large boneless, skinless chicken breast halves (1¼ pounds)

1 teaspoon sea salt

6 tablespoons sake (rice wine)

1 large egg white, lightly beaten until the thick part is completely broken up

1 tablespoon plus 1 teaspoon cornstarch or potato starch

2 teaspoons sesame oil

6 tablespoons Spicy Miso Sauce (page 102)

1 medium yellow onion (6 ounces)

3 scallions

3 tablespoons canola oil or vegetable oil

2 tablespoons chopped garlic

1¼ cups unsalted cashews, toasted

Cut each chicken breast crosswise into ¼-inch-thick strips. Place the chicken, ½ teaspoon of the salt, and 2 tablespoons of the sake in a large bowl and toss with a large spoon. Add the egg white and cornstarch and stir well. Add the sesame oil, stir well, and refrigerate for 20 minutes.

Mix the remaining ½ teaspoon salt, the remaining 4 tablespoons sake, and the Spicy Miso Sauce in a bowl. Cut the onion into ¼-inch-thick slices crosswise. Cut the scallions into ¼-inch-thick diagonal slices and separate the green and white parts.

Heat a medium pot of water over medium heat until it begins to simmer, then add the sliced chicken and cook for 1 minute. Use a fork to separate the chicken pieces as you drop them in the water so that they do not stick together. Drain the chicken in a colander, and discard the water.

Heat the canola oil in a wok over medium heat, add the onion, and cook for 1 minute, stirring. Increase the heat to medium-high, add the white part of the scallions and the garlic, and cook for 20 seconds, stirring. Add the precooked chicken and the prepared miso sauce, turn the heat to high, and cook for 1½ minutes, stirring. Add the cashews and scallion greens, and give several large stirs. Divide the food among serving plates and serve.

Juicy Chicken Katsu Burger with Spicy Miso Sauce

Everyone loves chicken *katsu*—bread crumb–dusted, deep-fried chicken—because it is golden in color, crispy, and rich tasting. So why not enjoy it on a traditional burger bun with Spicy Miso Sauce? Substitute chicken with pork, beef, or lamb to please your audience.

MAKES 4 SERVINGS

4 small boneless, skinless chicken thighs (14 ounces)

¼ cup all-purpose flour

2 large eggs, lightly beaten with ⅓ cup water

1½ cups panko bread crumbs

⅓ cup finely chopped walnuts

Canola oil or vegetable oil

6 tablespoons Spicy Miso Sauce (page 102)

2 tablespoons unsalted butter, softened

1 tablespoon grainy mustard

4 hamburger buns

4 iceberg lettuce leaves

4 slices large red onion

4 slices large beefsteak tomato

Make large, shallow checkerboard pattern cuts on the inner side of each chicken thigh. Place the flour in one bowl, the eggs and water mixture in another bowl, and the bread crumbs and walnuts in a third bowl. Using a fork, pick up one of the chicken thighs, transfer it to the flour bowl, and dredge the chicken on all sides with flour. Set on a plate. Repeat the process with the remaining pieces. Using a fork, pick up one of the floured chicken thighs and dip it in the egg mixture. Shake the chicken to remove excess egg liquid and then dredge in the bread crumb and walnut mixture. Repeat the process with the remaining pieces.

Heat 2 inches of the canola oil in a deep skillet over medium heat to 345°F. Add the chicken to the skillet, decrease the heat to medium-low, and cook the chicken for 6 minutes, or until it is golden. Turn the chicken and cook for 7 minutes, then increase the heat to high, and cook both sides until crisp. Drain the chicken on a wire rack set over a baking sheet.

Mix the Spicy Miso Sauce, softened butter, and mustard in a small bowl with a spoon. Lightly brown the cut surfaces of the buns in a heated skillet over high heat. Smear the bottom half of each bun with half of the butter-miso mixture. Stack the lettuce leaves, onion slices, tomato slices, and cooked chicken on the bun. Paint the top of each chicken with the remaining butter-miso mixture. Cover the chicken with the top part of the bun and serve.

Chicken Salad with Peanut Butter–Miso Sauce

Chicken is fun to prepare and eat because there are so many ways to enjoy it, and nearly everyone loves it. In this dish I boil chicken, slice it, and serve it along with vegetables bathed in Peanut Butter–Miso Sauce. To prepare tender and juicy chicken, I first immerse it in boiling water and cook it briefly over low heat. Then, keeping the pot covered, I let the chicken sit in the hot water for some time. Use any vegetables available in your refrigerator for the salad.

MAKES 4 SERVINGS

2 medium boneless, skinless chicken breast halves (1 pound)

Lemon juice

Sea salt

1 large avocado, pitted and peeled (8 ounces)

1 medium tomato (6 ounces)

1 medium Kirby cucumber (4 ounces)

½ cup Peanut Butter–Miso Sauce (page 103)

4 cups shredded romaine lettuce

1¼ cups finely shredded carrots

Olive oil

¼ cup chopped roasted unsalted peanuts

Place a large pot of water over high heat until it comes to a boil, decrease the heat to medium-low, and add the chicken. Cook the chicken for 8 minutes. Cover the pot with a tight-fitting lid, turn off the heat, and let it stand in the water for 18 minutes. Using a slotted spoon, transfer the chicken to a cutting board and cut the chicken into ⅔-inch cubes. Transfer the chicken to a medium bowl and toss it with squeezes of lemon juice and a pinch or two of salt.

Cut the avocado, tomato, and cucumber into ½-inch dice and add them to the bowl with the chicken. Add the Peanut Butter–Miso Sauce and gently toss the chicken and vegetables with a spoon.

Toss the romaine lettuce and carrots with a pinch of salt, a bit of olive oil, and lemon juice in a bowl until the vegetables are lightly seasoned. Divide the vegetables among salad bowls, and add the chicken salad on top of the lettuce and carrots. Garnish with the chopped peanuts and serve.

Miso-Braised Lamb

Mackerel, *saba*, comes first to my mind as an ingredient to use in miso braising. After moving to America, I tried to make this traditional dish with locally available mackerel from Maine and nearby waters, but the flavor was always disappointing. Mackerel in America does not have the same amount of fat or the rich flavor of the Japanese variety. So I said good-bye to my mackerel recipe and developed this one with lamb. The cooking time for this recipe is rather long because braising the meat to achieve a fork-tender texture takes more than an hour, but the process is very simple. Best of all, this dish has an exciting flavor and a clean finish. I suggest marinating the lamb the day before cooking.

MAKES 4 SERVINGS

2 pounds stew-cut lamb

½ cup Spicy Miso Sauce (page 102)

2 tablespoons canola oil or
   vegetable oil

1 thumb-size piece ginger, plus 2
   tablespoons finely grated ginger

½ cup sake (rice wine)

¼ cup mirin (sweet cooking wine)

4 large Brussels sprouts (4 ounces)

1 medium carrot (3 ounces)

4 cauliflower florets (4 ounces)

1 teaspoon shoyu (soy sauce)

Rub the lamb with the Spicy Miso Sauce in a large bowl. Cover with plastic wrap and refrigerate overnight.

Preheat the oven to 350°F. Prepare a full kettle of boiling water. Gently squeeze the lamb to remove any excess marinade, and reserve the marinade, even though there may be very little to save. Heat 1 tablespoon of the canola oil in a medium skillet over medium-low heat, add half of the lamb, and cook for 2 minutes or until the bottom is golden. Turn the lamb pieces over and brown the other sides. Continue turning the lamb pieces to brown all surfaces. Transfer the browned lamb to a large colander. Pour some of the water from the kettle over the lamb to quickly rinse and clean the lamb pieces (see page 31). Transfer the lamb to a bowl.

Add the remaining 1 tablespoon canola oil to the skillet (if the skillet is covered with too many burnt bits, rinse it with warm water) and finish browning the second batch of the lamb in the same manner. Transfer the lamb to the colander and quickly pour some more of the water from the kettle over the lamb to clean it. Then transfer the lamb to the bowl with the first portion.

Cut the piece of ginger (skin on) into thin slices about the size of a quarter. Place the sake, mirin, and sliced ginger in a medium ovenproof pot and bring to a simmer. Add the lamb and the remaining hot water in the kettle until the lamb is barely covered. Cover the pot with a tight-fitting lid and cook the lamb in the oven for 1½ hours.

Cut the Brussels sprouts in half. Cut the carrot into 8 pieces using the *rangiri* technique (see page 201). Bring a medium pot of water to a boil over medium heat, add the cauliflower, and cook for 2 minutes. Remove the cauliflower with a slotted spoon, add the Brussels sprouts and carrot, and cook for 3 minutes. Drain the vegetables and keep them warm.

Transfer the pot with the lamb to the stovetop. Add the remaining 2 tablespoons Spicy Miso Sauce, soy sauce, and the reserved Spicy Miso Sauce used to marinate the lamb to the pot. Cook the meat, uncovered, over low heat for 20 minutes. Using a slotted spoon, transfer the lamb from the pot to a bowl. Add the grated ginger to the pot, increase the heat to medium, and cook the lamb broth for 15 minutes or until it is reduced by half. Return the lamb to the pot, and toss with the broth to warm. Serve the lamb with the cooked vegetables on the side.

CHAPTER 5

BEST BASTING AND COOKING SAUCE

I developed the delicious special basting and cooking sauce called BBC Sauce that's featured in this chapter. It is a flavorful combination of shoyu and mirin that I created after my apprenticeship at a yakitori restaurant in Osaka City, Japan. Yakitori is a dish that uses almost the entire chicken. Bottom tail, chicken skin, neck meat, and/or breast or thigh meat is threaded onto bamboo skewers and cooked at high heat over Japanese *bincho-tan* charcoal (see page 136). BBC is the special sauce used to baste the skewers during cooking, creating a very flavorful and shiny coating on the chicken.

When I returned to New York after my training in Osaka, I was able to re-create the restaurant's BBC sauce in my kitchen. I modified the taste and formulation to make the BBC suitable to a broad range of recipes, including those in this chapter. I use BBC Sauce not only for yakitori but also in dishes requiring a high-quality, clean-tasting teriyaki-style sauce. The basic formulation of BBC Sauce and commercially available teriyaki sauces are somewhat similar, but the store-bought sauces tend to be too sweet, too salty, and unpleasantly gooey. Beyond the shoyu and mirin, the flavor elements of BBC Sauce come from scallions and dried red chile peppers, and the texture of my version is loose and smooth. In this chapter, I use BBC Sauce in traditional dishes and also extend its use to new recipes as well. BBC Sauce can wear many hats—as dipping sauce, cooking sauce, stir-frying sauce, and basting sauce.

BBC Sauce

MAKES 2 CUPS

1 cup mirin (sweet cooking wine)

½ cup sake (rice wine)

½ cup shoyu (soy sauce)

¼ cup sugar

2 scallions

2 *akatogarashi* (Japanese dried red chile peppers) or 1½ teaspoons red pepper flakes

Place the mirin and sake in a small pot over medium heat, and bring it to a simmer. Add the soy sauce, sugar, and scallions and cook the sauce for 8 minutes. Remove the pot from the heat and let cool. Discard the scallions and add the chile peppers. Refrigerate the sauce in a clean glass jar with a tight-fitting lid. There is no need to freeze this sauce; it will keep for 6 months in the refrigerator.

Technique

BINCHO-TAN: THE ULTIMATE CHARCOAL

Bincho-tan is an artisan-made, high-quality charcoal used at restaurants in Japan. It is known as the best heat source for grilling fish, fowl, other proteins, and vegetables. The steel-hard charcoal is made from a member of the oak family known in Japanese as *ubamegashi*. A unique aspect of *ubamegashi* is that the wood actually sinks in water due to its density. It is so hard and dense that when you handle the *bincho-tan*, no black powder comes off onto your hands. It burns at more than 1,000°F—much higher than conventional charcoals—and thereby produces both convective and copious radiated (infrared) heat. Because of this, the cooked food acquires a golden outside while retaining its moist and juicy inside.

Bincho-tan plays another role at my house. When friends and guests see my pitcher full of tap water with a couple of black small logs on the bottom, they ask me what these strange objects are. They are *bincho-tan*, and I use them to purify water.

BBC Cilantro Sauce

I created this sauce for the Steamed Tofu and Shiitake Gyoza (page 158). The rich flavor of BBC Sauce is further enhanced by the addition of aromatic cilantro, scallion, and garlic. It is excellent for steamed chicken, fish, or vegetable dishes such as Steamed Radicchio, Endive, and Lettuce (page 159). You will find many more ways to enjoy the sauce, I am sure.

MAKES ½ CUP

½ cup BBC Sauce (page 136)

2 teaspoons *rayu* (spicy sesame oil) or sesame oil

2 teaspoons shoyu (soy sauce)

2 tablespoons chopped fresh cilantro

2 tablespoons chopped scallion (white part only)

2 teaspoons minced garlic

Sea salt

Whisk together the BBC Sauce, spicy sesame oil, and soy sauce in a small bowl until well blended. Add the cilantro, scallion, and garlic. Add a pinch or two of salt to taste. Refrigerate the sauce in a clean glass jar with a tight-fitting lid, and use within 3 days for the best flavor.

BBC Tonkatsu Sauce

Tonkatsu sauce was commercially developed in the mid-1960s to accompany the classic Japanese deep-fried pork cutlet, *tonkatsu*. It is a spicier, sweeter, and gooier version of Worcestershire sauce. Commercially available *tonkatsu* sauce is made from many vegetables, fruits, and spices, but the first ingredient is usually some type of sweetener, and the last few ingredients are typically chemical additives. This recipe allows you to prepare your own simple, natural version of *tonkatsu* sauce. I'm sure you will also find many other uses for this delicious sauce besides its traditional use on deep-fried pork cutlets.

MAKES ¾ CUP

¼ cup BBC Sauce (page 136)

2 tablespoons water

2 tablespoons ketchup

1½ tablespoons Worcestershire sauce

2 teaspoons shoyu (soy sauce)

1 tablespoon sugar

1 teaspoon Dijon mustard

½ teaspoon freshly ground black pepper

1 tablespoon cornstarch mixed with 1 tablespoon water

Place the BBC Sauce, water, ketchup, Worcestershire sauce, soy sauce, sugar, Dijon mustard, and black pepper in a small pot over medium heat. Cook the sauce, stirring, until the sugar is dissolved. Decrease the heat to low, add the cornstarch slurry, and cook, stirring constantly, for 1 to 1½ minutes or until semitranslucent. Transfer the sauce to a clean glass jar, cool, cover with a tight-fitting lid, and refrigerate. Use within 3 days for the best flavor.

Vegetable Fried Rice

This recipe makes a quick lunch using a bag of frozen vegetables and frozen cooked rice (the rice should be defrosted before stir-frying). If you don't have any rice already made on hand, make it fresh, but rinse it under cold tap water before proceeding with the recipe. Serve this simple and pretty rice dish with a cup of miso soup, or use it as a side dish to accompany your main protein.

MAKES 2 TO 4 SERVINGS

2 scallions

3 cloves garlic

2 tablespoons canola oil or vegetable oil

2 large eggs with a pinch of sea salt, in a bowl

1 tablespoon finely julienned ginger

5 cups day-old cold cooked rice (short-, medium-, or long-grain)

1⅓ cups frozen corn, carrots, green peas, and string bean mix

¼ teaspoon sea salt

½ teaspoon freshly ground black pepper

3 tablespoons BBC Sauce (page 136)

Cut the scallions into very thin slices diagonally, and separate the green and white parts. Cut the garlic into paper-thin slices.

Heat 1 tablespoon of the oil in a wok or large skillet over medium-high heat. Add the eggs, break the yolks, give several vigorous stirs, and continue to cook until the eggs are slightly firm, about 20 seconds. Do not cook the eggs through. Transfer the eggs to a small bowl.

Add the remaining 1 tablespoon canola oil to the wok over medium heat. Add the white part of the scallions, the garlic, and ginger and cook for 20 seconds or until fragrant. Add the rice and continue to cook for 5 minutes, stirring continuously. Add the frozen vegetables and cook for 2 minutes. Add the salt and black pepper and cook for 2 more minutes. Add the BBC Sauce and cook for 1 minute. Return the cooked eggs to the wok and add the scallion greens. Break up the eggs and stir for an additional 30 seconds. Serve the rice in bowls.

Chicken Rice Bowl, page 144.

Tomato, Onion, Avocado, and Bacon Rice Bowl

Donburi—rice in a bowl with a wide variety of toppings—is a Japanese meal-in-one-bowl dish (see page 143). The rice bowl dishes popular at American Japanese and Asian restaurants are *gyu-don* (beef rice bowl), *katsu-don* (fried pork cutlet rice bowl), and *teriyaki-tori-don* (teriyaki chicken rice bowl). This rice bowl includes vegetables and bacon to enrich the flavor and texture of the dish.

MAKES 4 SERVINGS

2¼ cups short- or medium-grain rice

2 medium tomatoes

1 medium red onion, peeled

2 small avocados, pitted and peeled

9 bacon slices (7 ounces)

Sea salt

¾ cup BBC Sauce (page 136)

¼ cup chopped fresh parsley

Cook the rice according to the instructions on page 21.

Cut the tomatoes into ½-inch cubes. Cut the red onion in half lengthwise and then into thin slices crosswise. Cut the avocados into ½-inch cubes.

Heat a large skillet over medium heat and add the bacon in a single layer. Cook the bacon for 8 to 10 minutes or until it is crisp, turning each piece once. You may need to decrease the heat during cooking to avoid burning the bacon. Transfer the bacon to a paper towel–lined plate to cool, and discard the excess fat from the skillet. Cut the bacon into ½-inch squares.

Wipe out any excess oil from the skillet, but leave a thin coating of fat in the bottom. Return the skillet to medium heat and add the onion and a pinch of salt. Cook the onion for 2 to 3 minutes, until slightly wilted. Remove the skillet from the heat and add the BBC Sauce. Return the skillet to medium-high heat, add the tomatoes and avocados, and cook the sauce and vegetables for 2 minutes.

Divide the rice among bowls. Spoon the cooked onion, tomatoes, avocados, and sauce over each rice bowl. Garnish with the bacon and parsley and serve.

Beef Rice Bowl

Gyu-don, beef rice bowl, is a dish in which thinly sliced beef is cooked with onion and egg in a sweet shoyu (soy sauce) broth and served over a bowl of rice. It is one of several beef dishes created at the turn of the twentieth century, at a time when many Japanese people began to consume meat. In order to promote beef to the Japanese population, chefs had to devise recipes that included rice and were chopstick friendly. This is why many Japanese beef dishes are composed of thinly sliced or ground beef. Here in America, the norm is big cuts of meat meant to be eaten with a knife and fork, and it is difficult to find a butcher who carries thinly sliced beef. My beef rice bowl was born out of the beef cuts available in America, and I changed up the egg component of the dish as well. Instead of cooking the egg in the beef sauce, I make a sunny-side-up egg and serve it as a garnish.

MAKES 4 SERVINGS

2¼ cups short- or medium-grain rice

8 cherry tomatoes

1 pound round eye steak

Sea salt and freshly ground black pepper

3 tablespoons canola oil or vegetable oil

4½ cups small broccoli florets (10 ounces)

¾ cup BBC Sauce (page 136)

4 medium eggs

¼ cup sliced scallions (green part only)

Cook the rice according to the instructions on page 21. Cut each tomato in half and set aside.

Season both sides of the beef with salt and pepper. Heat 1 tablespoon of the canola oil in a medium skillet over medium heat, add the beef, and cook until the bottom is lightly golden, about 3 minutes. Turn the beef over and cook for an additional 3 to 4 minutes. You may need to adjust the cooking time depending on the thickness of the meat. Transfer the beef to a cutting board. It will be on the rare side (see page 143), but while resting it will continue to cook. The beef will also be cooked again in the sauce.

Quickly clean the skillet with hot water, put it back over medium heat, and add 1 tablespoon of the canola oil. Add the tomatoes, broccoli, and a pinch of salt. Cook the vegetables for 4 minutes, stirring from time to time. Add 2 tablespoons of the BBC Sauce and stir until the vegetables are well coated. Divide the cooked rice among bowls. Divide the vegetables and sauce into the bowls.

Quickly clean the skillet again with hot water. Put the skillet over medium heat, add the remaining 1 tablespoon of canola oil, and break the eggs into the skillet. After the bottom of the egg white sets (about 30 seconds), add 3 tablespoons cold water to the skillet and immediately cover it with a lid. Cook the eggs over low heat for 2 to 2½ minutes. Transfer the eggs to a large platter and keep covered with the lid.

Cut the beef into 1-inch cubes. Add the remainder of the BBC Sauce to the skillet and bring it to a simmer. Add the beef cubes to the skillet and coat them with the sauce. Divide the beef among the serving bowls. Spoon the remaining sauce from the skillet over each of the bowls. Top each with a sunny-side-up egg and scallion greens and serve.

Donburi: Necessity Is the Mother of Invention

Donburi—a simple bowl of rice with a topping—is a creation of our Japanese rice-based food culture. Just as Western culture produced numerous bread-based foods such as sandwiches and pizza, so did Japanese culture create many new foods with rice (Japan's main staple).

The story of the birth of donburi at the beginning of the Edo period (1600–1868) mirrors the Earl of Sandwich story for the creation of the sandwich. Necessity was the mother of invention for both. As the story goes, a traveler who was going to take a boat ride ordered a bowl of steamed rice and grilled eel for a quick lunch at a *chaya* (teahouse) by the river. Just as the waitress brought him a bowl of steamed rice and a plate of grilled, sauce-basted eel, he heard the boatman un-expectedly announce the last call for the departure of his boat. The traveler did not want to miss the boat, so he quickly put the plate of eel upside-down on top of the rice bowl to secure his food, making it easier to carry, and made a run for the boat. This caused the sauce-covered eel to land on top of the hot, steaming rice. He carried his meal in this fashion to the end of his journey. Although he wasn't at all happy that his meal had been ruined by the accidental mixing of his two dinner items, he consumed them anyway in the form of his newly invented eel rice bowl.

Of course, there is a happy ending to this tale. To his surprise, the flavor and texture were better than when the eel and rice were served separately, as was the common custom. He found that the eel, which had steamed in the closed rice bowl for some time, was velvety and tender, and that the rice had absorbed the rich-tasting sauce, making an absolutely delicious dish. The story ends with the traveler later returning to the teahouse and ordering the dish that he had invented. I wonder if this tale has any more truth to it than the story of the invention of the sandwich.

Technique

MEDIUM-RARE BY TOUCH

This is a popular and easy way to judge whether the steak that you are cooking is rare, medium-rare, or well-done: by touching the meat. First you need to calibrate your touch measuring technique. You do this using your hands and your nose (yes, I'm serious). Relax your left hand, and with the thumb of your right hand touch the area between the thumb and index finger of your left hand. This skin is very soft and not resilient. If a steak touched while cooking has this same feel, the steak is rare. Next, open the fingers of your left hand, strongly separating your thumb from the other four fingers. Then touch the same area between your thumb and index finger. Now you feel some resilience, but there is still a slight tenderness in the central area. This is the feel of medium-rare meat. A well-done steak has the same feel as when you press the tip of your nose.

Chicken Rice Bowl

You will find that refrigerated BBC Sauce is handy for many tasty dishes, including chicken. I usually brown chicken in a skillet and finish it in the oven, but this recipe calls for cooking the entire dish on the stovetop. I cut the cooked chicken into cubes, heap it on top of cooked rice, and drizzle slightly thickened BBC Sauce over the top.

MAKES 4 SERVINGS

2¼ cups short- or medium-grain rice

1 thumb-size piece ginger, peeled

1 sheet nori seaweed (optional)

6 thick or 12 thin asparagus spears, brown frills removed (about ½ pound)

4 large cremini or shiitake mushrooms (6 ounces)

4 small boneless, skin-on chicken breast halves (1 pound 10 ounces)

Sea salt and freshly ground black pepper

1 tablespoon canola oil or vegetable oil, plus more as needed

¾ cup BBC Sauce (page 136)

4 teaspoons white sesame seeds

Cook the rice according to the instructions on page 21.

Finely julienne the ginger. Cut the nori sheet, if using, into quarters lengthwise. Stack the nori strips and cut them into thin strips crosswise with scissors. Place the nori strips in a dry bowl, because even the slightest moisture will cause them to lose their shape. Cut the asparagus diagonally into ⅓-inch-thick slices. Cut off the hard bottom part of the mushroom stems, and cut each mushroom into thin slices.

Season both sides of the chicken with salt and pepper. Heat the canola oil in a skillet over medium heat, then add the chicken, skin side down.
After 1 minute, decrease the heat to medium-low, and cook the chicken for 8 minutes, or until the skin is golden. Turn the chicken over and cook for 8 minutes. Transfer the chicken to a cutting board, let cool slightly, and cut into 1-inch cubes.

Toss the asparagus and mushrooms with a little canola oil and a pinch of salt in a bowl. Wipe the skillet with a paper towel to remove any excess chicken fat, and return it to medium-high heat. Add the ginger and cook for 20 seconds. Add the asparagus and mushrooms and cook for 2 minutes, or until both vegetables are moist and the asparagus is bright green. Transfer the vegetables to a bowl. Add the BBC Sauce to the same skillet over medium-high heat, and cook the sauce for 1 to 2 minutes, or until it thickens a bit.

Divide the rice among bowls. Divide the chicken and vegetables into the bowls. Drizzle the sauce over each bowl. Garnish with the sesame seeds and nori strips, and serve.

Collard Greens Salad with BBC Tahini Sauce

Although I had never encountered leaves as tough and hardy as collard greens until I moved to America, I fell in love with their down-to-earth green flavor. I usually purchase a bunch or two of collard greens every week in season at my local farmers' market or at a nearby store. Because of the toughness of the leaves, many recipes call for cooking them for quite a long time, almost to the point of mushiness. Because the texture of firm greens reminds me of a firm and chewy New York bagel, my cooking time in this recipe is surprisingly short. If you prefer more tender greens, please increase the cooking time as needed. I have noticed that the outer leaves are tougher than the inner leaves, and, similarly, late summer and fall greens are also tougher than early spring greens, and they require 2 minutes or so additional cooking time.

MAKES 4 SERVINGS

¼ cup BBC Sauce (page 136)

¼ cup tahini

¼ cup warm water

½ cup chopped red grapefruit

½ cup chopped dried apricots

1 bunch collard greens (10 ounces), hard bottom part of the stems removed

½ teaspoon shoyu (soy sauce)

2 tablespoons white sesame seeds, toasted

Whisk the BBC Sauce, tahini, and warm water in a bowl until well blended. Add the grapefruit and apricot pieces and mix well. Set aside.

Bring a large pot of salted water to a boil over medium heat. Add the outer leaves of the collard greens to the boiling water. Grasp the remaining inner leaves in your hand or with tongs, and hold the stems only in the water for 1 minute, then submerge the leaves in the boiling water. Cook the leaves for an additional 4 minutes (if you prefer the leaves very tender, cook them for as long as 15 minutes). Drain the greens in a colander, and rinse them under cold water to cool. Pick them up by the stems, collect them in a bunch, and squeeze firmly to remove excess water.

Transfer the greens to a cutting board. Cut the leaves in half down the center of the stems. Cut the leaves again, lengthwise, into 2-inch-wide strips. Pile the strips, and cut the whole bunch crosswise into ½-inch-wide strips. Transfer the greens to a bowl and sprinkle them with the soy sauce. Massage and distribute the soy sauce into the collard greens. Again, squeeze the collard greens firmly to remove excess water. Divide the greens into small serving bowls and spoon the BBC Tahini Sauce over each portion. Garnish with the sesame seeds and serve.

Beef and Asparagus Roll

I used to teach Japanese cooking all across the country, and I was often asked by students, "How can I make that tasty beef roll with scallion stuffing that I enjoy at Japanese restaurants?" I had no idea what people were talking about, because this is not a very popular dish in Japan. It was only then that I learned that this humble dish had somehow become one of the signature dishes at many Japanese and Asian restaurants in America. So, after some research, I went to work on my own version of this popular preparation. In this recipe, I added asparagus for better flavor and appearance. A little cornstarch sprinkled over the sliced beef helps to bind the roll together during cooking. When preparing this dish, be sure that you make a tight roll.

MAKES 4 SERVINGS

1 pound round eye steak

12 medium asparagus spears, brown frills removed (about 1 pound)

4 scallions

2 teaspoons cornstarch, plus more for the beef

2 teaspoons canola oil or vegetable oil

¼ cup plus 2 teaspoons water

½ cup BBC Sauce (page 136)

Cut the beef into 12 thin 2½ by 4-inch rectangular slices (or you can ask your butcher to do the work for you). Cut each asparagus spear in half crosswise. Cut the white part of the scallions into thin strips lengthwise and the green part into thin disks. Bring a medium pot of salted water to a boil over medium heat, add the asparagus, and cook for 30 seconds. Drain the asparagus in a sieve and air-dry.

Spread the beef slices over the work surface, with the narrow edge near you and each piece slanted 15 degrees to the right. Using a pastry brush, paint the cornstarch over the surface of the beef slices. Place one top half and one bottom half of the asparagus spears next to each other on top of the beef, parallel to the work counter. Place them so they reach the left edge of the beef. Finish placing the asparagus on the remaining 11 slices. Place a portion of the scallion whites next to the asparagus on each of the 12 beef slices. Roll each of the beef slices tightly with the asparagus and scallions, completely covering the vegetables with the beef. Secure the end of each roll with toothpicks.

Heat the canola oil in a large skillet over medium-high heat and cook the beef rolls until all surface areas are lightly golden. Remove the toothpicks and cook the seam as well. Total cooking time should be about 3 minutes. Transfer the beef rolls to a large platter. Mix the cornstarch with 2 teaspoons of the water in a small cup.

Add the remaining ¼ cup water and the BBC Sauce to the skillet and cook the sauce over medium heat until the liquid is reduced to two-thirds of the original volume. Return the beef rolls to the skillet and spoon the sauce over the rolls. Remove the skillet from the heat, add the cornstarch water, and stir it until the cornstarch liquid is well blended with the sauce. Return the skillet to low heat and cook for 1 to 2 minutes, continuing to spoon the sauce over the beef rolls. Transfer the beef rolls to a cutting board and cut each in half diagonally. Transfer the beef rolls to a large plattter and spoon the remaining sauce over them. Garnish with the scallion greens and serve.

Kabocha and Lamb Wanton
Pot Stickers, page 197.

BBC Chicken Liver Pâté

What inspired me to create this dish is *yakitori rebaa* (Japanese people have difficulty pronouncing "L" and "R," so liver becomes *rebaa*), grilled chicken livers on a skewer basted with BBC Sauce. I always order that dish when I visit a yakitori restaurant. First, I thought of creating a recipe for cooked liver with BBC Sauce, but I found that not many people enjoy eating whole chicken livers. After some contemplation, I settled on a chicken liver pâté dish and wound up with a wonderful new creation. My family and friends are now crazy about this style of chicken liver pâté.

MAKES 6 SERVINGS

1 pound chicken livers

2 tablespoons olive oil

¾ cup chopped yellow onion

½ cup chopped celery

¼ teaspoon sea salt

¼ cup brandy

¼ cup BBC Sauce (page 136)

½ teaspoon Worcestershire sauce

Crackers of your choice (such as rye or water crackers)

Cut the chicken livers into approximately 1-inch slices. Bring a medium pot of water to a boil over high heat, add the livers, and cook over medium heat for 5 to 10 seconds or until the outside of each piece is white. Drain the livers in a colander, discarding the cooking liquid.

Heat the olive oil in a medium skillet over medium heat, add the onion, celery, and salt, and cook for 4 to 5 minutes. Add the liver pieces and cook for 2 minutes. Add the brandy and cook for 3 minutes, or until the liquid is 80 percent absorbed. Add the BBC Sauce and Worcester-shire sauce, increase the heat to high, and cook, stirring constantly, for 1 to 2 minutes. Allow some moisture to remain in the cooked mixture; otherwise when it is puréed, the pâté will be too firm. Transfer the mixture to a food processor and process until smooth. Serve the pâté with good crackers.

BBC Pork Chops with Oranges

Adding oranges to the BBC Sauce enhances the distinctive pork flavor in this dish. In August 2011, the United States Department of Agriculture lowered the minimum internal temperature for the safe cooking of pork to 145°F. At this temperature, pork chops remain juicy and moist. Be more cautious, however, when cooking ground pork, which requires a safe cooking temperature of 160°F. To check the temperature with a cooking thermometer, insert the point very close to but not touching the bone, where you will find the lowest temperature.

MAKES 4 SERVINGS

1½ cups BBC Sauce (page 136)

Zest of 2 large oranges

5 tablespoons orange juice

4 bone-in pork chops (each about 11 ounces and 1½ inches thick)

Sea salt and freshly ground black pepper

1 tablespoon canola oil or vegetable oil, plus more as needed

1 bunch watercress

20 orange segments

Mix the BBC Sauce, orange zest, and orange juice in a large bowl. Add the pork chops to the mixture and let stand for 30 minutes. Remove the pork chops from the sauce and wipe them dry with a paper towel, reserving the marinade.

Preheat the oven to 350°F. Lightly season the pork with salt and pepper. Heat the canola oil in a large skillet over medium-low heat, add the pork, and cook for 4 minutes, or until the bottom is golden. Turn the pork over and transfer the skillet to the oven. Cook the pork for 16 to 18 minutes. Pick the leaves from the watercress and place them in a medium bowl.

Remove the skillet from the oven and transfer the pork chops to plates. Add 2 tablespoons of water to the skillet and scrape the bottom with a spatula. Discard the water and scrapings. Return the skillet to medium heat and add the reserved marinade. Cook the marinade until it thickens slightly. Spoon a portion of the sauce over each pork chop. Toss the watercress in a bowl with a little bit of canola oil, just enough to coat the surface of the leaves. Sprinkle in a little salt and toss the greens thoroughly. Divide the watercress among the plates next to the pork, top each chop with 5 orange segments, and serve.

Salmon Teriyaki, BBC-Style

This is another super-easy preparation with great flavor. BBC Sauce does not mask the bad flavor of poor-quality fish, so choose salmon that is very fresh. Today I tend to trust frozen fish more than "fresh" fish, which may have been left on the fishmonger's counter for a couple of days and already looks tired. Freezing technology has improved dramatically, and so has the quality of frozen fish. I love the taste of wild sockeye salmon from Canada, and it is often available frozen at the supermarket. The natural sweetness of this fish is enhanced by the BBC Sauce. The best way to defrost frozen fish is to leave it in the refrigerator overnight.

MAKES 4 SERVINGS

¾ cup BBC Sauce (page 136)

Juice and finely grated zest of
   1 lemon cut into 4 pieces

2 pounds scaled, skin-on salmon
   fillet

Sea salt

1 bunch Swiss chard (about 1 pound)

2 tablespoons canola oil or
   vegetable oil, plus more as needed

Cooked brown rice, for serving

2 tablespoons water

Mix the BBC Sauce, lemon juice, and lemon zest in a small bowl. Set aside.

Season the salmon on both sides with salt and let it stand for 20 minutes (see page 94).

Carefully rinse the salmon under tap water to remove the salt. Wipe the salmon dry with a paper towel. Cut off the hard bottom part of the stems of the Swiss chard, and cut the remaining leaves in half along the center of the stems. Then, cut it into thin slices crosswise. Toss the Swiss chard with a little oil and a pinch or two of salt in a large bowl.

Lightly season the salmon with salt. Heat the canola oil in a large skillet over medium heat, add the salmon skin side down, and cook over medium-low heat for 5 minutes or until the skin is golden. Do not move the fish while it is cooking. Turn the fish over with a spatula, and cook for 5 minutes longer. Please make sure that the fish is cooked through. Transfer the fish to plates.

Wipe the excess oil from the skillet with a paper towel and return it to medium-high heat. Add the Swiss chard, and cook it until the leaves are wilted, stirring continuously. Place the Swiss chard next to the fish on the plates. Add the rice to the plate next to the fish and the Swiss chard. Wipe the skillet again with a paper towel and return it to medium heat. Add the water, bring it to a simmer, add the prepared BBC sauce, and cook it until the sauce is slightly thickened. Spoon the sauce over each piece of salmon and serve.

Beef and Broccoli

The stir-fried beef and broccoli that is served at Chinese and Asian restaurants in America is also a popular home-cooked dish in Japan. It is part of so-called *chuka-ryori*, "Japanized" Chinese cuisine that is very popular in Japan. Home cooks use shoyu (soy sauce), sake (rice wine), sugar, and/or oyster sauce along with potato starch as a thickener. My recipe includes rich-tasting BBC Sauce to produce a delicious version of the classic preparation. Flavorful and economical skirt steak is a good choice for the cut of beef.

MAKES 4 SERVINGS

1 pound skirt or flank steak

6 tablespoons BBC Sauce (page 136)

2 tablespoons sake (rice wine)

1 tablespoon cornstarch mixed with 1 tablespoon water

1 teaspoon sesame oil

3 scallions

4½ cups broccoli florets (10 ounces), including peeled and thinly sliced stems

2 tablespoons canola oil or vegetable oil

3 cloves garlic, thinly sliced

6 cups cooked brown or white rice

Cut the beef into slices measuring ¼ inch thick, 3 inches long, and 1-inch-wide slices. Mix the 2 tablespoons of BBC Sauce, the sake, corn-starch water, and sesame oil in a bowl. Add the beef to the bowl and massage with the sauce. Let the beef marinate for 10 minutes.

Cut the white part of the scallions into ½-inch-thick diagonal slices and the green part into very thin slices diagonally. Bring a large pot of salted water to a boil over high heat, add the broccoli, and cook for 45 seconds. Drain the broccoli in a colander and air-dry.

Add the canola oil to a wok or a large skillet over medium-high heat, add the scallion whites, and cook for 1 minute. Add the garlic and cook for 20 seconds. Add the beef and its marinating sauce to the wok and cook for 1 minute, or until the outside of the beef is white, stirring with a spatula. Add the broccoli and the remaining 4 tablespoons BBC Sauce and cook for 1 to 2 minutes. Turn off the heat, add the scallion greens, and give several large stirs. Divide the beef and broccoli among bowls and serve with the rice on the side.

Spicy Miso Chicken Wings,
page 119.

Potato and Beef Korokke

Korokke is the Japanese name and pronunciation given to "croquette" (see page 154), introduced in Japan at the end of the nineteenth century. The béchamel sauce–based croquette was intended to be eaten with a knife and fork and was a hit at expensive, white-tablecloth, "Western-style" restaurants called *Yoshoku-ya* in Japan. The potato-based croquette with minced meat eventually became a favorite dish at home because of its simple preparation and the easily accessible ingredients in the recipe. I tried many times to create a non-fried version, but despite my best efforts I concluded that the traditional deep-fried version tastes best. My *korokke* is a 2½-inch diameter patty, but you can make yours into other shapes and sizes.

MAKES 6 SERVINGS (36 PIECES)

3 large russet potatoes (3 pounds)

3 tablespoons canola oil, plus more for frying

4 cups diced yellow onions

2 teaspoons sea salt

½ pound ground beef mixed and loosened with 3 tablespoons water

½ to 1 teaspoon freshly ground black pepper

½ teaspoon ground nutmeg

¾ cup frozen or fresh corn kernels

¼ cup chopped fresh parsley

½ cup all-purpose flour

2 large eggs, beaten with 2 tablespoons water

2 cups panko bread crumbs

½ cup BBC Tonkatsu Sauce (page 138)

Bring a large pot of lightly salted water to a boil over high heat. Add the potatoes, then decrease the heat to medium-low and cook the potatoes for 50 minutes, or until they are quite tender. Drain the potatoes in a colander and, when they have cooled, peel them if that is your preference. Transfer the potatoes to a large bowl and mash them with a potato masher. If you do not have a potato masher, gently crush and mash the potatoes using the bottom of a small pot.

Heat the canola oil in a large skillet over medium heat. Add the onions and 1 teaspoon of the salt and cook for 4 minutes, or until the onions are soft. Add the beef, the remaining 1 teaspoon salt, the black pepper, and nutmeg. Increase the heat to high and cook until the liquid is absorbed, stirring continuously and breaking the beef into fine crumbles. Add the corn and parsley, and cook until the water is absorbed. Transfer the cooked beef to the bowl of mashed potatoes and, with a spatula, thoroughly mix the beef and potatoes. Cool the beef and potato mixture in the refrigerator for 15 minutes.

Divide the beef and potato mixture into 6 portions, and then form each portion into 6 small smooth balls. Place each ball on your palm and, using both hands, flatten it into a 2½-inch diameter patty. Repeat to finish making all 36 patties.

Heat 3 inches of canola oil in a heavy skillet to 360°F. Dredge each of the *korokke* patties in the flour in a bowl, patting away any excess flour. Dip each floured patty in the egg-water mixture in another bowl and then dredge each one in the bread crumbs in the third bowl, until you have finished coating all of the patties. At this stage, you can freeze some of the patties for consumption at a later time. They will keep for up to 3 months.

Add several patties at a time to the hot oil (see page 164) and cook for 2 to 3 minutes, or until they are golden, turning them over several times. Transfer the cooked patties to a wire rack and drain. Finish frying all of the patties. Serve the *korokke* patties with BBC Tonkatsu Sauce.

Korokke: A Snack from the Butcher

Korokke is a very nostalgic food for me. It reminds me of the local butcher who was on my way to my junior high school in Meguro-ku, Tokyo. I frequently dropped by that butcher shop with my friends for a treat. The butcher made fresh *korokke* fried in lard every day, and the toasty, deep-fried aroma permeated the street in front of his shop. Following after school sports club activities, my friends and I were so hungry that we could not pass the butcher without savoring one or two *korokke*, even though I knew that my mother's *korokke* was the best in the world. The *korokke*—slightly larger than today's smartphone in the shape of a fairly flat patty—was golden brown, crusty on the outside, and juicy, moist, and flavorful inside.

In Japan, butchers often sell *korokke* and other prepared food items to go. They make and sell *menchi-katsu* (a deep-fried ham-burger-like patty composed of beef, pork, or chicken), *hamu-katsu* (a thickly sliced deep-fried ham cutlet), *tonkatsu*, and whatever else they can produce within the capability of the operation. In addition to meat items, no matter the size of their operation, butchers always produce and sell potato salad. A butcher and potato salad sound like strange partners, but butchers find that making and selling potato salad can boost their sales. The salad uses nearly the same ingredients that they employ in *korokke* and other preparations. Sadly for me, American butchers do not sell *korokke*. But I gained much here with my local butchers that I could not have in Japan, such as a large variety of fresh sausages, game, hams cured by various methods, and other charcuterie products. And, of course, I can always prepare excellent *korokke* at home.

Chicken Katsu Sticks

This dish is a kid favorite, but it is also excellent for a casual party. I cut chicken into strips and coat them with peanut-laced bread crumbs before deep-frying them. Cutting the chicken into strips reduces the cooking time and creates a very appealing finger food. Be sure to read Frying Guidelines on page 164.

MAKES 4 SERVINGS

4 small boneless, skinless chicken breast halves (1 pound 10 ounces)

½ teaspoon sea salt

6 tablespoons cornstarch

1 cup unsalted raw or roasted peanuts

1 cup dried bread crumbs

½ cup chopped fresh parsley

2 medium eggs

Canola oil or vegetable oil, for deep frying

BBC Tonkatsu Sauce (page 138)

Cut each chicken breast across the grain into 5 strips (about 1¼ inches wide). Transfer the chicken to a large bowl and toss it with the salt. Massage the chicken and let it stand for 10 minutes. Then place the cornstarch in the bowl of chicken and dredge the strips with the cornstarch.

In a food processor, process the peanuts until they are finely crumbled. Add the bread crumbs and process them with the peanuts for 30 seconds. Transfer the peanut–bread crumb mixture to a medium bowl and mix with the parsley. Break the eggs in another medium bowl and beat them well. One at a time, dip each cornstarch-coated chicken strip into the eggs. Dredge each chicken strip in the bread crumb mixture until completely coated. Finish breading all of the strips, and transfer them to a large platter.

Heat 2 inches of the canola oil in a heavy skillet to 350°F. Add the chicken strips, 4 to 6 strips at a time, and cook them for 5 minutes or until golden, turning them several times. Transfer the cooked chicken strips to a wire rack set over a baking sheet. Finish cooking all of the strips.

Place a paper towel or piece of parchment paper over a deep dish and transfer the chicken strips to the dish, standing them up on end. Serve with the BBC Tonkatsu Sauce on the side for dipping.

Tsukune and Shrimp Yakitori

This is a colorful and fun dish that is perfect for a barbecue party. The traditional yakitori prep-aration uses thin, short bamboo skewers to hold the meat, but here I put all of the ingredients—chicken meatballs, shrimp, broccoli, red and yellow bell peppers, and brown mushrooms—on long steel skewers like those used for shish kebabs. This makes for easy and simple handling. Cooking this dish in the oven works, but the broiler or barbecue grill will better brown the yakitori. As a last resort, you can cook all of the ingredients in a skillet without a skewer if need be.

MAKES 4 SERVINGS

18 chicken meatballs from Glazed
  Chicken Meatballs (page 27)

Sea salt

18 large shrimp, shelled and
  deveined, with tail attached
  (21 to 30 count per pound)

1 medium red bell pepper
  (7 ounces)

1 medium yellow bell pepper
  (7 ounces)

5 large cremini mushrooms
  (5 ounces)

9 broccoli florets (2 inches long)

½ cup BBC Sauce (page 136)

Canola oil or other oil

Sea salt

Bring a pot of water to a boil and cook the meatballs in the water for 3 minutes, following the instructions on page 27. Transfer the meatballs to a plate. Add cold water and a little bit of salt to a medium bowl, add the shrimp, and clean them thoroughly. Drain the water, add more cold water to the bowl, and clean the shrimp again. Drain the shrimp and pat dry with a paper towel.

Cut the red and yellow bell peppers into 1½-inch square pieces. You will need 9 pieces of each. Cut off and discard the hard bottom part of the stem of the mushrooms, and then cut each mushroom in half. Have nine 12-inch-long steel skewers on hand (thinner is better). On two skewers, thread the ingredients in the following order: yellow bell pepper, chicken meatball, broccoli, chicken meatball, mushroom, chicken meatball, red bell pepper, and chicken meatball. For a colorful variation, reverse the order on the next two skewers, beginning with red bell pepper and then the chicken meatball. On the next two skewers, put the ingredients in the following order: broccoli, shrimp, red bell pepper, shrimp, mushroom, shrimp, yellow bell pepper, shrimp. On two of the remaining skewers, put the vegetables in the opposite order, beginning with yellow bell pepper and then the shrimp. On the last skewer use the remaining ingredients in the order you prefer.

Heat the broiler to high. Heat the BBC Sauce in a small saucepan over medium-low heat and cook for 3 minutes. Using a pastry brush, lightly paint the canola oil on a large baking sheet that is big enough to hold half or all of the skewers. Lightly sprinkle each side of each skewer with salt and place them on the baking sheet. Transfer the sheet to the broiler, 4 inches from the heat, and cook for 3 minutes. If your broiler cannot accommodate the 4-inch distance, cover the skewers with aluminum foil for part of the cooking time. Carefully remove the baking sheet from the broiler and baste the shrimp, meatballs, and vegetables with the BBC Sauce. Return the sheet to the broiler and cook for an additional 30 seconds to dry the sauce. Remove the baking sheet from the broiler and paint all the ingredients with the BBC Sauce, then turn the skewers and paint the other sides with the sauce. Return the baking sheet to the oven and broil for 2 to 3 minutes. Baste the skewers one more time with the sauce during broiling. Remove the baking sheet from the broiler and liberally paint the skewers again with the sauce before serving.

Steamed Tofu and Shiitake Gyoza

Gyoza, pot-sticker dumplings, are a popular menu item at ramen and "Japanized" Chinese restaurants in Japan. They also show up at ramen and Japanese restaurants in the United States. The stuffing may consist of vegetables, shrimp, pork, squid, fish, or chicken. The key to rich-tasting gyoza is the addition of a small portion of pork fat to each type of stuffing. In this recipe, I offer a vegetarian version that does not use pork fat. But, when the occasion allows, you can replace 20 percent of the tofu and mushroom mixture with pork fat for richer-tasting pot stickers. You won't regret it.

MAKES 4 TO 6 SERVINGS (48 PIECES)

½ block firm or extra-firm tofu (7 ounces)

1 cup plus 1 tablespoon finely minced shiitake mushrooms

½ cup frozen or fresh corn kernels

½ cup frozen or fresh green peas

¼ cup minced scallions (green part only)

1 tablespoon plus 1 teaspoon BBC Sauce (page 136), plus more for serving

2 teaspoons shoyu (soy sauce)

2 tablespoons minced ginger

1 clove garlic, grated

½ teaspoon freshly ground black pepper

2 small eggs, lightly beaten

1 tablespoon cornstarch

½ teaspoon sesame oil

48 gyoza wrappers

8 large iceberg lettuce leaves

1 cup BBC Cilantro Sauce (page 137)

Wrap the tofu in a paper towel, place it between heavy dinner plates, and let it stand for 20 minutes to remove the excess water. Remove the tofu from between the plates, discard the paper towel, and cut the tofu in half crosswise. Wrap each piece in a fresh paper towel and squeeze firmly to remove any excess water. Transfer the tofu to a large bowl and mash it with your hands until it has a smooth texture. Do not use a food processor; doing so will result in an unpleasant, pasty texture. Add the mushrooms, corn, peas, scallions, BBC sauce, soy sauce, ginger, garlic, black pepper, eggs, cornstarch, and sesame oil and mix all the ingredients thoroughly with your hands.

Spread 10 gyoza wrappers over your work surface at a time. Keep the remaining wrappers in their original packaging, because if they are left in the open air they will dry out quickly and become too brittle to handle. Using a pastry brush, paint half of the circular edge of each wrapper with water. Using a teaspoon, scoop 2 teaspoons of the tofu mixture and place it in the center of each gyoza wrapper. Fold the gyoza wrapper in half, creating a half-moon shape, and press the edges together. Cover the finished dumplings with a moist paper towel to keep them from drying out. Repeat the process, making only 10 dumplings at a time until you run out of filling.

Heat 3 inches of water in the bottom of a steamer over high heat and cover it with a lid. When adding or removing food items from a hot steamer, be sure to wear long oven gloves to protect yourself from the steam. When the steamer begins to produce copious amounts of steam, carefully open the lid and place the lettuce leaves on the steamer rack. Replace the lid and wait for high steam production to return. Carefully open the lid and place a batch of the dumplings on top of the lettuce leaves. Replace the lid and cook the dumplings for 8 minutes. Transfer the cooked dumplings to a warm platter and cover with a fitted lid or plastic wrap to keep warm. Finish cooking all of the dumplings. Serve the dumplings with BBC Cilantro Sauce for dipping.

Steamed Radicchio, Endive, and Lettuce

The United States Food and Drug Administration's new nutritional guidelines, called "My Plate," are very much like the way I eat at home. One-quarter of the plate is occupied by vegetables, another quarter by protein, another quarter by rice or other grains, and the remaining portion is for fruits. Most of the vegetables that I consume at home are cooked to remove any harmful natural chemicals in the vegetables. Cooking also allows their nutrients to be more easily absorbed by the body. In this recipe, I steam several vegetables with tofu and serve them with BBC Cilantro Sauce. Select any seasonal combination of vegetables for your version of this dish.

MAKES 4 SERVINGS

1 medium head radicchio (10 ounces)

2 medium heads endive (10 ounces)

1 small head iceberg lettuce
   (10 ounces)

1 block soft tofu (14 ounces)

1 bunch watercress

4 cipollini onions (5 ounces), peeled

¾ to 1 cup BBC Cilantro Sauce
   (page 137)

Cut the radicchio into quarters. Cut the endive heads into quarters. Cut the iceberg lettuce into quarters. Cut the tofu in half crosswise, then cut each piece of tofu into thin rectangles, producing 4 sheets. Cut each of these tofu sheets into quarters crosswise, for a total of 16 pieces. Cut off the hard stems of the watercress. Place a small pot of cold water over medium heat, add the cipollini onions, and bring to a boil. Decrease the heat to medium-low and cook for 4 minutes. Drain the onions in a sieve and air-dry.

Heat 2 inches of water in the bottom of a steamer over high heat. Make sure to wear long oven gloves for protection while using the steamer. Place all of the vegetables and the tofu in a container, and place the container in the hot steamer. You may need to do this in a couple of batches. Cook the vegetables and tofu for 3 minutes. Carefully remove the vegetables and tofu from the steamer and keep them warm. Finish cooking all of the vegetables and tofu. Divide the vegetables and tofu among salad bowls. Divide the BBC Cilantro Sauce into small bowls and serve alongside.

Sukiyaki in an American Kitchen

Sukiyaki is thinly sliced beef that is cooked in sake (rice wine), shoyu (soy sauce), and sugar. It is usually prepared at the table in a heavy iron pot over a portable gas burner, and it is one of the most celebrated dishes at Japanese restaurants in America. Though the preparation of sukiyaki is not difficult, sukiyaki has never become popular in the American home kitchen for a couple of reasons. First, thinly sliced beef is not a readily available cut of meat, and many butchers are unable to supply it. Second, the heavy iron pot and gas-fired tabletop burner are not typically found in an American kitchen. The lack of these special tools has been a barrier to the preparation and enjoyment of this delicious dish at home. However, due to the abundance and low cost of beef in America, it makes more sense to enjoy sukiyaki in this country than in Japan, where the price of beef is extremely high. I developed a version of this classic dish that can be readily prepared in a typical American home kitchen.

MAKES 4 SERVINGS

4 large cremini mushrooms
(4 ounces)

1 small yellow zucchini (5 ounces)

1 small green zucchini (5 ounces)

1 thin and long sweet potato
(8 ounces)

1 bunch watercress

4 cipollini onions (5 ounces), peeled

4 round eye steaks (2 pounds)

Sea salt and freshly ground
black pepper

2½ tablespoons canola oil or
vegetable oil

½ cup BBC Sauce (page 136)

½ cup sake (rice wine)

Remove the hard bottom part of the mushroom stems and cut the mushrooms in half. Cut the yellow and green zucchini into 6 pieces each (widest part is 1½ inches), using the *rangiri* technique (see page 201). Cut the sweet potato (skin on) into 8 pieces using the *rangiri* technique. Remove the hard bottom part of the stems of the watercress, and cut the bunch in half crosswise. Set the watercress aside.

Place the sweet potato pieces and cipollini onions in a large pot with cold water to cover over high heat, and bring it to a simmer. Add the mushrooms and yellow and green zucchini and cook for 2 minutes. Using a slotted spoon, transfer the mushrooms and zucchini to a colander to air-dry while the onions and sweet potato continue to cook for 5 more minutes. Using a slotted spoon, transfer the onions to the colander to air-dry while the sweet potato continues to cook for 7 minutes. Using a slotted spoon, transfer the sweet potato to the colander and air-dry.

Season the beef with salt and pepper on both sides. Heat the canola oil in a large skillet over medium heat, add the beef, and cook until both sides are golden; total cooking time is about 6 minutes. Transfer the beef to a cutting board. Add the vegetables to the skillet and cook until the surfaces of each vegetable are lightly golden. Remove the skillet from the heat, leaving the vegetables in the skillet. Cut each steak into 6 pieces. Push the vegetables to one side and return the beef to the skillet. Pour the BBC Sauce and sake over the beef and vegetables, and return the skillet to medium-high heat. Add the watercress and cook for 1 to 2 minutes, frequently basting the beef and vegetables with the sauce. Divide the beef and vegetables among deep bowls and serve.

My Father and Our Sukiyaki Dinner

My father, Hiromu Shimbo, passed away 20 years ago at the relatively young age of 70. He was a surgeon-turned-family-doctor and practiced to the very end of his life in a clinic/small hospital that was based in our home in Tokyo. My father always donned a crisp, starched white doctor's coat that set off his very gentle smile. He was hard-working and compassionate toward his patients and was, as a result, well loved. In contrast, he was not a family man who enjoyed spending his non-working hours with us, even at the dinner table for informal conversation. He was always quiet. This was partly because my mother—with her ebullient personality—dominated the conversation. My father concentrated on chewing his food very well—a custom that he persuaded us (and his patients) to adopt.

I do not remember a single instance when my father as much as stepped into the kitchen or went grocery shopping. In fact, he did not have much interest in food, including its history or the cultural relationships surrounding it. My mother was the complete opposite. She had (and still has) a tremendous interest in food. During the time my sisters and I were living at home and the clinic/hospital was in operation, she prepared breakfast, lunch, and dinner for our family daily, except for those rare occasions when we dined out. She also prepared meals for two live-in nurses and one maid, as well as my father's inpatients. It was hard work that she performed alone, with only a little assistance from the maid.

There was one major exception to this pattern in our family life. Just once a year, my father contributed his labor to the preparation of the family meal. This was the eagerly awaited sukiyaki meal every year on December 31, New Year's Eve. Beef was very expensive when I was growing up—more than ten times the price in the United States—and as a very special treat, my parents prepared and served sukiyaki. It was my mother's job to purchase the ingredients and do the prep work in the kitchen, arranging all the necessary items for the sukiyaki on large platters: the best-quality thinly sliced marbled Japanese beef, *shirataki* noodles, *naganegi* (long green onions), *shungiku* (chrysanthemum greens), tofu, and mushrooms. My father set up the dining table for this special occasion. When everything was ready with the gas burner and iron pot in place on the table, we were asked to take a seat, and my father began his show—first adding the beef suet to the heated iron skillet, lubricating the entire bottom of the heavy pot with its melting oil. He then added the beef slices and cooked one side. Then he poured into the skillet some sake (rice wine), shoyu (soy sauce), water, and sugar without precisely measuring each and without any hesitation. My father moved smoothly, like an experienced home cook who had been preparing sukiyaki meals and other dishes his entire life. After the beef was eaten, he continued adding the other ingredients, and the meal continued until everything was consumed.

When I married Buzz, I did not bring the New Year's Eve sukiyaki tradition to my new home. This year marks the twentieth anniversary of my father's death, and it is my plan to reproduce the sukiyaki dinner at our home on his memorial day. Buzz will take my father's role for the evening. I'm confident that he can do it.

Fried Chicken

Fried chicken was my mother's favorite, so it appeared on our table accompanied by stories from her childhood about chickens (see page 165). After my sister and I left home, and she became the grandmother of my two nephews, she frequently suggested that her little guests (now adults) make a trip with her to Kentucky Fried Chicken. My nephews' excited voices—they did not get such treats from my sister—still echo in my ears. It is amazing that such a common and simple food can play such an important role in our lives. The use of BBC Sauce and cornstarch in the marinade of this fried chicken recipe give it a rich flavor and a chewy crust. Be sure to read Frying Guidelines on page 164.

MAKES 4 SERVINGS

6 medium boneless, skinless chicken thighs (1½ pounds)

3 tablespoons BBC Sauce (page 136)

1 tablespoon grated ginger

1½ teaspoons garlic powder

1 teaspoon onion powder

½ teaspoon freshly ground black pepper

½ teaspoon hot paprika

¼ teaspoon ground nutmeg

¼ teaspoon sea salt

½ cup plus 2 tablespoons cornstarch

Canola oil or vegetable oil, for frying

Lemon wedges

Hot mustard paste from Japanese or Colman's mustard powder mixed with water

Cut the chicken into 1½ by 2-inch pieces. Mix the BBC Sauce, ginger, garlic powder, onion powder, black pepper, paprika, nutmeg, and salt in a large bowl. Add the chicken pieces to the bowl and stir with a large spoon. Let the chicken stand in the marinade for 30 minutes.

Place the cornstarch in the bowl with the chicken and dredge the chicken thoroughly in the cornstarch. Let the chicken stand in the bowl for 10 minutes.

Heat 3 inches of the canola oil in a heavy skillet to 340°F. Add the chicken, 6 to 8 pieces at a time, and cook them for 4 minutes or until golden. Transfer the fried chicken to a wire rack set over a baking sheet to drain. Finish cooking all of the chicken pieces.

Increase the temperature of the oil to 350°F and re-fry the chicken for 20 seconds, until crisp. Divide the chicken onto plates. Add a lemon wedge and a small mound of hot mustard paste to each plate and serve.

FRYING GUIDELINES

There are important guidelines for deep frying that should be followed to achieve the best results:

- Use a cooking pot that is thick, shallow, and has a flat bottom. A cast-iron or stainless steel–lined copper pot is an excellent choice for steady control of the temperature of the oil.

- Use a depth of oil that is two to three times the height of the items to be fried. When there is too little oil, the temperature will be poorly regulated. An ample volume of oil holds the oil temperature constant at the right level.

- To judge the temperature of the heated oil without a thermo-meter, add a tiny drop of batter to the surface. If it sinks and does not rise to the surface, the oil is not hot enough. When the temperature reaches around 340°F, the batter sinks near the bottom and then quickly rises to the surface. This is the temperature that I frequently use to fry shrimp, boneless fish and chicken, or vegetables. For high-temperature frying at 375°F, a drop of batter will fry immediately upon hitting the surface and will not sink. When the oil is too hot, it begins to smoke. Different oils have different smoking temperatures, so I recommend using canola oil.

- Do not crowd the oil: Leave half of the oil surface open and uncovered by the material you are frying. Crowding the oil with too much food produces poor cooking results. If you toss too many items at once into the heated oil, the temperature is dramatically reduced, and it takes some time for the oil to come back to proper frying temperature. During this time food items absorb larger amounts of oil, resulting in greasy foods. Also, when the oil is too crowded with frying items, too much steam is generated by the overabundance of cooking material, and this reduces and delays the production of a crisp outer surface.

- After using new oil, carefully transfer it through a strainer when it has somewhat cooled (but is still hot) to an appropriate container. Cover with a tight-fitting lid and store for later use. I reuse oil two or three times, depending on the condition of the oil. If you heat the used oil and see tiny bubbles busily coming up from it, it is a sign of tired oil. Discard it.

Chicken Cutlet, Chicken Soup, and Omelets

My mother, Tokuko Shimbo, was born in 1927 as the fourth child of six siblings of the Okada family in Takada. Takada is in Niigata Prefecture, on the western side of Japan, about 180 rugged and mountainous miles northwest of Tokyo. The area is famous for receiving the deepest snowfall in Japan. Her father, Ryuta Okada, was a local, well-to-do, highly respected pediatrician. Her father's love of literature, including Western works, led him to appreciate foods from America and Europe that were then newly introduced to Japan. My grandfather's wife, Setsu, frequently volunteered at a nearby Canadian mission and befriended the resident minister and his wife. Working with these foreigners at the church gave her a feeling of individual worth. This was very unusual in those days, when a woman was subservient and considered far inferior in all aspects to her husband and other men. (Unfortunately, some aspects of this old-fashioned male-female relationship persist in modern-day Japan.)

These encounters with Western culture not only brought new social concepts into my mother's home, but many new recipes and ways of cooking as well. Back then, my grandfather's patients, many of whom were too poor to pay him in cash, paid with some of the foods they produced on their farms. Chickens and eggs happened to be the most welcomed and frequent gifts at my grandmother's home. Whenever my mother arrived home from school and found her mother plucking chicken feathers in the kitchen, my mother and her siblings would jump for joy. They knew that dinner would be chicken cutlets, a newly discovered "modern" recipe (for rural Japan).

My mother also watched her mother prepare two other very Western dishes that were a favorite of her father's: chicken soup made from simmering chicken carcass, onion, carrot, and scallion, cooked all day in a large iron pot on the stovetop; and real French omelets with butter. In addition to these delicacies, my grandparents, though deep in the traditional countryside, also enjoyed French cheese that came to Japan by way of the Russian railway across Eurasia and then by boat across the Japan Sea to the port city of Niigata. In the early part of the twentieth century, just after Japan began embracing European ingredients and food preparations, my mother's home and kitchen was an oasis of fine Western cuisine and dining in the midst of rural Japan.

Though my father was a very traditional Japanese man, my mother's love of Western cuisine persisted in our house as I grew up, and my mother's appetite to this day remains strong for KFC, which is called "Ken-tuk-ee-Furaido-Chik-n" in Japan. But although McDonald's is literally everywhere in Japan, she never has become a serious fan of hamburgers. Unfortunately, my grandmother died when my mother was a teenager, so I did not have an opportunity to meet her. But my mother's repeated stories about her are deeply engraved in my memory, and perhaps in some way they are responsible for my own career and the way I live my life.

Gingered Pork Burger

Buta no shoga-yaki, gingered sautéed pork, is one of our most popular lunch items at home and in restaurants across Japan. Thinly sliced, lightly marinated pork is cooked in a skillet until golden and flavored with ginger and Japanese staples such as shoyu (soy sauce), mirin (sweet cooking wine), and sugar. The cooking time is very short. I have revised this quick-and-easy traditional recipe so that it has more appeal to a wider American audience. I serve my *buta no shoga-yaki* on a hamburger bun, just like a classic sloppy joe.

MAKES 6 SERVINGS

1 pound pork sirloin

¼ cup BBC Sauce (page 136)

1 tablespoon Worcestershire sauce

2 tablespoons honey

2 tablespoons finely grated yellow onion

2 tablespoons finely grated apple, skin on

2 tablespoons finely grated ginger

1 large clove garlic, grated

½ teaspoon sea salt

2 teaspoons sesame oil

1 salsify, 10 inches long and 1 inch in diameter (3 ounces), or 3 ounces portobello mushrooms, stems removed

1 small carrot (3 ounces), peeled

2 scallions (green part only)

½ small head romaine lettuce

1 tablespoon canola oil or vegetable oil

2 tablespoons white sesame seeds, toasted

6 hamburger buns

Unsalted butter (optional)

Pound the pork sirloin with a meat mallet or the bottom of a saucepan until it is thin and has spread out to about 50 percent larger in diameter than the original steak. Cut the pork diagonally into about 28 slices.

Combine the BBC Sauce, Worcestershire sauce, honey, onion, apple, ginger, garlic, salt, and sesame oil in a large bowl. Add the pork slices, massage them with the marinade, and let them stand in the marinade for 20 minutes.

Peel the salsify by rubbing its skin with a hard brush, or use a vegetable peeler, then shave it into thin strips about 4 inches long. Using the vegetable peeler, shave the carrot in the same way. Cut the scallions into very thin slices diagonally. Cut the romaine lettuce into thin strips crosswise.

Transfer the pork slices to a colander placed over a bowl, and, with the back of a soupspoon, gently press them to remove excess liquid, reserving the marinade in the bowl. Heat the oil in a skillet over medium-high heat, add the pork slices in a single layer, and cook for 3 minutes or until lightly golden. Turn the pork slices once or twice during cooking. Turn off the heat and transfer the pork to a plate. Add the salsify and carrot to the skillet and return it to medium heat. Cook the vegetables until they are wilted, stirring. Return the cooked pork and the reserved marinade to the skillet. Increase the heat to medium-high, and cook the mixture until the sauce thickens and the pork and vegetables are coated with the sauce. Add the sesame seeds and scallions and give several large stirs. Turn off the heat.

Toast the cut sides of the hamburger buns and spread the butter, if using, on the bottom half of each bun. Divide the lettuce among the 4 buttered buns. Divide the pork and vegetables on top of the lettuce. Cover the pork with the top of each bun. An exciting new burger!

CHAPTER 6
SUPER SAUCE

Super Sauce is the name I gave to one of the most useful sauces in my refrigerator. By mixing Super Sauce with varying proportions of water, I can make numerous broths and sauces such as tempura dipping sauce, cold noodle dipping sauce, hot noodle broth, vegetable simmering broth, and many other derivatives simply by flavoring it with additional readily available ingredients such as rice vinegar, sesame paste, sugar, and more. Super Sauce is made from a few key ingredients, including *katsuobushi* (skipjack tuna fish flakes), kombu (kelp), mirin (sweet cooking wine), and shoyu (soy sauce). Super sauce adds rich consistency and flavor to dishes such as Simmered Branzino (page 195), Chicken Namban (page 188), and Japanese Beef Stew (page 199).

Super Sauce

MAKES 1⅓ CUPS

1 cup mirin (sweet cooking wine)

1 cup shoyu (soy sauce)

3 cups tightly packed *katsuobushi* (skipjack tuna fish flakes)

1 ounce kombu (kelp) (about two 4 by 7-inch pieces), cut into 4-inch-long pieces with scissors

Place the mirin in a small saucepan over medium heat and bring it to a simmer. Add the soy sauce and bring the mixture to a gentle simmer again. Add and submerge the fish flakes and turn off the heat. Let the sauce sit for 15 minutes.

Strain the sauce through a fine-mesh strainer, and discard the fish flakes. Transfer the sauce to a clean glass jar and add the kelp. Refrigerate the sauce, covered with plastic wrap, for 4 hours, then remove and discard the kelp.

The Super Sauce will be very concentrated. Store it in a freezer-friendly jar with a tight-fitting lid. The Super Sauce will not solidify in the freezer, so portions are easily removed with a spoon. Use the sauce within 3 months.

Ponzu Sauce

Ponzu is made from yuzu juice (see below), shoyu (soy sauce), mirin (sweet cooking wine), rice vinegar, skipjack tuna fish flakes, kelp, sugar, and salt. Yuzu provides the distinctive flavor for this sauce, but because yuzu, a Japanese citrus fruit, is not readily available in America, I have replaced it with a blend of lemon and grapefruit juices. The result is very good, and is certainly better than commercially available bottled ponzu sauce, which may contain unnecessary chemical ingredients. Ponzu Sauce is excellent as a non-oil salad dressing and for making dipping sauce for steamed chicken, meat, seafood, vegetables, and dumplings. You will find many ways to enjoy it using the recipes in this chapter.

MAKES 1 CUP

½ cup Super Sauce (page 170)

¼ cup water

2 tablespoons grapefruit juice

4 teaspoons rice vinegar

1 tablespoon lemon juice

1 tablespoon sugar

Place the Super Sauce and water in a small saucepan over medium heat and bring it to a gentle simmer. Remove the pot from the stove and add the grapefruit juice, vinegar, lemon juice, and sugar. Stir the mixture until the sugar is dissolved. Cool the sauce and store it in a clean jar with a tight-fitting lid. Refrigerate and use the sauce within 1 week for the best flavor.

Yuzu: The Aromatic Citrus

The popular saying, "*Momo, kuri san'nen; kaki hachinen; yuzu no oobaka juhachi-nen*" means that it takes three years for peach and chestnut trees to bear fruit, and eight years for persimmon trees to bear fruit after their first bloom. But when it comes to slow-growing yuzu, it takes 18 years, so many farmers take a shortcut by grafting branches from yuzu trees onto other citrus trees. Yuzu harvested from grafted trees have a diluted, poor flavor, while the fruit from an un-grafted tree, called *Misho yuzu*, is the real yuzu. Farmers who inherited yuzu trees from their ancestors take great pride in their fruit and strive to pass the trees on to the next generation. Yuzu trees that are 200 years old continue to produce gorgeous fruit. So if you are planning to plant a yuzu seed in your garden, you should think of the next and succeeding generations; you need a long-term plan. Furthermore, according to one *Misho yuzu* farmer, his tree bears flowers and fruit only every other year. This one-year hibernation perhaps contributes to the longevity of the tree. The tree produces deep green fruit that turns golden yellow at the time of the harvest in late fall.

   In food preparations, only the juice and rind of the fruit are used to flavor and garnish the many dishes in which it is used. The highly aromatic scent and golden yellow color heighten the enjoyment of our traditional winter dishes. So what that popular saying really implies is that it takes a long time, great care, and hard work for our dream to bear fruit. Patience is golden.

Hot Noodle Broth

Hot noodle broth, *kake-jiru*, is a clear, light brown, highly fragrant brew because its base includes kelp, fish flakes, and shoyu (soy sauce). This Hot Noodle Broth can be used with udon (wheat noodles), soba (buckwheat noodles), or as a tempura dipping sauce.

MAKES 4½ CUPS (4 SERVINGS)

4 cups water

3 tablespoons plus 1 teaspoon
   Super Sauce (page 170)

1 tablespoon sugar

¼ teaspoon sea salt

Place all of the ingredients in a small saucepan over medium heat and bring to a simmer, stirring to dissolve the sugar. Turn off the heat. Refrigerate and use the broth within 3 days for the best flavor.

Cold Noodle Sauce

Compared to the Hot Noodle Broth, this sauce is darker in color, higher in sodium content, and more robust in flavor. It can be used as a cold noodle sauce or as a dressing for cooked greens like spinach or kale.

MAKES 1½ CUPS (4 SERVINGS)

1 cup water

2 tablespoons Super Sauce (page 170)

2 tablespoons shoyu (soy sauce)

Place all of the ingredients in a saucepan over medium heat and bring to a simmer. Turn off the heat and let the sauce stand until cool. Refrigerate and use the sauce within 3 days for the best flavor.

Ginger-Walnut Butter Sauce

Blending Super Sauce with walnut butter creates a rich-tasting sauce that is great to use on cold noodles or as a dressing over simmered vegetables like broccoli, cauliflower, asparagus, or grilled eggplant. Replace the walnut butter with peanut butter if you prefer.

MAKES 1½ CUPS (4 SERVINGS)

½ cup warm water

6 tablespoons walnut butter

¼ cup Super Sauce (page 170)

1 to 2 tablespoons ginger juice from freshly grated ginger

Whisk the water and walnut butter in a bowl until smooth. Add the Super Sauce and ginger juice and mix until well blended. Refrigerate and use within 3 days for the best flavor.

Cold Udon Noodles with Ginger-Walnut Butter Sauce

In Japan, cold udon (wheat) noodles or soba (buckwheat) noodles are perennial favorites, especially during the sweltering hot summer months. No matter the season, I prefer cold noodles to hot ones because I can better detect the subtle but fragrant flavor of wheat or buckwheat flour and the firmer noodle texture. In this recipe, I serve udon with Ginger-Walnut Butter Sauce. Be sure to read Noodle Cooking Techniques on page 59.

MAKES 4 SERVINGS

14 ounces dried udon (wheat) noodles

1 medium Kirby cucumber (3½ ounces)

4 cherry tomatoes

2 scallions

1½ cups Ginger-Walnut Butter Sauce

¼ cup finely chopped walnuts, or 2 tablespoons white sesame seeds, toasted

Bring a large pot of water to a boil over medium heat and cook the udon as instructed on the package. Drain the noodles in a colander and rinse them under cold tap water until they are cold and no longer starchy. Drain and reserve the noodles in the colander.

Cut off the ends of the cucumber and cut it, skin on, into thin 3-inch-long strips. Cut the cherry tomatoes in half. Cut the scallions into very thin slices diagonally.

Divide the Ginger-Walnut Butter Sauce among noodle bowls. Then divide the noodles into the bowls. Garnish with the cucumber, tomatoes, scallions, and walnuts. Advise your guests to stir the sauce, noodles, and toppings together before consuming.

Soba Seafood Salad

Cold Italian pasta dishes made from shorter pasta varieties such as spirals, shells, bow ties, and penne are popular in America, but long pasta like spaghetti or linguini is usually served hot. I hope you will try this recipe and enjoy cold soba (buckwheat) noodles—long noodles—especially when the weather is very hot. This dish of soba, squid, and shrimp tossed with Ponzu Sauce is cooling and refreshing, and the flavor and texture are delightful. Be sure to read *Te-Uchi* Soba, Serious Business, on page 175 and Noodle Cooking Techniques on page 59.

MAKES 4 SERVINGS

14 ounces dried soba (buckwheat) noodles

1 tablespoon olive oil or vegetable oil

¾ cup Ponzu Sauce (page 171)

2 scallions

12 medium shrimp, shelled and deveined, with tail attached (about ½ pound)

8 squid (½ pound), cleaned

1 cup frozen corn kernels

1 cup shelled frozen edamame

Bring a large pot of water to a boil over medium heat and cook the noodles as instructed on the package. Drain the noodles in a colander and rinse under cold tap water until they are cold and no longer starchy. Drain the noodles, transfer them to a large bowl, and toss them with ½ tablespoon of the olive oil and half of the Ponzu Sauce. The oil prevents the noodles from sticking together as they cool. Set aside.

Cut the scallions into very thin diagonal slices and set aside. Cut each shrimp crosswise in half diagonally. Cut the squid into ½-inch-wide rings. Bring a medium pot of salted water to a boil over high heat. Place the corn in a small sieve that will fit inside the pot. Decrease the heat to medium, lower the sieve into the water, and cook the corn for 1 minute. Remove the corn from the water, air-dry, and transfer to a bowl. Add the edamame to the sieve and cook in the boiling water for 3 minutes. Remove the edamame from the water, air-dry, and transfer them to the bowl of corn. Cook the squid in the same water for 2 minutes. Using a slotted spoon, remove the squid from the cooking water, drain, and air-dry. Transfer the squid to the bowl of vegetables. Cook the shrimp in the same water for 3 minutes. Using a slotted spoon, remove the shrimp from the cooking water, drain, air-dry, and transfer to the bowl of vegetables.

Add the remaining ½ tablespoon of the olive oil and the remaining Ponzu Sauce to the bowl, and toss the vegetables and seafood with the sauce. Divide the noodles among bowls. Add the vegetables and seafood to the bowls. Garnish with the sliced scallions and serve.

Te-Uchi Soba, Serious Business

In Japan, there are many chef-owned and -operated soba restaurants that make homemade soba noodles, called *te-uchi* soba, from scratch every day. Each chef uses his own combination of soba noodle flours for his creation. Soba flour is not a simple product. After milling, the buckwheat flour passes through five different gradations of sieves, each with its own size holes. This produces five different flours, each with a different texture, aroma, and flavor. Chefs blend these components in order to create their own noodles. Soba chefs must have a complete understanding of the flour they use—its origin, seasonal factors, and other variable characteristics. Unfortunately, high-quality soba noodles like this are very hard to find in America, but New York City is an exception. In New York City, there are a dozen or so places that sell homemade *te-uchi* soba, and there is stiff competition among the local chefs who operate these restaurants. Home cooks have to rely on store-bought dried soba noodles. Here are some tips and advice on how to select the best product from among the many choices.

- Buckwheat has no gluten to help hold the noodles together, so some starch is usually added during production (wheat, mountain yam, or another starch). However, if you search hard enough, you may find 100 percent buckwheat soba noodles. These noodles have a coarse texture and a strong buckwheat flavor.

- Always read the ingredients list on the package. The list should be short: buckwheat flour, wheat flour (or other gluten-containing starch), and salt. If another starch is added, the buckwheat flour should still be the first ingredient listed; otherwise, you will be eating wheat noodles with a little added buckwheat flour.

- When shopping for *soba* noodles, look for *juwari* soba—100 percent buckwheat flour noodles; *nippachi* soba—80 percent buckwheat flour noodles; *hikigurumi* soba—flour that contains almost every part of the buckwheat, including endosperm and the brownish outer layer, resulting in robust flavor, darker color, and rough texture; or *yama-imo* soba—noodles with mountain yam.

Soba Sushi Rolls

This fun roll is for those who have graduated from inside-out roll preparation and want to extend their sushi repertoire. To keep the soba noodles from becoming tangled, bind one end of the dry noodles together with a rubber band. After cooking, pull the bound end of the noodles from the hot water and you should find a bundle of straight, cooked soba. Drain the noodles well, and dry them with a paper towel to remove excess water before laying them on top of the nori sheet. Nori sheets lose their shape easily even with a tiny drop of water. Soba noodles are not as sticky as sushi rice, so make a tight roll when rolling. Be sure to read Noodle Cooking Techniques on page 59.

MAKES 4 SERVINGS (24 PIECES)

9 ounces dried soba noodles

1 medium mango (14 ounces)

1 medium Kirby cucumber
(3½ ounces), peeled

½ medium avocado (3 ounces),
pitted and peeled

3 ounces smoked salmon

4 sheets nori seaweed

¼ cup Cold Noodle Sauce
(page 172)

Bring a large pot of water to a boil over high heat. Divide the soba noodles into 4 portions and bind one end of each together with a rubber band, being careful not to break the noodles. Add the noodles to the pot of boiling water and, using chopsticks, quickly separate the noodles to prevent them from sticking together. Cook the noodles over medium heat as instructed on the package. Drain the cooked noodles in a colander with the rubber bands still in place. Rinse the noodles under cold tap water until they are no longer starchy. Drain them well and pat dry with a paper towel. Set aside.

Peel, pit, and cut the mango into ½ by 3½-inch sticks. Cut off the ends of the cucumber and cut it (skin on) into ½ by 3½-inch sticks. Cut the avocado into 8 strips. Stack the smoked salmon and cut it into 1-inch-wide strips.

Place a bamboo rolling mat on your work surface. Place one of the nori sheets on top of the rolling mat, positioning it so that the edge of the nori sheet is at the edge of the rolling mat nearest you. Pick up one bundle of cooked noodles and place it at the near edge of the nori sheet with the tied end protruding from the right side.

Cut off the tied end of the noodles and discard. Spread the noodles up and down the sheet until two-thirds of the sheet is covered, leaving the top uncovered.

Place 2 sticks of the avocado across the end of the nori sheet closest to you. Place 3 sticks of mango next to the avocado. Follow the mango with the 3 sticks of cucumber and one-quarter of the smoked salmon. Roll the nori sheet tightly around the soba noodles and stuffing. Make the other three rolls.

Cut each roll into 8 pieces. Serve with Cold Noodle Sauce for dipping.

Winter Vegetables with Ponzu Sauce

Ponzu Sauce, which blends the complex flavors of citrus juice, rice vinegar, kelp, fish flakes, mirin (sweet cooking wine), and shoyu (soy sauce), is perfect with winter vegetables, which can sometimes lack flavor. For this dish, choose vegetables that are small in size and appear moist and heavy.

MAKES 4 SERVINGS

2 medium turnips (5 ounces), peeled

1 medium red potato (7 ounces)

1 medium carrot (6 ounces), peeled

1 medium parsnip (6 ounces), peeled

4 large Brussels sprouts (5 ounces)

3 tablespoons canola oil or vegetable oil

½ teaspoon sea salt

5 tablespoons Ponzu Sauce (page 171)

¼ cup chopped fresh parsley

Cut the turnips into quarters. Cut the potato (skin on) in half lengthwise, then cut each piece, lengthwise, into 3 pieces. Cut the carrot and parsnip into 1½-inch pieces using the *rangiri* technique (see page 201). Cut off the stems of the Brussels sprouts, and cut each sprout in half.

Place the turnips, potato, carrot, and parsnip in a medium pot and add cold water to cover. Put the pot over medium heat and bring it to a simmer. Cook the turnips and carrot for 3 minutes, remove them with a slotted spoon, and transfer them to a medium bowl. Cook the potato and parsnip for 2½ minutes longer, then add the Brussels sprouts and cook for 30 seconds. Drain the potato, parsnip, and Brussels sprouts in a colander. Transfer the vegetables to the bowl of turnips and carrot, add the canola oil and salt, and toss thoroughly.

Heat a large heavy skillet over medium heat. Add the vegetables and cook for 5 to 6 minutes, or until the vegetables are golden, turning them every 1½ minutes. Remove the skillet from the heat and add the Ponzu Sauce. Put the skillet back over medium heat and toss the vegetables with a spatula. Divide the vegetables among bowls. Garnish with the parsley and serve.

Udon Noodles in Hot Broth with Kakiage Pancake

Every udon noodle shop in Japan sells tempura udon. *Kakiage* is one type of tempura preparation, consisting of chopped ingredients tossed with thick tempura batter and deep fried. The thick batter holds the small chopped ingredients together during cooking, producing a kind of round tempura pancake. Popular ingredients used for *kakiage* are shrimp, scallops, and herbs like *mitsuba*. In my recipe, I use readily available frozen corn and peas. Be sure to read Frying Guidelines on page 164 and Noodle Cooking Techniques on page 59.

MAKES 4 SERVINGS

14 ounces dried udon noodles

½ cup frozen corn kernels

½ cup frozen green peas

8 medium shrimp, shelled and deveined (about 5 ounces)

2 cups watercress leaves

1 cup plus 2 tablespoons tempura flour or a blend of 80% cake flour and 20% cornstarch

¾ cup ice water

Canola oil or vegetable oil, for deep frying

4½ cups Hot Noodle Broth (page 172)

2 tablespoons grated ginger

¼ cup thinly sliced scallions (green part only)

Bring a large pot of water to a boil over medium heat and cook the noodles for 30 seconds to 1 minute less than the suggested cooking time on the package. Drain the noodles in a colander and rinse them under cold tap water until they are cold and no longer starchy. Drain the noodles and keep them in the colander. Set aside.

Bring a medium pot of water to a boil. Put the frozen corn and peas in a sieve that will fit inside the pot. Lower the sieve into the water and cook the corn and peas over medium heat for 30 seconds. Remove the sieve and let the corn and peas drain.

Cut the shrimp into ⅓-inch pieces crosswise. Mix the shrimp, watercress, corn, peas, and 2 tablespoons of the tempura flour in a medium bowl. In another bowl, mix the remaining 1 cup tempura flour with the ice water, and stir until smooth.

Heat 3 inches of the canola oil in a heavy skillet to 350°F. Place a slotted spoon in the oil and allow it to heat to the temperature of the oil to prevent the dough from sticking. Add the shrimp mixture to the tempura batter and mix with a large spoon.

Using the large spoon, scoop one-quarter of the shrimp mixture from the bowl and pour it into the slotted spoon that was warming in the oil (use an oven mitt if necessary).

Continued

181

Immediately lower the slotted spoon into the heated oil and submerge the shrimp mixture. Cook the mixture (*kakiage*) for 1 ½ minutes or until the bottom side is cooked.

Using a steel spatula or a clean spoon, remove the *kakiage* from the slotted spoon and let it float free in the oil. Cook the *kakiage* for about 4 minutes, or until lightly golden, turning it a few times during cooking. Transfer the cooked *kakiage* to a wire rack set over a baking sheet, and let drain. Repeat the process for the remaining batter, adding the next portion of *kakiage* batter to the hot slotted spoon.

Prepare a kettle of boiling water. Pour the boiling water over the cooked noodles to rewarm them. Drain the noodles and divide them into bowls. Bring the Hot Noodle Broth to a simmer in a medium pot over medium heat. Pour the hot broth into the bowls. Divide the *kakiage* tempura among the bowls. Garnish with the ginger and scallions and serve.

Chicken and Egg Udon Noodles

Oyako udon, a popular dish at Japanese noodle restaurants, is a hot noodle soup topped with chicken and egg. The name comes from the Japanese words *oya* and *ko*, or parent and child, represented in this recipe by the chicken and the egg. In the traditional preparation, chicken is cooked with onions and green vegetables in a noodle broth. Beaten eggs are added to the broth, and it is gently heated until the eggs are barely cooked, giving this dish the appearance of cloudy eggs mixed with chicken and noodles in brown broth. After living in America for thirteen years, I came to the conclusion that this look is not particularly appealing. Therefore, in this recipe, I have replaced beaten eggs with poached eggs. Be sure to read Noodle Cooking Techniques on page 59.

MAKES 4 SERVINGS

1 small bunch spinach (10 ounces)

14 ounces dried udon noodles

2 boneless, skinless chicken thighs (1½ pounds)

Sea salt and freshly ground black pepper

4 scallions

2 teaspoons canola oil or vegetable oil

1¼ cups Hot Noodle Broth (page 172)

4 large eggs

Lemon zest from ½ lemon

Bring a medium pot of salted water to a boil. Cook the spinach in the water for 1 minute, then drain the spinach and cool it under cold water. Squeeze the spinach to remove any excess water. By hand, form the spinach into a cylinder, transfer the spinach to a cutting board, and cut it into four 2-inch-long portions.

Bring a large pot of water to a boil. Cook the udon noodles in the pot over medium heat for 30 seconds to 1 minute less than the suggested cooking time on the package. Drain the noodles in a colander, and rinse them under cold tap water until they are cold and no longer starchy. Drain the noodles again and keep them in the colander. Set aside.

Season the chicken thighs with salt and pepper. Cut the white part of the scallions into 1-inch pieces diagonally. Cut the green part of the scallions into thin diagonal slices. Heat the canola oil in a medium skillet over medium heat, add the chicken, and cook for 3 minutes, or until the bottom surface is lightly golden. Turn the chicken over, add the white part of the scallions, and cook for 3 minutes. Transfer the chicken to a cutting board and cut the chicken into 1-inch cubes.

Bring the Hot Noodle Broth to a simmer in a medium pot over medium heat. Transfer the chicken and the scallion whites to the Hot Noodle Broth and cook, covered, for 4 minutes. Poach the eggs (see page 84) and carefully set aside.

Prepare a kettle of boiling water. Pour the boiling water over the cooked noodles to rewarm them, then drain and divide the noodles into bowls. Pour the Hot Noodle Broth into the bowls. Add the chicken, spinach, and poached eggs to the bowls. Garnish with the scallion greens and lemon zest and serve.

Agedashi-Dofu

Agedashi-dofu is potato starch–coated tofu that is deep fried and served in a dashi broth. You may think that the crispy fried tofu would quickly become soggy, but it does hold its unique texture even after soaking in the hot broth. *Agedashi-dofu* can be found in nearly every kitchen—school, office, or casual restaurant—in Japan. You may also find it on the menu of Japanese restaurants in America. My version of *agedashi-dofu* has added sweet potatoes to increase its appeal. Be sure to read Frying Guidelines on page 164.

MAKES 4 SERVINGS

1 block firm tofu (14 ounces)

1 medium sweet potato (9½ ounces)

7 tablespoons cornstarch

1 teaspoon Old Bay seasoning or *shichimi togarashi* (Japanese seven-spice powder)

Canola oil or vegetable oil, for frying

1½ cups Hot Noodle Broth (page 172)

2 tablespoons grated ginger

2 tablespoons thinly sliced scallion (green part only)

Place the tofu between heavy plates. Put a bowl full of water weighing about 1 pound on top of the upper plate and let the tofu stand for 30 minutes. You want to remove about ½ cup water from the tofu using this process.

Cut the sweet potato (skin on) into 1-inch cubes. Place the sweet potato in a medium pot of water over medium heat and bring it to a simmer. Cook the sweet potato in the simmering water for 3 minutes. Drain and transfer to a paper towel–lined bowl to remove excess water.

Remove the tofu from between the plates, and discard the water. Gently wipe the tofu with a paper towel to remove any excess water, and transfer it to a cutting board. Cut the tofu in half crosswise, then cut each block into 2 thin sheets, and cut each sheet crosswise, making 3 blocks. You will have 12 blocks total.

Mix the cornstarch and Old Bay seasoning in a medium bowl, dredge the tofu and sweet potato in the starch mixture, and let them stand for 10 minutes.

Heat 3 inches of the canola oil in a heavy skillet over medium heat until it reaches 350°F. Add the sweet potato and cook for 2 minutes, or until golden. Using a slotted spoon, remove the sweet potato from the oil and transfer to a wire rack set over a baking sheet. Decrease the temperature of the oil to 340°F, add the tofu, and cook for 3 to 4 minutes, or until the outside is lightly golden. Using a slotted spoon, remove the tofu pieces from the oil and transfer them to the wire rack.

Bring the Hot Noodle Broth to a simmer in a small saucepan over medium heat. Divide the tofu and sweet potato among soup bowls. Pour the piping-hot broth into the bowls. Garnish with the ginger and scallion and serve.

Grilled Smoky Eggplant

Height-of-the season eggplant, grilled over an open fire and served with a simple dashi stock flavored with shoyu (soy sauce), is called *yakinasu* in Japan. Eggplant cooked in this manner acquires a pleasant smokiness and a moist and tender texture. With nothing to mask the true flavor of the eggplant, diners may taste the slight but pleasant astringency for which this vegetable is known. *Yakinasu* is often garnished with julienned fish flakes.

The cooking time for eggplant varies depending on the season, length of storage, skin thickness, and eggplant variety. Use the cooking time shown in this recipe as a guide, and modify it if necessary. Choose eggplant that is smooth and shiny.

MAKES 4 SERVINGS

2 small slender American eggplant (1½ pounds)

2½ tablespoons Ponzu Sauce (page 171) or Peanut Butter–Miso Sauce (page 103)

2 tablespoons finely grated ginger

2 tablespoons thinly sliced scallion (green part only)

¼ cup *katsuobushi* (skipjack tuna fish flakes; optional)

Make a very shallow circle cut along the top part of each eggplant, and remove the frills. Then, make very shallow lengthwise cuts from the top to the bottom of the eggplant, leaving about 1 inch between each cut. Place an open mesh grill over a gas burner set to medium heat. (You can use a broiler; heat the broiler until hot and arrange the eggplant close to the fire.) When the grill is hot, put one piece of the eggplant on the grill and cook for 3 minutes, or until the skin chars and the eggplant begins to steam. Turn the eggplant over and cook the other side of the eggplant for 2 to 3 minutes. The cooked eggplant should feel tender when gently squeezed between tongs. Transfer the eggplant to a cutting board and finish cooking the remaining eggplant.

Peel off the skin of each eggplant without using any water in order to preserve the smoky flavor of the eggplant. Cut each eggplant in half lengthwise, then cut each half into 4 pieces crosswise. Divide the eggplant among plates. Pour the Ponzu Sauce over the eggplant on each plate. Top with the ginger, scallion slices, and fish flakes, if using, and serve.

Summer Vegetables in Namban Sauce

In the summer, when vegetables are abundant, I often cook them *namban* style (see page 189). *Namban* is a preparation technique where vegetables, fish, or meat are cooked in oil and then marinated in a vinegar-flavored, soy sauce–based marinade. This cooking method was introduced to Japan in 1543 by the Portuguese who were the first Europeans to visit Japan. Choose vegetables that are very fresh and moist to minimize cooking time and to help preserve the natural flavors and vitamins of each ingredient. You also can serve the dish cold the next day.

MAKES 4 SERVINGS

¼ cup rice vinegar

¼ cup water

3 tablespoons Super Sauce
(page 170)

2 tablespoons sugar

1 small American eggplant
(12 ounces)

1 medium red onion (7 ounces)

1 medium red bell pepper (7 ounces)

1 medium yellow bell pepper
(7 ounces)

1 large green zucchini (11 ounces)

4 large cremini mushrooms
(4 ounces)

Canola oil or vegetable oil

Place the vinegar, water, Super Sauce, and sugar in a saucepan over medium heat and bring it to a gentle simmer, stirring with a spatula to dissolve the sugar. Transfer the marinade to a medium bowl and let cool.

Remove the stem of the eggplant and cut it into 8 wedges. Then cut each wedge into 2 pieces crosswise. Cut the red onion crosswise into ⅓-inch-thick slices. Remove the seeds and membranes of the red and yellow bell peppers and cut each lengthwise into ⅔-inch-wide strips. Cut the zucchini into ½-inch-thick diagonal slices. Remove the hard bottom part of the stem of the mushrooms and cut each mushroom in half.

Heat 1 inch of the canola oil in a heavy skillet over medium heat to 340°F. Add the eggplant pieces and cook for 2 to 3 minutes or until the bottom is golden. Turn the eggplant over and cook for 2 to 3 minutes, or until the other side is golden. Transfer the eggplant to the bowl of vinegar marinade. If necessary, add an additional ½ inch of canola oil to the skillet, then add the red onion and cook for 2 to 3 minutes, or until the bottom is lightly golden. Turn the onion over and cook for 3 minutes. Transfer the onion to the bowl with the marinade. Add the red and yellow bell peppers to the skillet and cook for 3 minutes, or until the bottom is golden. Turn the bell peppers over and cook for 3 minutes. Transfer the bell peppers to the bowl with the marinade. Add the zucchini to the skillet and cook for 3 minutes, or until the bottom is golden. Turn the zucchini over and cook for 2 to 3 minutes. Transfer the zucchini to the bowl with the marinade. Add the mushrooms to the skillet and cook for 3 to 4 minutes, or until lightly golden, turning them over once. Transfer the mushrooms to the bowl with the marinade. Gently stir the vegetables in the marinade and let them stand for at least 20 minutes before serving.

Chicken Namban,
page 188.

Chicken Namban

This is a chicken version of a *namban* dish (for a vegetable version, see page 186). In Japan, we prepare this kind of dish a day in advance and allow the *namban* flavor to penetrate the cooked item overnight. Although we typically enjoy it the next day, consumed cold, I suggest this recipe be served hot to appeal to American diners.

MAKES 4 SERVINGS

¼ cup rice vinegar

3 tablespoons Super Sauce (page 170)

2 tablespoons water

2 tablespoons sugar

6 tablespoons all-purpose flour

2 teaspoons Japanese curry powder or Madras curry powder

1 teaspoon paprika

8 boneless, skinless chicken thighs (2 pounds)

1 large Japanese sweet potato or other variety (12 ounces)

Canola oil or vegetable oil, for frying

Sea salt

2 tablespoons thinly sliced scallion (green part only)

In a bowl, combine the vinegar, Super Sauce, water, and sugar and set aside. In another bowl, combine the flour, curry powder, and paprika. Dredge the chicken in the flour mixture and let it stand for 10 minutes.

Cut the sweet potato into 1 by 3-inch matchsticks. Place the potato in a medium pot and cover with cold water. Bring to a simmer over medium heat and cook for 2 minutes. Drain the potato in a colander and air-dry. Transfer the potato to a paper towel–lined platter to remove any excess water.

Heat 2 inches of the canola oil in a deep ovenproof skillet over medium heat to 350°F. Add the potato and cook for 2 minutes or until golden, stirring from time to time. Transfer the potato to a wire rack set over a baking sheet to drain and sprinkle with a pinch or two of salt.

Preheat the oven to 350°F. Remove most of the oil from the skillet, reserving 2 tablespoons in the skillet. Heat the oil over medium heat, add the chicken, and cook for 3 minutes, or until the bottom is golden. Turn the chicken over and transfer the skillet to the oven. Cook the chicken for 25 minutes.

Remove the skillet from the oven and discard the excess oil from the skillet, reserving the chicken in the skillet. Put the skillet back over medium heat on the stovetop and add the vinegar sauce. Cook for 2 minutes. During cooking, baste the chicken in the skillet with the sauce. The sauce should reduce and become thick, coating the chicken with a velvety layer of sauce. Divide the chicken and sweet potato among plates. Garnish with the scallion and serve.

Namban: Southern Barbarian

Many art lovers have heard of Japanese *Namban* Art. *Namban* Art includes artistic crafts like elaborate folding screens, food boxes, gunpowder bottles, and intricate chests that were produced in the sixteenth and seventeenth centuries in Japan. All of these items depict the people and lives of the first European visitors, the Portuguese, who arrived in Japan in the mid-sixteenth century during Portugal's age of global exploration. Japanese artists represented the Portuguese in caricature-like exaggerated manner wearing baggy pants; loose blouses with frilled, round white collars at the neck; and tall hats. Their faces are depicted with big noses and big eyes, and many sport extensive mustaches and beards. The name *namban,* or "southern barbarians," was given to them because the Portuguese reached Japan via Southeast Asia, arrived from the south, and looked nothing like the neighboring Asians whom residents had known for centuries. The Japanese were initially amazed by these very different people, and Japanese artists were excited and anxious to use these new figures in their works. Portugal's influence was not limited to the art world; the Portuguese introduced guns and gunpowder that changed our political system, eventually resulting in a unified country that grew from the fighting among regional feudal lords. The Portuguese also introduced new cooking techniques and ingredients that greatly enriched our food culture. The deep-frying technique of tempura, sugar, biscuits, kabocha squash, bread, and a pound cake called *kasutera*—a corruption of the Portuguese expression *pão de Castela*, meaning "bread from Castile"—accompanied the Portuguese visitors. Many of the culinary words that were borrowed from the Portuguese continue to survive in Japanese, Portuguese, and English: *pan*, *pão*, bread; *kyarameru*, *caramelo*, caramel; *koppu*, *copo*, glass cup; and *booro*, *bolo*, biscuit. How about "thank you" (*arigato* in Japanese, *obrigado* in Portuguese)? Historical records show that the Japanese word *arigato* predates the arrival of the Portuguese in Japan, and most linguists agree that the similarity is a linguistic coincidence.

Oysters on the Half-Shell with Ponzu Jelly

Ponzu jelly is a new food fad that has become popular in Japan over the past several years. Adding conventional Western gelatin to ponzu sauce transforms it into a jelly, giving a new and modern face to this traditional sauce. Restaurant chefs and home cooks have created new dishes, such as prosciutto-wrapped melon with ponzu jelly, beef *tataki* (very rare thinly sliced beef) with ponzu jelly, sashimi with ponzu jelly, tempura shrimp with ponzu jelly, and pork cutlet with ponzu jelly. After observing the entire country's enthusiasm for ponzu jelly, food manufacturers began producing ponzu jelly products packaged and sold in tubes like toothpaste. My version is a new, quick-to-prepare, chemical- and food additive-free sauce for your kitchen, and I can assure you it will be a delightful experience for those dining at your table. In this recipe, I serve oysters on the half-shell with this modern sauce. Create your own ways to use ponzu jelly.

MAKES 4 SERVINGS

½ cup Ponzu Sauce (page 171)

½ cup water

1 (¼-ounce) package gelatin powder

1 teaspoon honey

Ice cubes

24 oysters of your choice

3 tablespoons minced red radish

2 tablespoons thinly sliced fresh chives

1 teaspoon finely grated lemon zest

Place the Ponzu Sauce, water, gelatin powder, and honey in a small saucepan. Bring the mixture to a simmer over medium heat. Turn the heat to low and cook, stirring with a spatula, for 4 minutes. Transfer the liquid to a small bowl. Cool the liquid and refrigerate until it sets.

Fill a large serving bowl with ice cubes. Using an oyster knife, carefully open all of the oysters and cut the muscle attached to the bottom shell. Place the oysters on the half-shell on the ice cubes.

Crush the Ponzu jelly into small pieces with a teaspoon. Spread ¼ teaspoon of jelly over each oyster. Top with the radish, chives, and lemon zest and serve.

Funny, Fanny Bay Oysters

During the colder months, we enjoy Fanny Bay oysters from Vancouver Island at the famous Oyster Bar in the lower level of Grand Central Terminal in New York City. If you love oysters, you must go and sit at the counter and watch the crew open oysters by the dozen. Choose a mix from the wide selection and eat your fill!

On vacation in Canada, I was excited to pass Fanny Bay on our way to the town of Tofino, a small west coast town. I was determined to try authentic Fanny Bay oysters. En route, we saw several billboards advertising local oysters and many buildings that looked like oyster processing facilities. We continued to look for a store or restaurant that might sell oysters for immediate consumption, but most places looked strangely quiet, with empty parking lots. We finally drove out of Fanny Bay without finding a restaurant or retail vendor selling oysters. We returned to one of the large buildings we had passed, entered, and found one person on duty behind a counter with no oysters in sight. When we asked to purchase some, we were told that no Fanny Bay oysters are harvested in August. This is because oysters spawn in August, and at that time of year, the water is warm, resulting in increased chances of bacterial contamination. Days later when we were in Vancouver City, we read an article in the local paper about an oyster contamination scare on Vancouver Island. So from then on, I went back to following the old "r" rule—enjoying raw oysters only in the months that contain the letter "r."

Vegetable Tempura

When prepared and served correctly, tempura is an excellent way to enjoy the peak flavor of vegetables in season. After discovering many different types of beets at my local farmers' market—purple, golden yellow, and one variety that has a whirlpool pattern on its cut surface— I could not wait to prepare them tempura style. Traditionally, the vegetables for tempura are cut into ⅓-inch-thick slices, but I cut them into much thinner slices so that the vegetables cook faster and stay crispier. We serve tempura on tempura paper (see page 193) to absorb excess oil, accompanied by dipping sauce and a small cup of grated daikon radish on the side. Daikon cleanses the oil from our palate and is rich in digestive enzymes. Be sure to read Pre-Battering Technique on page 93 and Frying Guidelines on page 164 before moving to the preparation. Each beet variety has its own distinctive taste, but if you cannot find the three varieties of beets called for, regular red beets will suffice.

MAKES 4 SERVINGS

1 medium purple beet (5 ounces)

1 medium golden beet (5 ounces)

1 medium Chioggia beet (the inside has a whirlpool pattern) (5 ounces)

1 small green zucchini (5 ounces)

4 zucchini blossoms

4 small cremini mushrooms

4 small okra

Canola oil, for frying

1¼ cups tempura flour or blend of 80% cake flour and 20% cornstarch

¾ cup cold water

4½ cups Hot Noodle Broth (page 172), at room temperature

1 cup finely grated daikon radish

Scrub the beets with a hard brush under cold water. Using a vegetable slicer or mandoline, cut the beets (skin on) into thin slices crosswise (about ⅛-inch thickness). Using the vegetable slicer, cut the zucchini lengthwise into thin slices. Remove the pistils from the zucchini blossoms. Cut off the hard stems of the cremini mushrooms. Cut off the stem ends of the okra.

Heat 3 inches of the canola oil in a heavy skillet over medium heat to 340°F. Whisk 1 cup of the tempura flour and the cold water in a bowl until blended. Add additional water if needed to achieve a texture similar to that of crêpe batter.

Add the remaining ¼ cup of tempura flour to another bowl. Add a few vegetables at a time to the bowl of flour and dredge them thoroughly. Transfer the flour-coated vegetables to a platter and continue to dredge until all of the vegetables are coated. One at a time, dip each flour-coated vegetable into the batter, shake off any excess, and carefully drop it into the oil. Add the vegetables until 50 percent of the oil's surface is covered. Cook each vegetable slice for 4 minutes, turning each a few times but not too frequently. Transfer the fried vegetables to a wire rack set over a baking sheet pan to drain, and continue frying until all the vegetables are cooked.

Divide the Hot Noodle Broth into small sauce bowls. Add a portion of the daikon radish to each bowl. Divide the tempura among tempura paper— or paper towel–lined plates. Serve while hot and crisp.

Whoops! You Don't Do That!

Our lives are a succession of happy celebrations and occasions of grief. Our ancestors created rituals and rules surrounding celebrations and funerals so that each occasion—happy or sad—is more meaningful and is celebrated in a way that is appropriate to our own society. The precise art of folding tempura paper can determine whether a person really knows Japanese culture and understands the "rules" that govern tempura paper folding (although younger generations may not care or may not have been brought up with the rules).

Tempura is always served on tempura paper to absorb oil from the deep-fried food. Tempura, especially vegetable tempura, is served at both celebratory events and at funerals. In order to distinguish between these two occasions, tempura paper is folded in two different ways. It is inappropriate to serve tempura at a celebratory occasion on paper that has been folded in the manner appropriate for a sad occasion. For ordinary meals and celebratory occasions, first place the tempura paper on the table with the shorter edge toward you. You are not going to fold the paper precisely in half, but must push the left corner of the front edge toward the right so that the tip protrudes above the far edge of the paper. Now complete the fold. The folded edge slants from the far left to the near right. For funeral occasions, you should fold the paper the other way.

Technique

PRE-BATTERING TECHNIQUE

We dust sliced vegetables or other foods for deep frying in dry tempura flour (or a mixture of cake flour and cornstarch) before dipping them in prepared tempura batter. The dusting process helps the batter adhere to the surface of the food. If you skip this step, the tempura will not pick up the proper thickness of batter coating.

Tempura Fish and Chips

It was not surprising several years ago to see one of my American friends feeding her children deep-fried frozen fish sticks. My mother never did this, but today, even in Japan, many young mothers are busy with work or are in search of cooking shortcuts, and so they buy items like frozen fish sticks for their children. I hope this recipe will help to counter this trend and show that spending a little more kitchen time is easy and still quick to do. So here is my recipe for homemade tempura fish sticks. I like to use tilapia because it is farm-raised in freshwater with a vegetarian-based diet and is therefore a sustainable choice. You may also use cod, halibut, or any other white fish. If the fish is frozen, thoroughly defrost it overnight in the refrigerator. Be sure to read Pre-Battering Technique on page 193 and Frying Guidelines on page 164.

MAKES 4 SERVINGS

1 pound tilapia fillets

12 medium shrimp, shelled and deveined, with tail attached (about 8 pieces)

1 teaspoon sea salt

1¼ cups tempura flour or blend of 80% cake flour and 20% cornstarch

¾ cup plus 2 tablespoons ice water

¼ cup finely chopped fresh parsley

2 to 3 teaspoons Japanese curry powder or Madras curry powder

Canola oil or vegetable oil, for frying

A small bag of potato chips or home-made potato chips (see page 15)

1 cup Ponzu Sauce (page 171)

2 scallions, very thinly sliced (green part only)

Cut the tilapia fillets diagonally into 1½-inch-wide sticks. You will have about 16 pieces. In a large bowl, gently toss the fish and shrimp with the salt. Place ¼ cup of the tempura flour in a medium bowl and dredge the fish and shrimp until well coated. Transfer the fish and shrimp to a large platter. In another medium bowl, whisk the remaining 1 cup tempura flour, ¾ cup of the water, the parsley, and curry powder until well blended.

Heat 3 inches of the canola oil in a heavy skillet over medium heat to 340°F. Pick up one fish stick, dip it in the tempura batter, shake off any excess batter, and place it in the hot oil. Continue adding additional fish pieces until 50 percent of the oil's surface is covered. Cook the fish for 2 to 3 minutes, or until the outside is lightly golden and the fish is just cooked through. Remove the fish from the oil and drain on a wire rack set over a baking sheet. Continue until all of the fish is cooked. Then cook the shrimp using the same method.

Divide the fish and shrimp among tempura paper— or paper towel—lined dinner plates. Add the potato chips to the plates. Divide the Ponzu Sauce into small saucers and add the scallions to the sauce. Serve the fish and shrimp tempura with the dipping sauce.

Simmered Branzino

The Japanese simmering or braising technique called *nimono* is the second most popular cooking technique next to grilling. In this dish, I use whole branzino (also known as Mediterranean sea bass) because it has a distinctively sweet flavor. I braise the fish in shoyu (soy sauce), mirin (sweet cooking wine), sake (rice wine), and ginger-flavored water. The ginger suppresses any strong fishy flavor that might otherwise be present in the prepared dish. Here is a checklist for selecting a whole fish: The fish should have clear eyes; the scales should be intact; the body of the fish should look moist and plump in the belly; and the flesh should be springy to the touch, without leaving a depression. You can ask your local fishmonger to scale and clean the fish, but leave the fins, head, and tail attached.

MAKES 4 SERVINGS

¼ cup finely julienned peeled ginger plus 8 slices peeled ginger

2 small whole branzino, cleaned with head on (about 2 pounds total)

½ cup sake (rice wine)

3 tablespoons mirin (sweet cooking wine)

2½ tablespoons Super Sauce (page 170)

¼ to ⅛ teaspoon sea salt

1 bunch spinach leaves (10 ounces)

1 teaspoon shoyu (soy sauce)

1 lemon

Have a large bowl of ice water on hand. Bring a large pot of water to a boil, place the julienned ginger in a sieve, and lower it into the boiling water. Cook the ginger for 1 minute. Transfer the sieve to the bowl of ice water and cool. (Keep the water boiling.) Drain the ginger and transfer it to a bowl. This will be used for garnishing the cooked fish.

Cut each branzino in half crosswise. Make an "X" cut on the surface of both sides of each piece of fish. Place one fish piece at a time on a large slotted spoon and lower the fish into the boiling water for 30 seconds, until the outside of the fish becomes white. Carefully remove the fish from the water and drop it into the bowl of ice water. Use your fingers to clean the fish in the ice water to remove any impurities or any scales that may have been left. Transfer the fish to a large platter. During handling, be careful not to damage the fish. Finish blanching and cleaning all of the remaining fish.

Bring a kettle of water to a boil. Cut a piece of parchment paper to make a disk 1 inch larger than the diameter of the pot you will use for braising the fish, and make a ½-inch hole in the center of the parchment paper. Place the sake in the braising pot over medium heat and bring it to a gentle simmer. Add 3 cups of boiling water from the kettle and the ginger slices. Carefully add the cleaned fish pieces to the pot in a single layer, and cover them with the parchment paper lid. Push the paper down into the pot directly on top of the fish, with the excess diameter of the paper folded up against the inside of the pot. Cook the fish at a gentle simmer for 10 minutes. Add the mirin beneath the lid and cook for 5 minutes. Add the Super Sauce and salt and cook for 5 minutes. Baste the fish with the braising liquid several times.

Continued

Bring a large pot of salted water to a boil over high heat, add the spinach, and cook for 1 to 2 minutes. Drain the spinach in a colander and rinse it under cold water. Drain the spinach again and squeeze it firmly to remove any excess water. Spread the spinach leaves on a cutting board and sprinkle them with the soy sauce. Massage the spinach for 30 seconds and again squeeze it firmly to remove any remaining excess water and soy sauce. Form the spinach into a 2-inch diameter cylinder and cut it crosswise into 4 pieces.

Place the fish and spinach next to each other in soup bowls. Divide the braising liquid among the bowls. Garnish with the julienned ginger, squeeze a little lemon juice on the fish, and serve.

My Mother's "Fish Tail" Life

I was raised in the traditional Japanese way that required women to take care of the men in their family. In our house, my father was the bread-winner and the only man, so my mother made sure that we paid him ultimate respect. At meal-time, my mother also treated him to the best culinary elements of the meal. Whether the meal included fruits, vegetables, fish, chicken, meat, cakes, or cookies, my mother always served my father the very best part of every food on the table. When it came to fish, the head part that included the collar, eye gelatin, cheek and neck meat, and succulent body meat was always served to my father. My mother was always content to eat the tail end of the fish again and again.

My father has now been gone for almost 20 years, and at last, my mother is enjoying the head part of the fish. When I have a chance to share a meal with her—sadly because of distance it is not so often now—she recalls her years in a "fish tail" life. This does not just mean that she missed out on the most delicious part of the fish for so long, but also that she recognizes the role and status of women that she experienced in her home life and in Japanese society. It was a life of sacrifice and devotion to her spouse and any other men who were important in her life and the life of her family.

Today my sister, Keiko, who is married and lives in Japan, follows in my mother's footsteps as a dedicated, devoted Japanese wife and mother. She has her own interesting and successful life as a published author, but the remnants of the "fish tail" life still govern her interactions with many people, including her family. My life at home with Buzz is different. If we are sharing a whole cooked fish, we share every part of it without argument. We split the fish lengthwise, and each of us enjoys the fish collar, cheeks, neck meat, and fillets, although Buzz generally gives me his portion of the eye gelatin. As for my mother, she is pleased to hear of the democracy at my home, the seeds of which were planted long ago by her strong mother, Setsu.

Kabocha and Lamb Wanton Pot Stickers

I created this dish with leftover kabocha squash after preparing Spiced Kabocha Squash Soup (page 18). The sweetness of the kabocha moderates the strong flavor of the lamb, making a dish well suited to autumn dining. Wonton wrappers are thinner and smaller than gyoza (pot sticker) wrappers, so using wonton wrappers results in a lighter dish.

MAKES 4 TO 6 SERVINGS (32 PIECES)

1 cup cooked and mashed kabocha squash

5 ounces ground lamb

1 large egg

½ tablespoon minced scallion (white part only)

1 tablespoon minced fresh parsley

2 teaspoons grated garlic

½ teaspoon sea salt

¼ teaspoon ground nutmeg

2 teaspoons Super Sauce (page 170)

2 teaspoons rice vinegar

32 wonton wrappers

3 tablespoons canola oil or vegetable oil

1 teaspoon sesame oil

Ponzu Sauce (page 171)

Place the kabocha, ground lamb, egg, scallion, parsley, garlic, salt, nutmeg, Super Sauce, and vinegar in a medium bowl, and thoroughly mix all of the ingredients with a spatula.

Spread 10 wonton wrappers on a work surface. Using a pastry brush, paint the edge of the wrapper farthest away from you with water. Using a spoon, scoop 2 teaspoons of the stuffing mixture and drop it in the center of the wrapper. Roll the wrapper firmly around the lamb mixture, as if rolling a cigar. Gently press the roll to flatten, but do not press so hard that the lamb filling begins to spill out of the tube. Leave the ends open so that the orange color is visible. Repeat with the remaining wrappers and filling to finish making all of the rolls.

Heat 1 tablespoon of the canola oil in a medium nonstick skillet over medium-high heat. Add 10 of the wontons in a single layer to the skillet, decrease the heat to medium-low, and cook the wontons until the bottom is golden. While the wontons are cooking, boil 2 cups of water and the sesame oil in a small pot. Turn the dumplings over and carefully ladle the water-sesame mixture into the skillet until one-third of the thickness of the dumplings is submerged. Be careful, because it will sizzle and splatter. Cover the skillet with a tight-fitting lid, turn the heat to low, and cook the dumplings for 8 minutes.

Remove the lid. If any water remains in the skillet, increase the heat to high and cook off the moisture that remains. The bottom of the wontons should be crisp and easy to remove from the skillet. Transfer the cooked wontons to a serving platter. Add another tablespoon of canola oil to the skillet and repeat the process to cook another batch, continuing until all the rolls are cooked. Serve the wontons with the Ponzu Sauce for dipping.

Japanese Beef Slew

This recipe was inspired by my mother's beef stew, which I have enjoyed for many years. My goal was to create a light and clean taste that acknowledges the flavor of each ingredient in the pot. Serve the dish with crusty country bread to soak up all of the sauce.

MAKES 6 SERVINGS

2 pounds beef shoulder

Sea salt and freshly ground black pepper

1 large carrot (10 ounces), peeled

3 small Yukon gold potatoes or other similar variety (10 ounces)

3 tablespoons canola oil or vegetable oil

12 cipollini onions (7½ ounces), peeled

1 cup sake (rice wine)

2 tablespoons grated ginger

¾ cup Super Sauce (page 170)

2 tablespoons cornstarch mixed with 2 tablespoons water

2 tablespoons chopped fresh parsley

Cut the beef into 2-inch cubes and season with salt and pepper. Cut the carrot into 1½-inch pieces using the *rangiri* technique (see page 201). Cut the potatoes into 1½-inch pieces.

Prepare a kettle of boiling water. Heat 2 tablespoons of the oil in a medium skillet over medium heat, add the beef, and cook until all sides are browned, 3 to 4 minutes. Transfer the beef pieces to a colander and pour the boiling water over them (see page 31).

In a stew pot, heat the remaining 1 tablespoon oil over medium heat, add the onions, and cook for 1 minute. Add the sake and bring to a simmer. Add the beef and pour hot water into the pot until it barely covers the beef. Bring the mixture to a simmer. Skim the foam from the surface of the water until it no longer appears. Then reduce the heat to low and cook, covered, for 30 minutes.

Using a slotted spoon, remove the onions and transfer them to a bowl. Add the carrot and potatoes to the pot and cook, covered, for 30 minutes or until the meat is tender. Add the ginger, Super Sauce, and the cooked onions back to the pot. Cook the stew, uncovered, for 15 minutes. Add the cornstarch slurry to the pot to thicken the broth. Cook the stew for an additional 5 minutes. Divide the stew among bowls. Garnish with the parsley and serve.

"DISORDERED" ROLL CUT

When we cut cylindrically shaped vegetables such as carrots, burdock, salsify, eggplant, or cucumbers, we often use the *rangiri* cutting technique. *Rangiri* literally means "disordered cut."

To make a *rangiri* cut, place the vegetable in front of you with the long edge facing you, hold the knife diagonally, and, keeping the angle of the knife fixed, rotate the vegetable a quarter turn before making each cut.

The "disordered" cut is actually a very strict "ordered" cut.

Rangiri cutting results in each piece having a large surface area. This facilitates quick, even cooking and flavoring.

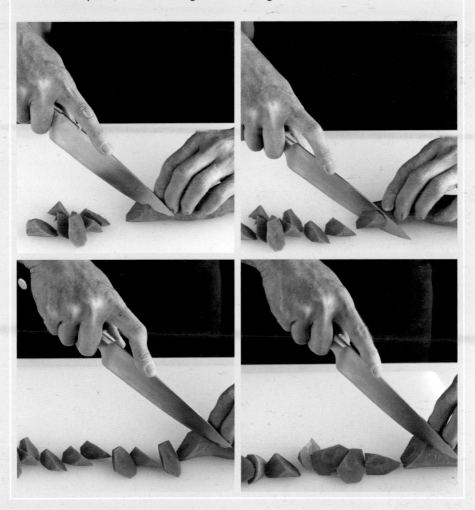

Acknowledgments

In the past years I have been blessed to work with many highly qualified and generous people, companies, government organizations, and professional cooking schools promoting Japanese cuisine in the United States. Each experience has challenged me and helped me grow. My first book, *The Japanese Kitchen*, is the foundation I have built on as a devoted explorer, practitioner, and promoter of classical Japanese cuisine. My heartfelt gratitude goes to all whom I contacted and worked with in the past years to develop the expertise that is the cornerstone of this book.

While writing this book the voice of my mother, Tokuko Shimbo, and what she taught me about cooking and life in general were always on my mind, even though she is far away in Tokyo. The seed for what I have grown into, where I am now, and what I am doing was planted by her mother, Setsu Okada. She was a great cook who 90 years ago in rural Japan was already deeply immersed in mastering many aspects of international cuisine. She was decades ahead of her time. Indeed I feel the influence of all of my family members and their ancestors on what I have written here.

For the development of recipes in this book I was fortunate to have the devoted assistance of a group of talented, young volunteers who, as trained cooking professionals, are becoming competent and confident chefs and are also my dear friends. Special thanks to Christina Wang, Georgia Wand Freedman, Anna Yeung, and Jennifer Batts.

I am indebted to photographer Frances Janisch, food stylist Michael Pederson, and Executive Art Director Tim Lynch, of Andrews McMeel Publishing, LLC, for the creative, high quality, and very useful photographs in the book.

Jean Lucas, my editor, patiently heard and respected my voice in the work during the editing and jacket design process. It was Dorothy Kalins who kindly introduced me to Andrews McMeel publisher Kirsty Melville, who made the book a reality. A special thanks also to my agent, Janis Donnaud, who always stands by me

Finally, this book is a product of my marriage to Buzz. As he did for my previous two books, Buzz played the roles of in-house editor and critic of early recipe developments, which by necessity have to be repeated several times to get them "right." Buzz's love and care about food and his experience of living in Japan for fourteen years enable him to be the best person for these roles. Big love and thank you. We look forward to watching this third book-child grow by opening a new and delicious Japanese world of flavors for you.

Sources for Japanese Food Products

ARIZONA

New Tokyo Food Market
3435 W. Northern Ave.
Phoenix, AZ 85051
602-841-0255

99 Ranch Market
668 N 44th St., Ste 188
Phoenix, AZ 85008
602-225-2288

CALIFORNIA

Mitsuwa Marketplace
665 Paularino Ave.
Costa Mesa, CA 92626
714-557-6699

675 Saratoga Ave.
San Jose, CA 95129
408-255-6699

333 S. Alameda St.
Los Angeles, CA 90013
213-687-6699

3760 Centinela Ave.
Los Angeles, CA 90066
310-398-2113

515 W. Las Tunas Drive
San Gabriel, CA 91776
626-457-2899

4240 Kearney Mesa Rd. #119
San Diego, CA 92111
858-569-6699

21515 Western Ave.
Torrance, CA 90501
310-782-0335

Suruki Supermarket
71 East Fourth Ave.
San Mateo, CA 94401
650-347-5288

99 Ranch Market
651 N. Euclid St.
Anaheim, CA 92801
714-776-8899

15333 Culver Dr. #800
Irvine, CA 92714
949-651-8899

5402 Walnut Ave.
Irvine, CA 92604
949-651-8888

CONNECTICUT

Fuji Mart Corporation Greenwich
1212 East Putnam Ave.
Old Greenwich, CN 06878
203-698-2107

FLORIDA

Kyoya Japanese Market
1956 E Sunrise Blvd.
Fort Lauderdale, FL 33304
954-761-8010

Japanese Market
1412 79th St. CSWY
N. Bay Village, FL 33141
305-861-0143

GEORGIA

Tamato Food Store
2086 B Cobb Pkwy.
Smyrna, GA 30080
770-933-0108

HAWAII

Marukai Wholesale Mart
2310 Kamehameha Hwy.
Honolulu, HI 968819
808-845-5051

Nijiya Market
1009 University Ave., #81
Honolulu, HI 96826
808-979-8977

ILLINOIS

Mitsuwa Marketplace
100 E. Algonquin Road
Arlington Hts., IL 60005
847-956-6699

KENTUCKY

Smith's Oriental Food Store
1587 North Dixie Blvd.
Radcliffe, KY 40160
270-351-9588

MARYLAND

Han Ah Reum Asian Mart
12015 Georgia Ave.
Wheaton, MD 20902
301-942-5071

800 North Rolling Rd.
Catonsville, MD 21228
443-612-9020

MASSACHUSETTS

Mirim Oriental Groceries
152 Harvard Ave.
Allston, MA 02134
617-783-2626

NEVADA

99 Ranch Market
4701 S. Cameron St. #F
Las Vegas, ND 89103
702-252-0666

NEW JERSEY

Han Ah Reum Asian Mart

260 Bergen Tpke.
Little Ferry, NJ 07643
201-814-0400

321 Broad Ave.
Ridgefield, NJ 07657
201-943-9600
25 Lafayette Ave.
Englewood, NJ 07631
201-871-8822

1720 Route 70E
Cherry Hill, NJ 08003
856-489-4611

Mitsuwa Marketplace

595 River Rd.
Edgewater, NJ 07020
201-941-9113

Nippon Daido USA, Incorporated

1385 16th St.
Fort Lee, NJ 07024
201-944-0020

NEW MEXICO

A-1 Oriental Market

1410-H Wyoming Blvd.
NE, Albuquerque, NM 87112
505-275-9021

NEW YORK

Han Ah Reum Asian Mart

29-02 Union St.
Flushing, NY 11354
718-381-5595

Katagiri

224 E. 59th St.
New York, NY 10022
212-755-3566

Sunrise Mart

4 Stuyvesant St. 2nd Fl.
New York, NY 10003
212-598-3040

494 Broome St.
New York, NY 10013
212-219-0033

Mutual Trading Inc.

(restaurant supply)
25 Knickerbocker Rd.
Moonachie, NJ 07074

NORTH CAROLINA

Hatoya Market

605 E. North Polk St.
Pineville, NC 28134
704-889-6600

Tokyo Shokuhin

784 A East Chatham Square
Cary, NC 27511
919-319-1620

OREGON

Uwajimaya

10500 Southwest
Beaverton, Oregon 97005
503-643-4512

PENNSYLVANIA

Han Ah Reum Asian Mart

7320 Old York Rd.
Elkins Park, PA 19027
215-782-1801

SOUTH CAROLINA

Oriental Import

1305 Laurens
Greenville, SC 29607
864-235-6089

TENNESSEE

Oriental Best Market

3588 Ridgeway
Memphis, TN 38115
901-366-1570

TEXAS

Nippon Daido USA, Inc.

11146 Westheimer Rd.
Houston, TX 77042
713-785-0815

VIRGINIA

Han Ah Reum Asian Mart

10780 Lee Highway
Fairfax, VA 22030
703-273-0570

8103 Lee Highway
Fairfax, VA 22042
703-573-6300

Naniwa Foods

6730 Curran St.
McLean, VA 22101
703-893-7209

WASHINGTON

Asia Oriental Market

2408 Meridian St.
Bellingham, WA 98225
360-671-0446

Sunrise Asian Market

70 W. 29th Ave.
Eugene, WA 97405
541-343-3295

Uwajimaya, Seattle

600 5th Ave. South
Suite 100
Seattle, WA 98104
206-624-6248

Uwajimaya, Bellevue

15555 NE 24th &
Bel Red Road
Bellevue, WA 98007
425-747-9012

Metric Conversions and Equivalents

To Convert	Multiply
Ounces to grams	Ounces by 28.35
Pounds to kilograms	Pounds by .454
Teaspoons to milliliters	Teaspoons by 4.93
Tablespoons to milliliters	Tablespoons by 14.79
Fluid ounces to milliliters	Fluid ounces by 29.57
Cups to milliliters	Cups by 236.59
Cups to liters	Cups by .236
Pints to liters	Pints by .473
Quarts to liters	Quarts by .946
Gallons to liters	Gallons by 3.785
Inches to centimeters	Inches by 2.54

OVEN TEMPERATURES

To convert Fahrenheit to Celsius, subtract 32 from Fahrenheit, multiply the result by 5, then divide by 9.

Description	Fahrenheit	Celsius	British Gas Mark
Very cool	200°	95°	0
Very cool	225°	110°	¼
Very cool	250°	120°	½
Cool	275°	135°	1
Cool	300°	150°	2
Warm	325°	165°	3
Moderate	350°	175°	4
Moderately hot	375°	190°	5
Fairly hot	400°	200°	6
Hot	425°	220°	7
Very hot	450°	230°	8
Very hot	475°	245°	9

APPROXIMATE METRIC EQUIVALENTS

Volume	
¼ teaspoon	1 milliliter
½ teaspoon	2.5 milliliters
¾ teaspoon	4 milliliters
1 teaspoon	5 milliliters
1¼ teaspoons	6 milliliters
1½ teaspoons	7.5 milliliters
1¾ teaspoons	8.5 milliliters
2 teaspoons	10 milliliters
1 tablespoon (½ fluid ounce)	15 milliliters
2 tablespoons (1 fluid ounce)	30 milliliters
¼ cup	60 milliliters
⅓ cup	80 milliliters
½ cup (4 fluid ounces)	120 milliliters
⅔ cup	160 milliliters
¾ cup	180 milliliters
1 cup (8 fluid ounces)	240 milliliters
1¼ cups	300 milliliters
1½ cups (12 fluid ounces)	360 milliliters
1⅔ cups	400 milliliters
2 cups (1 pint)	460 milliliters
3 cups	700 milliliters
4 cups (1 quart)	0.95 liter
1 quart plus ¼ cup	1 liter
4 quarts (1 gallon)	3.8 liters

Weight	
¼ ounce	7 grams
½ ounce	14 grams
¾ ounce	21 grams
1 ounce	28 grams
1¼ ounces	35 grams
1½ ounces	42.5 grams
1⅔ ounces	45 grams
2 ounces	57 grams
3 ounces	85 grams
4 ounces (¼ pound)	113 grams
5 ounces	142 grams
6 ounces	170 grams
7 ounces	198 grams
8 ounces (½ pound)	227 grams
16 ounces (1 pound)	454 grams
35.25 ounces (2.2 pounds)	1 kilogram

Length	
⅛ inch	3 millimeters
¼ inch	6 millimeters
½ inch	1¼ centimeters
1 inch	2½ centimeters
2 inches	5 centimeters
2½ inches	6 centimeters
4 inches	10 centimeters
5 inches	13 centimeters
6 inches	15¼ centimeters
12 inches (1 foot)	30 centimeters

COMMON INGREDIENTS AND THEIR APPROXIMATE EQUIVALENTS

1 cup uncooked white rice	185 grams
1 cup all-purpose flour	140 grams
1 stick butter (4 ounces • ½ cup • 8 tablespoons)	110 grams
1 cup butter (8 ounces • 2 sticks • 16 tablespoons)	220 grams
1 cup brown sugar, firmly packed	225 grams
1 cup granulated sugar	200 grams

Information compiled from a variety of sources, including *Recipes into Type* by Joan Whitman and Dolores Simon (Newton, MA: Biscuit Books, 2000); *The New Food Lover's Companion* by Sharon Tyler Herbst (Hauppauge, NY: Barron's, 1995); and *Rosemary Brown's Big Kitchen Instruction Book* (Kansas City, MO: Andrews McMeel, 1998).

INDEX

S

Hiroko Shimbo

is a chef-consultant for restaurants
and food companies, a trained sushi
chef, an award-winning author,
a media performer, and a chef-
instructor. She is also a frequent
guest chef at the Worlds of Flavors
Conference at the Culinary Institute
of America. Hiroko appears in the
media and online through her own
Web site, blog, and Twitter account
(@hirokoshimbo), as well as on
such services as About.com. She
is a member of the Women Chefs
and Restaurateurs and the Author's
Guild, and is a sushi adviser for the
Blue Ocean Institute.